WOMEN AND RESERVATION IN INDIA

Dr. Jyotirmay Mandal

PUBLICATIONS

KALPAZ PUBLICATIONS
DELHI - 110052

WOMEN AND RESERVATION IN INDIA
[*Women Studies*]

ISBN: 81-7835-145-5

Published in 2003 in India by
Kalpaz Publications
C-30, Satyawati Nagar
Delhi-110052
e-mail: kalpaz@hotmail.com

Laser Typeset at: Alphabet, Delhi
Printed at: Mehra Offset Press, Delhi

WOMEN AND RESERVATION IN INDIA

Contents

Preface

Keeping in view political uproar and motivating reports in different news-papers regarding Women's Reservation Bill, for the last three years, I have gone into detailed studies on practical position of women in Indian society. In that, even I had taken help of religious books on Hindus, Muslims and Christians to find out the causes attributable to build the present social status of women. However, the Adivasies could not be interrogated in this context. Similarly, keeping in view the present trend in Indian Society, the probable ways of betterment of women have also been examined.

What my studies and practical observation revealed, I have made an attempt to discuss the same in comprehensive manner. I have also made efforts to point out the exact nature of social behaviour of men towards women in a family as a unit and largely of a nation.

All my studies and observations were always in relating to the benefits of Women's Reservation Bill which is still held in abeyance. Before the bill become a law, what a layman should know, I made an endeavour to reflect those points in my writing.

According to my studies and knowledge about the position of women in our society, I found the causes of their degradation which I have discussed in a comprehensive language, so that no point of ambiguity is raised by any reader. The illustrations made in the discussion vindicate properly the causes of women's degradation in Indian society irrespective of religion and caste. However, the readers will find that caste distinction and religious taboos predominantly attribute to the miserable condition of women.

The palatable and prudent ways of improvement in status of women have also been described in this book with the intention to exhibit and encourage women to adopt these instead of longing for political reservation. I have also tried to explain that, political reservation cannot improve the status of women in male dominated Indian society. To establish respectable entity of women, they should acquire standard education, possess power of determination, bravery and instinct of competition in them.

In this book I made all possible endeavour within the limit of my practical observation and knowledge, to make the readers to be thoughtful about the consequences of political reservation for women in the present position of India. The illustrations made under different headings will perhaps make our readers to encourage the women to adopt all those measures instead of political reservation, to improve their status and entity.

I shall be grateful, if this book may impress the readers and logically make awareness among women category of Indian citizens and also I will be indebted to those readers who will suggest any modification and correction in the book.

It is my earnest appeal to the readers to forgive me for any discrepancies observed in the language I used to communicate my thoughts, and ommission, and also for any statement found to be hurting anyone's feelings, since I am not a professional writer or a meticulous linguistic person.

Dr. Jyotirmay Mandal

Abbreviations

A.F.S.W.C.	-	Anti –Facist Soviet Women's Committee.
A.I.R.	-	All India Reporter.
A.I.W.C.	-	All India Women's Conference.
A.I.W.C.A	-	All India Women Conference Association.
A.M.S.	-	Arya Mahila Samaj.
Art.	-	Article.
A.W.P.	-	Association for Women in Psychology.
B.B.C.J.	-	Bombay British Criminal Journal.
B.C.	-	Backward Class.
B.J.P.	-	Bharatiya Janta Party.
B.M.	-	Bachelor of Medicine.
B.M.P.	-	Bharat Mahila Parishad.
B.P.W.C.	-	Bombay Presidency Women's Council.
B.S.M.	-	Bharat Stri Mahamandal.
Cr.LJ.	-	Criminal Law Journal.
C.R.P.	-	Central Reserve Police.
D.A.W.N.	-	Development of Alternatives for Women of the New Era.
Ed.	-	Edition.
F.R.G.	-	Federal Republic of Germany.
G.B.M.C.	-	Graduate of Bengal Medical College.
I.C.S.D.W.	-	International Council of Social Democratic Women.
I.I.P.S.	-	Indian Institute of Physical Science.
I.L.O.	-	International Labour Organisation.
M.D.	-	Doctor of Medicine.
M.P.	-	Member of Parliament or Madhya Pradesh.

N.D.A.	-	National Democratic Alliance.
N.C.W.I.	-	National Council of Women in India.
N.G.O.	-	Non-government Organisation.
N.F.I.W.	-	National Federation of Indian Women.
N.F.W.W.	-	National Federation of Women Workers.
O.B.C.	-	Other Backward Classes.
P.	-	Page.
P.P.R.	-	Polish People's Republic.
S.C.	-	Scheduled Castes.
S.T.	-	Scheduled Tribes.
U.P.	-	Uttar Pradesh.
U.S.	-	United States.
U.S.A.	-	United States of America.
U.S.S.R.	-	Union of Soviet Socialist Republic.
V. or Vs.	-	Versus.
V.L.M.S.	-	Vernacular Licentiate in Medicine and Surgery.
W.I.A.	-	Women's Indian Association.
W.P.P.L.	-	Women's Protective and Provident League.
W.T.U.L.	-	Women's Trade Union League.

Introduction

Present day scientifically advanced countries are deeply concerned with their history of civilization. Since civilization makes a country to devise its further programme of development, no country can exist without civilization in modern world. Now the question arises about the constituents of civilization. Though I am not going to the terminology and definition to scientifically define civilization and its essential elements like learned sociologists and political thinkers. Simple and comprehensive language to define civilization is one, by which we understand the social, political, economic and environmental inter-action of public including habitation, regular biological needs. Thus to improve any nation's civilization its population is the foremost important element. Since the population can be divided into two distinct categories according to biological structural differences from the very day of birth, country's civilization depends on both the categories (men and women).

Here we are confronted with another complicated question as to how women influence the civilizations? Though it seems to be little bit difficult question but it has numerous answers which vary from individual to individual. For a layman it is easy to determine that a woman has a stretched area of activities in her family. On the other hand an educationist or a philosopher will find the women a prominent figure in management of a family. As such we can conclude that women has a lion's share in forming a good society because family is the basic element of society.

All the civilized countries of the world prove to have civilized societies. Thus country's civilization is founded on society and in the root, on women. This truth can also be adjudged by analysing the role performed by a woman in her family in relation to her father, husband, children, brothers and sisters. Therefore, the quality of her activities help in changing the civilizations of the country at large. But the quality of activities depends upon women's own mental faculty and sophistication. Any race, clan or species can also be compared in the present days and it will confirm that its development is proportionate to the status of women of that particular race or clan. Hence for a country like India where female population is about to exceed the male population, special care should be taken as a measure to enhance civility of women of the country to keep pace with other developed countries.

Keeping in view the above object there have been numerous endeavour at Government level as well as non-governmental social institutions to provide facilities for women to equate them with men. Now at this stage the ruling party of the country (B.J.P.) has taken a stand to provide political reservation to women to the extent of 33 per cent of the total membership in parliamentary political institutions. Therefore, it has become a matter of concern for every section of society to examine the merits and demerits, and also the way how women can really be upgraded. Some of the important aspects of women's status and the relative matter of facts about the Women's Reservation have been discussed in succeeding paragraphs:

Position of Women in Hindu Society

Hindu society is one where Hindu Law applies and Hindu Law is a branch of Dharma as understood by the Hindus and it signifies duty. The sources of Hindu Dharma Ved, Shruti, Smriti, Upanishads, commentaries and customs. In the scriptures of Hindu, based on the above sources the position of women has been painted as most virtuous but the real practice in Hindu society reduces a woman to the position of slave or a personal property of man. According to Hindu religious injunction women have been created to become mothers later (p-29 & 30, Modern Hindu Law of UPD Kesari). In Ramayana wife has been considered to be the soul of her husband and in Mahabharata she is stated to be half part of her husband and the best friend. Here we can charge the statement with the practical differences - in Ramayana Ram indicated Sita without considering her to be the soul of him and compelled her for fire-test (Agni Pariksha). Similarly the best friend and half part of King of Principles (Dharma Raj) Yudhisthira used Draupadi as his property in bate of dice (gambling). In Hindu Marriage the daughter is given away to a man - that signifies a daughter to be a matter of value to be gifted to a person. According to Manu once a daughter is given in marriage she remains as the wife of that man for ever, whatever may be the conditions thereafter, she cannot severe the marriage tie though later Narad and Parasar have accepted five conditions when wife can abandon the marriage. These conditions of course do not relate to their mutual disliking and other disputes. Thus before the enactment of Hindu Marriage Act 1955 there was no way out to get rid off the atrocities committed by a Hindu husband on his wife. The more deplorable condition is of a Hindu widow who according to Manu after death of husband has to lead her whole life simply on vegetation and in abstinence emaciating herself to minimal - thus leading a life of celebacy and chastity. A widower husband has every liberty to remarry, take food according to his choice and to enjoy company of others (male & female) but woman has no right. In the ancient age the Hindu religion accepted the very heinous form of marriage in which the girl was kidnapped or ravaged. Even today the Hindu Law & religion approve the marriage in which the bridegroom pay money, to the parents of the girl i.e. to say the girl is bought. In Hindu society atrocities on married women is prone even after the enactment of Dowry Prohibition Act 1961, demanding of dowry from the parents or relation of the bride is in abundance. This shows how the Hindu society treats a girl.

The coparcenary property devolve upon the surviving member according to Section 6 of the Hindu Succession Act 1956 but when the surviving member is a female this law does not apply. That is to say a woman cannot hold any interest on the coparcenary property after the death of coparcenar. The Hindu female can become a Mahant of a Math but she is not authorised to perform the spiritual, and religious rituals according to Hindu Law. In a Hindu joint family the widow cannot represent the joint family in any suit as per the verdict of Patna High Court in a case (AIR 1978 Pat.258)

In Hindu society woman is degraded or looked down upon the event of sexual relationship before marriage at the same time men are not stained. Hindu law though impose condition of monogamy at the time of marriage but the Hindu society allows bigamous marriage for men, at the same time vehemently oppose bigamous marriage to women. Society demands woman's predominant chastity. Hindus society has drifted towards the women's beauty shows and artful performance to amuse the public. The beauty contest, fashion show and lively or rhythmical movement have now consummated commercially. Thus it is apparent that women in Hindu society is used as all object of amusement to a great extent. As women by biological ingredients is made amorous, her caress for the splendour further adorn her to be fondling object for men.

In the family female child from the childhood as a general trend has to bear the neglectful attitude of parents and relations. There are frequent reports of family coercion upon the female children in India. Specially in rural areas even in these days of global advancement girls are deterred from educational development. If we look into the family affairs, the females are subjected to perform all the dismal work of the household. Indian society is man dominated. Here women are depressed or deterred. The general feelings of Indian society is that women are physically weak and mentally dull. They cannot shoulder responsibilities in the same manner as men can do.

Position of Women in Muslim Society

The degradation of women is prevalent not only in Hindu society but also in Muslim community. Muslim Law (Quran) depicts the picture of women in society in the following manner.

According to Quran Muslim women's condition is like a chatel as regards marriage because Muta marriage is also permitted which is a temporary agreement for sexual relation permitted for the amount paid to the woman. The duration of such marriage may be fixed or may be uncertain. According to Muslim religious doctrine the husband can dissolve the marriage by pronouncing talaq three times. Thus the woman's married life last at the discretion of man. The procedure of talaq under Muslim Law signifies that a man after enjoyment of conjugal happiness can get rid of a woman by paying some compensation agreed upon, at his sweet will. Purdah system prescribed in Islam makes women bound to remain within certain limit and curtail her freedom of movement, whereas, no such restrictions are imposed upon the males. As regards religious performance the women's status is lowered discriminately by not allowing them to approach the Mosque. The Muslim law though permits a woman to hold the office of a Mutawalli but restraint the right to perform religious rituals. In the family life woman as a tradition has to remain subjected to obey the men. Their willingness has no meaning as they are supposed to do the household task. In these days of scientific development the Muslim female children are rare seen to attend higher educational institutions. Women go for service outside the periphery of their habitation are considered a sin by Islam.

Position of Women in Christian Society

The religious differences from Hindu and Muslim are of the spiritual ideology, in Christianity. There are differences of customs and tradition as regard spiritual and religious observance. But the social status created for women by the religious customs and tradition of Christianity is not far better than that of Hindu or Muslim. Christianity also lays down norms of distinction between male and female from the very childhood. The female children in Christian society are poised in adverse position of the male children in every domestic or social activity. Thus from the childhood the female child develops a sense of inferiority and insecurity in her and gradually in adolescence she becomes solely dependent on male for her self protection.

The practical life of women in Christian community if analytically examined, it would come to light that their status except in the context of education, in the same as in Hindu and Muslim communities. Christian religion has also not given them equal rights with man to perform the religious acts and rituals. Thus it can be concluded that in Indian Christian society the status of women is not far better than the women in Hindu and Muslim society. Only in matrimonial home Christian women enjoy greater liberty than Hindu and Muslim women as their marriage is considered as a social contract.

Attributable Causes of Women's degradation

The position of women in Indian society as stated in preceding paragraphs are attributable to the causes mentioned below:

(a) Tradition
(b) Religion
(c) Servile mentality
(d) Political aspects
(e) Education
(f) Role of Media
(g) Role of Film Industries.

The above causes of attribution to women's degradation are being discussed in the succeeding paragraphs.

(a) Tradition

For the miserable condition of women in India, first cause we find is the traditional behaviour in society. In Hindu society when a female child is born the customary ceremony performed by the family distinctly indicates the birth of a female because of the differences in observance and degree of amusement. Thereafter the mother inculcates all those servility in the day to day movement of the child which keeps her depreciated in society in comparison to a male. Parents administer upon her all those rules and procedures in the family life which arrest her physical robustness, mental fertility and courage. At the adolescence the girls are taught and guarded by the mother and other female relations in the direction to feel that she needs protections. Thus a recoiling tendency develops in them in every walk of life. The parents and relatives very much encourage the female grown up children to make their bearing more beautiful and delicate. Thus they develop habit of meeckness and allurement.

When a girl in married and transferred to the family of her husband, the in-laws make her to perceive that she is only the humble servant of her husband and in-laws even the younger in-laws frequently cast a disgusted look on her slight deviation from their choice and liking they expect from her. These sorts of activities at the beginning days of matrimonial home are nothing but the rot tradition of which knowing fully well to be derogatory and inhuman unpalatable in the present day world still repeat as a traditional norm. Though now a days women are being imparted education in academic/ technical fields but they are compelled to do other house hold work which the male children are not required to do. There are enormous practical instances in the surrounding where girls being more brilliant than the boy are not getting full support from parents for education and self improvement, whereas the dull and disobedient boy gets everything from parents at his whims. There are plenty of instances in different section of society which evince that tradition to a larger extent prejudice against the women. Women's identity changed after marriage is also a traditional degradation.

(b) Religion

Religion in the Indian soil has also a great impact on atrocities committed on women. In Hindu religion woman is called Vaama (left). This word in other sense denotes what is rejected or refused or useless. That is to say, the neglected one in the human society. In Hindu Dharmashastra like Ved, Vedanga and Smriti woman is called Sudrani which means the maid-servant (female slave or wife of a slave). Word 'Sudra' in Hindu religion derived from the name of a varna which is the lowest in social strata and the classification enjoins upon women of this varna all sorts of service to men of upper strata. Hindu religion directs the women to be obedient to the command of their husbands and remain under the shelter and protection of the husband. None of religions Hindu, Muslim or Christian has allowed women to take part in religious rituals and worship though a slight difference is noticed in Christianity. Nuns have some rights to participate in religious propagation, preaching and performance of rites. Here I quote a verse from Al-Quran in which Holy Mother Mary (Sura Mariyum) is addressed with an honour which is not to be found given to Mary in Christian Bible—

> O 'Mary'
> God Huth chosen thee
> and purified thee
> Above the women
> of all Nations" (Al-Quran 3:42)

But I ask my Muslim brethren, can they show me the practical' use or adherence of the above verse in their daily family or social life? So far my practical experience directs me to state that, though in Quranic verses women have been treated with honour and utmost dignity but in natural leading life in Muslim community comparatively degrade women more than the Hindu and Christian communities. As far as the religious status of women is concerned the Sikh only in India has raised the status of women equal to men. A lady became the Chairperson of the Shiromani Gurdwara Prabandha Committee in the recent past signifies my above statement. Another Quranic verse very lucidly states, the male should not forget all important roles which a female performs. It says, the mother who bore us must have our reverence. The wife through whom we enter parentage have our reverence.

"You demand your mutual rights
and (Reverence) the wombs
(That bore you)" (Al-Quran 4:1)

Almost all the Muslim disobey this verse of Quran in practice.

Similarly there are numerous prose and verse in Hindu religious scriptures but the real practices entirely give opposite results.

(c) Servile Mentality

The Indian social structure has been erected in such a way from the time immemorable that, women themselves weaken their capability. They develop incapacity, insecurity, shyness and gradually loses enthusiasm. The moment they get a chance to demonstrate their intelligence, bravery and sense of responsibility, hesitate to avail the opportunity of self aggrandisement. Some of the Indian women are plunged into religious dogmas and taboos so deep that they consider themselves as an object to be offered for the comfort of male and procreation to keep continue the clan. Some of the Hindu women are found to be made for worshipping male and to fulfil their unreasonable desires. In the field of economy these women press themselves hard to save the balancing state of economic stability of the family, while the male members become extravagant in their daily expenses.

As regards progress in educational field, it is prevalent in Indian society that when the parents and teachers aspire for a excellent career of a female students according to her performance in lower academic duration she recoils herself either for her lack of confidence or due to the social taboos. Most of female youths have been found to love feminish move and to be more inclined towards the characteristics of prudent submissive personality. They very often become victim of sexual exploitation due to their own impulses and fallible imagination.

(d) Political aspects

In the political field Indian women are though being accepted now but very few, because the stages a politician has to pass through from the day of joining the party generally does not suit a female instinct. Scarcely enough the rural guardians approve political participation of their female children. On the other hand there are pretermitted remarks prevalent in society against the female who engender political enthusiasm and enfranchisement, which quite often discourage female to take part in political activities.

The other side of political backwardness of women is due to the political stalwarts' attitude towards women. It is glaring defect in political parties that only the affluent members or the one who has political family back grounds are given political avenue. Hence female from the mediocre family spontaneously loses interest in politics.

(e) Education

In India as it has been recorded in world, the literacy rate is the lowest resulting in more than 50% people are illiterate. But the position of Indian women as regards literacy is quite admirable. According to census report, the literacy rate of women in 1991 was 46.01% and it has enhanced to 60.22% in 2001 and particularly in Kerala State the percentage has raised in 2001 to 90.92% (Bahujan Nayak, 15th April 2001). Despite recording the greater degree of talents in women the Indian society tame women according to the sweet will of the men in almost all sections of society. This is really a stigma on man dominated Indian Society. The educational status of women has failed to improve their social status. Daily newspaper contains enormous reports of atrocities on women in the country. International organisations on protection of human rights and creation & maintenance of amicable relationship in human society, continuously have been preparing various devises to grant equal right to women with men have been proved a farce, since condition of women in Indian society has not changed an Inch. The coercive dominating attitude of men against the women has made them submissive to men in every field. In urban area most of the families between age group of 18 to 25 years females are more educated than males even then the higher educated wife has to act on the tune of her lower educated husband.

The practical happenings in a large number of family depict the coercive state of domination of husband over a wife. If one studies the proceedings of divorce cases, he will come to know the degree of cruelty is practical upon the women. Education alone cannot save the women from men's atrocities, here is an instance of a rape case committed by a blood relation in Sehore District of Madhya Pradesh upon a girls hostel student recently. Despite the higher literacy rate of women than men in India a UNICEF report confirms that among the entire world's population of prostitutes or flesh market, Indian ratio is 6:6 (Dainik Jagran 4th April, 2001). We frequently read in newspaper the police atrocities on women like rape in custody, nude parade etc.

All the above descriptions direct to conclude that education alone cannot improve the status of women.

(f) Role of Media

It is evident from the world history of renaissance that media plays an unequivocally important role to change the social environment and history of human race. This media when pays a partisan role the history changes un-noticed to the artificial state. This is the theory, the Indian media adopted in the case of depicting picture of Indian women. Media over emphasise in highlighting the weakness of women. Whenever a case of women's depression or derogation comes to the notice of media it sarcastically gives colour to the story in such a way that the public amuse on the undignified impulses of the women displayed in the media report. Our Indian mentality is so poor that no body takes pains to reach the truth either in imagination or physical verification of the incident. Media is very perfect to articulate the instances to hide the truth and vindicate the falsified aspects of it. In this way woman character is blemished before the public so that a rational view of public goes against the reputation of women thereby making them always subjugated before the men. The media report some times reflects the character of women in ridiculous way so that common intention goes against women's character. Thus when any atrocity is committed upon a woman by a man the woman stands on the discredited state. Media also fabricates amusing stories at the cost of women's dignity. The general picturesque of women by media allure the male to commit ravaging act against women whereby, women remain as the puppet in the hands of reputed & notorious men with the hope of escaping with reputation unstained. But such an act on the part of woman derogates her further. In this context it will not be exaggeration to say that media to a great extent distort the image and reputation of women in Indian environment. Most of the disgruntled women are prey in the hands of media. Good quality and genius of women are not properly high-lighted to enable them to earn reputation but easily goes against it. This is because the media personnel are the tools in the hands of corrupt aristocrats and politicians.

(g) Role of Film Industries

Film industries and advertising agencies' role to lower the dignity of women in Indian society is not a less. The fashion show, beauty contest and other physical features display in India are inadvertently over emphasised by business magnates with the help of media. The Film industry to attract public demand create obscure scenes on woman character. Repeated display of sexy pose by the film industry in cinema not only lower the dignity of women but also encourage men to commit offences. Thereby the young women are misguided to be attractive towards modeling and dancing in the aspiration to be promoted to Heroine. Model is though an artful performance and a talented work but it creates feminish and servile attitude in women. The women develop in themselves a sense of self beautification and lose other talents capable of rebutting the superiority of manhood. The present trend of women participating in beauty contest, modeling and acting in cinema have made them more or less to feel that they are creature of God on the earth to appease men. They being a matter of fiddling consider them to be an amorous object for men. They never compare them with men to earn reputation. On the contrary they become more and more concerned about the tactic they can employ to draw attention of men. Film industries are exploiting women to be a commercial object out of which millioners earn profits for their own betterment. There area many obscene pictures of women in advertising material which diminish the prestige of women in society. I don't know what impresses the public when a sample item of new products is advertised for sale by a woman, whether the product or the beauty or the artful movement of the lady? It is observed that majority of spectators draw their attention towards the impulsive artful appearance of the lady. Thus we can more or less form an opinion that beauty of the model appeals to the public and not the quality of product. That is why almost all the advertising agency prefer to employ beautiful young ladies in advertisement programs. This directly creates a sense among people to adore women as the source of amusement. Naturally the women do not care to develop their personality in other fields but to become beauty conscious. As a result it becomes an inherent character to allure male in every action of a woman. Regarding the question of equal status and rights in society for the women, it needs competitive attitude which is rare in women's character in India till now. Equality therefore cannot be earned by women with men until they themselves strive for the same.

Political Reservation and its meaning

Sardar Gyan Singh (Meerut) mentioned in his article titled "Nari Rajniti Aur Arakshan" that, on 26 July 1997 a Women Seminar on Women - Politics and Reservation was organised at Bombay Bazar in Meerut. The bill of 33% reservation for women though was introduced at the beginning of the Parliament Session in 1997 but it could not be passed because, some MPs suggested modification to grant quota to SC/ST and backward class women proportionate to their population. The women who organized the seminar expressed their displeasure or this suggestion of allotment of SC/ST & BC quota in the bill. They upheld that women are only women (one identity). They also declared that if the Parliament fails to pass the Bill of 33% reservation for women before 15 August 1997, they would resort to agitate on the street.

Now it is matter of concern for the women of SC/ST & BC communities in India that, when our benevolent patriotic political stalwarts are very anxious to give political rights to women so that they can improve the status of women, then what is harm if proportionate quota is allotted to SC/ST & BC according to population. The declaration and expression of anguish by women in the seminar of Bombay Bazar at Meerut can be considered as the result of perpetration of savarn ruling class because, on the one hand they consider SC/ST & BC women as women but cannot give then their dues.

In reality our upper caste leaders do not want to give equal right to women nor do they want to improve the status of women in society. This 33% reservation for women has a different intention. It is worthy of mentioning here a statement of a lady (Chandra Prabha Solanki) of the Seminar held at Meerut. She said, "I consider women's demand for reservation a wrong notion, because the reality is that the reservation for SC has not benefited the dalits as only the shrewd and affluent dalits have been benefitted by it. Similarly reservation for women will benefit the savarn shrewd and rich ladies. The common women will not be benefited. Therefore we should demand for all round facilities for development."

The statement of Prabha Solanki gives vent to the real intention of the political magnates. The intention behind the woman's reservation is to capture parliament by installing upper caste women by reducing the reserved seats for SC/ST. The present state of Parliament compel them to formulate policies and programme taking into consideration the interest of lower castes people. But if they can form the absolute majority by their own men then they can fulfil their desire by depriving 85% population of India (SC/ST/BC & Minority) whom they consider their born enemy.

This reality has been clearly proved in the same Seminar by instigating two little girls to say that, by giving reservation to SC/ST & BC illiterate uncivilized women in politics and public administration should the nation go to dog?

The upper caste former Speaker of the Lok Sabha B. Rai has vehemently supported the women's reservation but supported allotment of proportionate quota to SC/ST & BC. Whenever the sufferers of backwardness demand their right the manuwadi elements oppose it either on the pretext of unity or religion. When our generous savarn women consider that woman are all one, there is no distinction then why they perpetrated innocent girls to abuse dalit and backward class women calling illiterate and uncivilized. Suppose the reservation bill was introduced by BJP with a generous thought of providing equal right to improve the condition of women then proposal for allotment of proportionate quota according to population to SC/ST & BC should have been accepted by them. But when it is vehemently opposed at every level upto their reach, it is crystal clear that in the name of women they want to bag the seats for savarn politicians. Savarn women only will get the chance to be elected by context since backward women are still not in a position to compete with upper castes women, not because of their lack of capability and intelligence but because of their lack of unfair means like criminal force, money, immoral practices and shrewdness to apply.

Women themselves are confused about what they are going to achieve out of the reservation. Savarn women if succeed in getting 33% reservation, have to submit to the cruelty of partymen of their own caste. They will have to work as proxy of the male. Their independent opinion will have no say. But without reservation when a woman wins a poll she can maintain her entity to a larger extent. Reservation also will play all those defective roles which they described to refute the suggestion of allotment of quota. Even if 33% reservation without quota for SC/ST & BC women is allowed, capable and intelligent woman leaders, who really love the country will not find place in parliament because the vaidik politicians appreciate stooges and become worst inimical to able personalities.

Present Hindu political tendency is never a women's supportive one. Hindu religious doctrine teaches to make the women their slaves. This has already been explained under heading "Position of women in Hindu society". If these politicians really respect the women they should have first discarded those religious taboos and teaching which degrade worsen before men. The Hindu religion teaches women to worship men and to be always busy for the comfort of their husbands. Hindu religious philosophy teaches:

"Pujiye Vipra Sheel Gun Heena
Na Hee Sudra Gun Gyan Praveena
Dhol, Gavar sudra Pashu Naree
Ye Hain sab taran ke Adhikari".

Upper caste Hindu political leaders have the same view that is why, they will not treat the women colleagues with respects. This reservation will give them opportunity to strengthen the upper caste in parliament. They will be able to pass the bill easily in parliament with full support, despite the facts that the bill may be against the interest of majority population of the country. Therefore, women's Reservation Bill can be termed as Second Device to establish permanent supremacy of upper caste, the first one being Review of Constitution. The provisions of the existing constitution prevent the upper caste ruling class from doing arbitrary act and its amendment is also not easy for them because of reserved seats for SC/ST in parliament. Hence if 33% reservation can be given to women without allocating seats categorically for SC/ST & BC, 1/3rd majority will easily be with them. Thereby they will be able to amend the constitution according to their whims. When one demand quota in Women's Reservation Bill the savarn women oppose it on the plea that women have no separate identity, all are women only. But where this advocacy vanish when a Hindu woman hate a Muslim, Kori, Chamar, Bhangi, Mushar or Mahar. Why they cannot seat together and eat together? When a question of right arise this shrewd section wants to encroach upon the rights of others on the pretext of equality and similar identity.

An important question may arise here that, were not our constitution makers competent to examine & understand the Indian society? If they were learned and expert politicians then why the provision of reservation for women was not incorporated in the largest constitution of the world when provisions of reservation for SC/ST and even BC were incorporated. If our predecessor politicians thought it expedient for the country then they would have done it since there were many renowned woman politicians very active like Sarojini Naidu, Vijay Laxmi Pandit, Sushila Kaur, Hansa Mehta etc. at that time. Even a woman Prime Minister remained continuous in power over 10 years but never felt its requirement.

Women are not outside the caste hence the caste quota served the women's interest. However, if our politicians are so concerned about the interest of women they should provide reservation according to the caste quota or the reservation should be given out of residual seats after allotment of reserved quota to SC/ST/BC & Minority. In this context I would like to warn the SC/ST/BC & minority about the real intention of Women's Reservation Bill. Draw your attention to the parliamentary events of the past; when Dr. B.R. Ambedkar was Law Minister he brought a Hindu Code Bill, this bill was clarion call for emancipation of women from the cluster of man's atrocities. The bill incorporated enormous rights for women like equal right to wife and sons on father's property, marriage according to own choice, divorce, adoption of child by widow and so on. But not a single Indian women of that time have supported the bill and now their present generation is shouting for reservation. It is all farce show to deceive majority population.

Merits and Demerits of Women's Reservation Bill

In the succeeding paragraphs the merits and demerits of the women's reservation have been discussed in the context of Government's intention and its implication upon the majority population in India. The points discussed have to be taken into consideration by the readers keeping in view the larger interest of major population and unity, integrity and prosperity of the Nation as a whole.

(a) Merits

Merits of this Women's Reservation Bill as per my conscience and belief, go to the ruling class. This reservation will make the upper caste permanent ruler of the country. Majority in parliament can be formed by the upper castes by placing their candidates on compulsory 33% seats. The women will get chance to excel in politics. The reservation will ensure their participation in formulation of laws of the country. The interest of the women population could be protected. But this is the virtuality of the women's reservation in principle. Practically the upper caste ruling class specially Brahmins who introduced varnashram in society to become the permanent ruler will be benefitted. Whatever they lost during British regime and after independence, will soon be restored back by their one act play of supremacy in Parliament. Gradually the allies of Brahmin will also lose their dominant role in Government of the country. Though people belonging to many castes who consider themselves superior to SC/ST will find some opportunity to sit in parliament but will soon find themselves under the claws of Brahmanism. The strategy of government is devising though initially will benefit all upper castes but in the long run the Brahmins will be benefitted. This bill is the primitive stage of establishing Brahman Raj in India. Other upper castes will gradually be adversely affected after some time as is evident from the past history of Aryan.

Women's reservation drastically curtails the rights of SC/ST & BC & minority and protect the absolute interest of upper castes. All those women who vehemently advocated in favour of women's reservation are savarn and are well versed to deceive others. Real intention of caste Hindu is not to give reservation to women but to lead their own women ahead to capture and control administrative machinery and impose slavery upon women as prevailed in the past.

(b) Demerits

Reservation for women without allotment of quota for SC/ST/BC and minority will not be beneficial to all women but only to a particular class. Women are not equal in every class. The dalit women have not yet received the basic education to improve their personalities. An illiterate woman cannot compete with a literate. Similarly dalit women being economically deprived can also not compete with an affluent woman. A beautiful woman cannot always be defeated by a moderate beautiful or ugly woman. The conditions of dalits/ ST/BC section of women are worst than that of a upper caste Hindu woman. Upper caste women are educationally advanced, they are more beautiful because of their comfortable life free from hard labour, protection from sun and rain and possession of modern appliances of comfort and rest. These inequalities will never allow any benefit of equal reservation to SC/ST & BC women. Dalit women cannot incur expenditure for beautification and development of delicacy. Thus they cannot develop their health properly and look ugly. Political parties as a general trend enrol beautiful and glamarous women candidates, as such women of the backward classes can hardly stand against the savarn women in competition. On the other hand money gives men of the modern days all the courage & strength to undertake any venture, which dalit/ST/BC women lack. Thus savarn women find themselves in better position to defeat the dalits in every field.

The prevailing untouchability in India makes the dalit/ ST women mentally feeble in front of savarn women hence equitable reservation for them will be meaningless. Education which has the most important role to help them reach at the peak of advancement, is lacking in dalit women. As stated earlier the educationally, economically and socially backward women cannot properly comprehend the meaning of policies/ programmes decided by the party high command. Hence the interest of their own community or class cannot be safeguarded by them even if they find a place in party or in parliament.

On the other hand when quota for SC/ST/BC and minority women is not allotted, almost all the seats will be contested by savarn women suppressing the rights of others and finally bagged by them. Consequently the parliament will be captured by savarn. Even if the caste Hindu legislators be pleased to improve the status of women, they will take into consideration only the interest of savarn women and not for the common category. Normally men's atrocities are suffered by low caste women but they never get justice because they have no representative of their own in Assemblies and Parliament to safeguard their interest.

As stated earlier woman is not a caste and Indian society is caste ridden. Therefore, all women cannot be taken at par. Their problems are different in one caste from that of another caste. Hence uniform treatment as regard reservation will not help lower caste and minority community women to ameliorate their grievances. Castism in India occupies every field of human activities. Hence women's progress in the field of education, employment, economy, socio-culture and politics depends upon the progress of their own caste. As such if the caste based quota is not allotted to women, lower caste women's interest cannot be protected against the prejudices of savarn women and men. Low castes women's position can only be improved if they themselves can seat in parliament to high-light their problems.

Reservation for women without allocation of quota to SC/ST/BC & minority women will certainly defeat the aim for improvement of common women and make a permanent supremacy of higher caste women over lower castes and minority. It will not at all prevent atrocities upon women in lower strata of society by men of every class or caste.

One

Women: Law and Legal Procedure

After independence of the country the supreme law of the land "the Constitution of India" which was drafted by a special committee of experts, political magnates, learned men and luminaries of the time provides many provisions to safeguard the interests of women. The modernization of the country in the face of world civilization had made the political and administrative experts to think over the role of women in shaping the civilization of the country. Therefore, according to their past experience and the foresight on political phenomena based on the prevailing situation, had recorded their opinions and provided certain safeguards and privileges which can be discussed as follows:—

Before we talk about the special provisions relating to women in our constitution we have to bear in mind the prospects which induced our constitution makers to provide those special articles. The prospectives which our politicians and law-makers thought of India were reflected or incorporated in the Preamble of the Constitution. Here one thing must be clear to readers that, *Preamble* is the theme of Statute as like "face is the index of mind". Preamble gives the clear view, what our constitutional pundits have done and wanted to do. Now let us see what they have given us to possess to rule a sovereign country. We find the statement of eminent legal experts of Lucknow University Dr. V. N. Shukla in his explanatory book on "Constitution of India" about the Preamble as under—

"The Preamble to the Constitution sets out the aims

and aspirations of the people of India and these have been translated in the various provisions of the Constitution. The objectives before the Constituent Assembly were to constitute India into a Sovereign Democratic Republic and to secure its citizens justice, equality and fraternity. The ultimate aim of the makers of the Constitution was to have a Welfare State and an egalitarian society projecting the aims and aspirations of the people of India, who made the extreme sacrifice for attainment of the country's freedom".[1]

The above statement of the legal expert make us to understand that our country is ruled on the principle of Sovereign Democratic Republic with a view to establish a welfare State which will make endeavour to provide its citizens with justice, equality and brotherhood. When the basic and fundamental principle of government is democratic republic then rights of the female population cannot be undermined because in democracy, population play an important role and our Constitution does not give any right to any authority to discriminate population based on sex. Thus women population have a significant role in democracy. But to make the democratic state functioning smooth and progressive, women should be capable to discharge their responsibilities properly in democratic role. Therefore, they need to be properly developed side by side with male population.

In this context our constitution makers have taken considerable pains to examine their position in society of the past and present exhaustively and then determined certain ways and means to equalize them in future to male and laid down certain special provisions in the Constitution. These provisions are :—

(i) Equality before law. (Art. 14)

(ii) Prohibition of discrimination on grounds of religion, race, caste, sex or place of birth. (Art. 15)

(iii) Equality of opportunity in matters of public employment. (Art. 16)

(iv) Protection of certain rights regarding freedom of speech, movement, religion etc. (Art. 19)

(v) Protection of Life and personal liberty. (Art. 21)

(vi) Prohibition of traffic in human beings and forced labour. (Art. 23)

(vii) State to secure a social order for promotion of welfare of the people. (Art. 38)

(viii) Right to work, to education and to public assistance in certain cases. (Art. 41)

(ix) Provision for just and humane conditions of work and maternity relief. (Art. 43)

Equality before law in Art. 14 of the Constitution implies a declaration of equality of all persons within the territory of India, it has the national effect of English common law i.e. absence of any special privilege in favour of any individual. Legally it means, every person whatever his rank or position be, is subject to the jurisdiction of the ordinary courts. One of the prominent legal expert of English Law has explained the legal concept of the word "equality" as follows :—

> "With us every official, from the Prime Minister down to a constable or a Collector of taxes, is under the same responsibility for every act done without any legal justification as any other citizen".[2]

The constitution makers have laid down the law in Art. 14 and the language used says – "The state shall not deny to any person equality before the law or the equal protection of the laws within the territory of India". So the article provides two distinct phrases "Equality before law" and "equal protection of law", as a layman can construe. But our legal experts have different view, they say the second phrase is the deduction of the first.

The Constitutional experts have construed the article with the guiding principles that, all persons and things similarly conditioned shall be treated alike both in privileged and liabilities imposed. The above principles guide us to conclude in the context of women's position before law equal to that of men. The women have the same right with men if both have the same status and circumstances whereas, this right was not granted to women according to the ancient Hindu Law or other personal laws in India. Indian women as I have stated earlier, according to religious obligations, are placed in submissive condition before men. This aspect of discrimination on women did not permit them to develop themselves; as a result the society and entire nation was affected.

To bring change in the status of women in modern age our democrats have devised the system of law in the administration of justice giving equal rights, to be treated alike with men, so that the population of the country become self-conscience and developed. Now-a-days the position of women even without any special privilege in politics is far better than that of the past, when there was no such law on Indian land. However, we find the laid down principles of the apex court that, equal treatment to unequals is as bad as unequal treatment to the equals. The rule of the law under Art. 14 is that, like should be treated alike and unlike should be treated differently.[3] As a matter of fact, all persons are not alike or equal in all respects. Here we have a point to be understood that, the judicature accept that Indian public are not equal in all respects and justice cannot be given on equal term to all, only the equal can be treated alike in law.

From the above guiding principles of justice we very well can infer that, women of this country cannot be always treated alike even with women, because, the circumstances they live in, are not same with all. But they can avail similar rights with men even, if the circumstances are same. Thus the question of reservation in politics in no case can be beneficial or helpful to improve the status or safeguard the interests of low caste women. Caste discrimination in Indian Society is a devil den against equality, and that cannot be demolished by giving special rights to women in politics. Despite all possible measures provided in constitutional law, the supreme law of the land, the male population have not yet become equal since the equality before law is limited to the equals and not provided to unequals either of circumstances or status. In the context of the construction advanced by the judicature and legal experts of the country, the improvement in the status of women to bring equality, special privilege should be given to women based on the reasons for inequalities. These reasons are mostly, lack of education, economic austerity religious taboos and the very vast caste discrimination. Till such time the sociologists, historians and philosophers of excellent reputation have not considered the political representation as an essential element to bring change in women's status.

We have to remember that our constitution aims at establishment of a welfare State and to do welfare to its subjects, at the same time we happen to be with the interpretation given or the inference drawn by the law courts. In one of judicial decision, the court has laid down the principles as under:—

> "In fact, public welfare requires that persons, property and occupations be classified and be subjected to different and appropriate legislation. Government is not a simple thing. If encounters and must deal with the problems which come from persons in an infinite variety of relations. Classification is the recognition on the relations and, in making it a legislature must be allowed a wide latitude of discretion and judgement."[4]

The principle of equality, as mentioned in preceding paragraphs, does not mean that every law must have universal application for all persons who are not by nature, attainment or circumstances in the same position. But the Article 14 forbids class legislation and accepts classification or differentiation which are based on reasonable grounds of distinction.[5]

As regards classification, the principle laid down by law courts for administration of justice stipulates that the classification must be reasonable to be valid and it should fulfil two conditions to satisfy reasonableness:—

(1) The classification must be founded on an intelligible differentia which distinguishes persons or things that are grouped together from others left out of the group and

(2) The differentia must have a rational relation to the object sought to be achieved by the statute in question.

Taking into consideration the legal aspect of classification we can very well declare that, Indian women population suffer varied distinctions in them which a layman can observe in the contexts of any particular object to achieve. For example if any law is enforced to bring economic equality among the women, we are confronted with the question of classification because we find women in varied circumstances; thus the same law to govern all the women needs classification. As a woman from a landless family cannot achieve the object with the same privilege which are provided to a woman of bureaucrat family. Similarly a down caste women needs separate and special facility to improve her educational standard in comparison to a woman of higher caste or Brahmin family. Thus if any government feels that political reservation for women without classification can bring equality and improve their status, will be a myth. But the present BJP led NDA government of India is vehemently advocating the same.

Under Article 15 of the Constitution law has been framed to deter discrimination of citizens by the Government's executive, judiciary and the legislature based on religion, race, caste, sex or place of birth. The second clause of the article is to remove any restriction, disability and liability to approach any place of public entertainment public places maintained wholly or party out of public fund and dedicated to use of the public, based on religion, race, caste, sex etc. This law implies that the women have no disability or restriction in approaching the public place of entertainment and use of public property. According to this law women have the same rights as that of men. This right has made the women to feel equal to the status of men, as there is no bondage on their movement and use of public places. Without these laws they would have been at the mercy of male domination as directed in their religious orders or dicta.

The aspect of untouchability in society which were in force intensively in the past has been removed by this provision of article 15. Despite enforcement of this provision of law even after 52 years, the social phenomena provides us instances of disability and restriction on members of the Scheduled Castes and Scheduled Tribes. They still are treated as socially disabled by many sections of the society. The religious edicts have made the women disabled in many respects. Even then, if we consider all women equal, there will be a big force. Though men and women are given the equal rights by the provisions of Indian Constitution but in actual practice the men and women of one caste of class are treated with discrimination by other castes. Thus besides being provided with right to equality under the Art. 14 and removal of all disabilities and restrictions all male or female are not equal among them. Even women of the same religion and place of birth are treated differently if they belong to different castes. Thus women of India are victims of caste systems. Therefore, uniform policy of reservation for women in politics may not at all be beneficial for all women. On the contrary inequality and exploitation will increase day by day. When equal facility or privilege will be given to population of different groups or class having vast differences, the inequality will inevitably be increased. The rich will be richer and educated will be more educated. On the other hand poor will be poorer and illiterate will remain dull. The political reservation if granted uniformly to women without classification or distinction, the lower caste, poor and illiterate will never be able to enjoy this privilege and improve themselves. But our present government is insisting on the device.

Although clause 3 of the Art. 15 of the constitution authorizes the State for making special provision for the advancement of women and children and clause 4 of the said article authorizes the State to make special provision for socially and educationally backward classes, our government is not following the same. Even the apex court in several decisions had upheld that the caste of a group of person cannot be the sole or predominant factor though it may be a relevant test for ascertaining whether a particular class is backward or not.

Backwardness under Art. 15(4) must be social and educational and that social backwardness is, in the ultimate analysis, the result of poverty. The occupation and place of habitation could not be the relevant factors in determining social backwardness. Thus castes and tribes placed in the Schedule for special privileges for advancement had due consideration to be treated differently from the general class.

Accordingly, the parliament or legislature while framing any statute which may effect all, should have the special privileges for so called classified backward classes. If such provisions are not included in the statute, that statute violates the rights granted to weaker section under clause 4 of the Art. 15. In this pretext, the present attempt of the BJP led NDA government to provide reservation for women in politics is a step further to enhance inequalities between the upper castes women and lower castes women, because by granting such a privilege to women the higher castes women who are already in better position in all respects than the women of the backward classes, scheduled castes and scheduled Tribes, will be in far greater state of superiority and equality among the women will be a farce and myth in reality. By this act the over all inequality will be embedded in Indian society, which is already inequal for centuries.

The preamble of the Constitution of India aims at bringing equality into the Indian public, whereas, the present government strive to negate the aims and objectives of our constitution makers. The common public have to take serious view about such acts of the representative government of

India because, the results of the government actions have to be endured by the public for several years.

There is further evidence of legal recognition of inequality in Indian society. When the inequality exists in society then it is inevitable to exist inequality in same sex and caste. Thus the women of India cannot be termed equal in every respect. Consequently, our constitution makers, the makers of the supreme Law of the land, with a view to remove inequality have provided special privilege for certain sections of population of India and classified them as Scheduled Castes and Scheduled Tribes. Yet they were not satisfied instantly by providing special privilege under constitution and made an attempt to find out further inequality and disabilities in any other groups of people in comparison to mainstream of people found to be on the surface layer of developed people by contemplating under Article 340 the appointment of a commission to investigate into the conditions of socially and educationally backward classes and such other matters as may be referred to the commission by the President.

In fact, our President had exercised his power under this provision twice, first in 1953 under the Chairmanship of Kaka Kalelkar and the second time in 1978 under the Chairmanship of B. P. Mandal. Both the commissions had taken caste as the dominant if not the sole factor in determining the backwardness and no decision could yet be taken because, each State is experimenting different tests influenced by social and political considerations as well as judicial decision.[6]

However, it cannot be denied that there is backwardness in population besides Scheduled Castes and Scheduled Tribes. As such remaining population excluding Scheduled Castes and Scheduled Tribes are also not equal. Therefore, implementation of uniform rules or policies of the government will not be conducive to orient equality. In several cases the apex court of the country has either rejected or upheld the backwardness of certain classes of people while examining the basis of classification. But in no case it has been confirmed by the courts of laws and the legal experts of the country that, there is no backwardness in people except Scheduled Castes and Scheduled Tribes. And the apex court in the case of P. Rajendran Vs. State of Mysore has accepted the criteria adopted by the Mysore Govt. for ascertaining the backwardness of a class and it upheld the test of backwardness, which was predominantly based on caste. It said—

"Now if the reservation in question had been based only on caste and had not taken into account the social and educational backwardness of the caste in question, it would be violative of Article 15 (1). But it must not be forgotten that a caste is also a class of citizens and if the caste as a whole is socially and educationally backward, reservation can be made in favour of such a caste on the ground that it is socially and educationally backward class of citizens within the meaning of Article 15 (4)."[7]

Taking into consideration the above principles of law laid down by the apex court, women's reservation in politics without taking into consideration the prevailing discrimination among them, will be unjustified and against the ultimate objects of the constitutional law of the land. In its practical effect, the inequality in women population as well as in the entire population will accelerate rapidly. Thus political reservation without special privilege to SC, ST and OBC will not be conducive.

The laws laid down under Article 16 of the Constitution also affirm that there is differences among the citizens. Therefore, provisions of reservation for socially and educationally backward class of citizens are made to remove the inequality. When the supreme law of the land, the Constitution of India prescribes reservations for certain classes of citizens, we can take it as granted that, there exists inequality among the citizens and special care should be taken to remove the inequality. Here it is worthy of mention that, the principles laid down by Supreme Court with majority view in the case of

State of Kerala Vs. N. M. Thomas, regarding relationship of Articles 14, 15 and 16 that,

> "Article 16 (1) permitted reasonable classification and did not forbid the State from rendering social justice to backward classes. Its opinion rested on the promise that, the impugned exemption had been granted only for a temporary period. Chief Justice Ray stated categorically that Articles 14, 15 and 16 form part of a string of constitutionally guaranteed rights supplementing each other. Article 16 was explained as an incident of guaranteed equality contained in Article 14 and therefore, permitted reasonable classification of the employees in matters relating to employment or appointment. Article 16(1) using the expression "equality" made it relatable to all matters of employment and permitted classification on the basis of object and purpose of law or State action except classification involving the discrimination prohibited by Article 16(2); Article 16(4) indicated, one of the methods of achieving equality embodied in Article 16 (1) and explained that classification on the basis of backwardness did not fall within Art. 16 (2)".[8]

The entire expression of the views of the judges as mentioned above have one common and predominant point of consideration is that the law framed by our legislators and constitution and the views possessed by our learned judges admit that, there is inequality in Indian citizens and the government has to make all possible endeavour to remove this inequality. Naturally we understand and should; there is inequality even among the women themselves. Their equality with men can be expected only when they themselves are equal.

The rights granted under Art. 19 of the Constitution make endeavour to improve the status of women to equate with men. The personal laws in force in Indian system of jurisprudence, the ancient customs and traditions did not permitted women alike men to freedom of speech, form association and move freely. But the laws have been framed under constitution with a view to bring equality and improve the status of citizens of India and also to give opportunity to women for their self-development. Thus law and justice have admitted that Indian citizens are not equal in every respect and provided discriminatory provisions of law to bring equality by way of reservations to weaker sections i.e. socially and educationally backward classes.

It is a matter of great concern for the common people of India to examine the government's proposals for laying down any rule or law which has implication upon them. Thus the recent government bill of political reservation for women should have drawn the attention of public to substantiate, whether it will be beneficial for women at par or by this bill the ruling party wants to establish supremacy of a particular class. It is very clear from the notional effect of reservation without classification at the present state of unequal society that, women of higher castes, who are almost educated, culturally advanced economically sound and already have an inclination towards politics, will be benefitted. On the other hand women belonging to Scheduled Castes, Scheduled Tribes and other backward classes, who are socially, educationally and economically poor will remain far behind in the political fray if they are not given special privilege among women in the proposed bill. Now at the present situation we can hope and see the public reaction on this bill. Even if the bill becomes a law in the long run when inequality will be multiplied in society a massive movement against this law will be imminent.

The position of our women as the laws of the land admit is that, a woman now-a-days can live with human dignity with necessities of life like-adequate nutrition, clothings, shelter, facilities for reading, writing and expressing and freely moving. Art. 21 of the Constitution provide protection of life and personal liberty. The article runs as under—

> "No person shall be deprived of his life or personal liberty except according to procedure established by law".

While interpreting the above article in the judgement in various cases the learned judges have given different explanation by which the citizens of India are not only protected against deprivation of life and liberty but also given certain facilities of life and liberty. The interpretation given by justice Bhagwati in the case of Francis Coralie Vs. Union Territory of Delhi is noteworthy to examine the position of Indian citizens which the law permits. Justice Bhagwati held—

> "We think that the right to life includes the right to live with human dignity and all that goes along with it, namely, the bare necessaries of life such as adequate nutrition, clothing and shelter over the head and facilities for reading, writing and expressing oneself in diverse forms, freely moving about and mixing and comingling with fellow human beings".[9]

From the above statement of the learned judge it becomes clear to us that, the legal position of Indian citizens are quite well, whatever may be the practical condition. Thus position of Indian women is also good according to legal aspect, although reality in Indian society is quite different. Yet it is evident from the comparative studies of medieval time and the present time that, women's position has improved a lot. Now in India, it is the fundamental right of every one in the country to live with human dignity free from exploitation. The right to live with human dignity enshrined in Art. 21 is strengthened by the Directive Principle of State Policy.

Under the provision of Art. 23 the citizens are protected against traffic in human beings and begar and other similar forms of forced labour. Traffic in human beings means to deal in men and women like goods, such as to sell or let or otherwise disposed. It also includes traffic in women and children for immoral and other purposes.[10] To make the women free from such atrocities and exploitation the suppression of Immoral

Traffic (Prevention) Act 1956 has been enacted by the Parliament under Art. 35 of the Constitution of India for the purpose of punishing acts resulting traffic in human beings. Though slavery has not been expressedly mentioned under Art. 23 but there is no doubt that the expression "traffic in human beings" would cover it.[11] Thus the present social condition of women and children in comparison to past has improved a lot by providing legal protection formulating preventive or deterrent law by the Parliament. However, we cannot firmly uphold that the real social position of women is equal to position guaranteed by law.

While examining the legal aspect of women's social position in independent India we have to keep in mind the comments offered by Hon'ble Member of the Drafting Committee in Constituent Assembly, Mr. K. M. Munshi—

> "Look at Hindu Law; you get any amount of discrimination against women; and if that is part of Hindu Religion or Hindu religious practice, you cannot pass a single law which would elevate the position of Hindu women to that of men".[12]

The above comments of the Hon'ble member make us to understand that personal laws discriminate women in comparison to men and restrict their independence and have very limited scope for self improvement to equate with men in society. On the other hand though the constitution of India provides right to equality for all citizens yet it permits and accepts the personal laws, to govern the citizens in many respects according to their religious traits; thus position of women in their respective religious community is lower than men and submissive to men. Accordingly we can assert that, despite our Constitution makers' efforts women of India in almost all religions remain subordinate to men.

Although Article 38 of the Constitution lays down that State shall strive to promote the welfare of the people by securing and protecting social order in justice, social, economic and political life and strive to minimize the inequalities in income, status, facilities and opportunities not only amongst individuals but also amongst groups of people residing in different areas or engaged in different vocations, the inequalities have not yet been removed. The Indian women have not yet reached the position of men in society. Women still lack many rights to avail in practice. Thus even legal protection could not improve the position of women in society.

Again we find legal provision under Art. 41 of the Constitution to improve the condition of citizens. According to this article the State is supposed to make effective devices for citizens for securing the right to work, to education and public assistance in cases of unemployment, old age, sickness and disablement. According to this provision we can conclude that when right to work and right to education have been the part of Directive Principles of State Policy to provide all citizens, keeping in view the economic capacity of the State, the position of women in society will be improved. But the practical experience shows that though women are being provided with job and education yet they have not come to the state of competing with men due to certain discrepancies of personal laws and socio-cultural tradition. Despite all efforts though legally women seem to be equal to men but caste distinction and religious edicts have kept the women within certain limitation, thereby arrested their development.

Even the laws framed by the legislature recognize some distinctions and inequalities in society as far as women are concerned. The social customs and traditions could not yet be ignored by laws to bring equality among the people either of different sex or of the same sex and caste. Section 132 of the Civil Procedure Code lays down that, women who according to the customs and manners of the country, ought not to be compelled to appear in public shall be exempted from personal appearance in the court. This clearly indicates that, even all women of the country cannot be treated alike in law; and our constitution proposed equality before law and to provide special privileges to certain weaker sections to bring equality. Thus we have sufficient evidence with us to prove that inequality still prevails in Indian Society and at this stage uniform rule of reservation for women will not be beneficial for all women irrespective of social, economic and educational back-ground and the caste they belong. Hence to bring equality and to ameliorate the miseries, if political reservation for women is considered inescapable, it should invariably be discriminatory based on caste classification and backwardness. Specific quota should be fixed for women of Scheduled Caste, Scheduled Tribes, Other backward class and minority to ensure that political benefits are not bagged only by the elite group or higher castes or the existing developed sections. To ensure equitable distribution of political power and benefits among the women, specific quota should be allotted to weaker sections so that the women of these sections can avail the opportunity and keep pace with the elite section.

References

1. V.N. Shukla's *Constitution of India*, 9th Ed. p. A 24.
2. *Ibid.*, 1994 Ed., p. 37.
3. AIR 1990 SC 1607 (V.N. Shukla's Constitution of India 1994 Ed. p. 38).
4. Tinga. Vs. Texas (1940) 310 US 1417.
5. V.N. Shukla's *Constitution of India*, 1994 Ed., p. 38.
6. *Ibid.*, p. 76.
7. *Ibid.*, p. 77.
8. AIR 1976 SC 490 (V.N. Shukla's Constitution of India, 1994 Ed.) p. 89).
9. AIR 1981 SC 746 (V.N. Shukla's Constitution of India, 1994 Ed.) p. 165).
10. Raj Bahadur Vs. Legal Remembrancer, AIR 1953 Cal. 522 (VN Shukla's *Constitution of India*, p. 201).
11. Dubar Vs. Union of India, AIR 1952 Cal. 496.
12. *Constitution of India*, 1994 Ed., by V.N. Shukla, p. 38.

Two

Equality of Rights

Since 18th century there has been a long advocacy throughout the world especially in Western countries for equality of rights to women with men. Women gradually demanded equal rights in every field of human society with men. India also joined this stream in the beginning of 19th Century. Indian woman and the liberal social reformists had deliberate discussion on the roles of women in the development of the nation. As a result reformists, nationalists and elite groups started encouraging women to participate in public life and advocated for equal rights to women with men. The aim of this advocacy was to provide women equal rights with men to bring women to equal footing with men and enjoy:

(a) Political Equality
(b) Legal Equality
(c) Educational Equality
(d) Economic Equality
(e) Social Equality

The present position of women in India in the context of above equalities have been discussed in the succeeding paragraphs with the above headings. However, based on the prevailing situation of India I have discussed the inequalities faced by women based on their sex.

Political Equality of Women

In the modern world women's participation in socio-economic field especially in production, acquiring higher educational, professional and cultural position in society they have grown self consciousness. The various measures taken by the developed and developing countries and growing self-consciousness of women have permitted them to combine family life with the social productive labour. All these things enable the women to participate successfully in the social and political life of the country including public service at all levels. They have become trustworthy of the society in their shouldering the responsibilities, initiative and contribution to the formulation and implementation of the internal and external policies of the state.

The analytical studies carried out by authors of "Women Today" about the women's position in the world, during International Women's Year (1975) declared by UN General Assembly give us the women's political phenomena as follow.

In Bulgaria for example the latest election gave 18.75 per cent of the seats in the National Assembly. In People's Council women made up one-quarter of all elected deputies. In Hungary's National Assembly women secured 23.8 per cent of seats of the deputies and 24.3 per cent of the deputies elected to local Councils. In German Democratic Republic the number of locally elected women officials rose from 53, 000 in 1965 (25.8 per cent of all deputies) to 65, 000 (more than 30 percent of the present total). In Poland among the members of the Sejm (Parliament) elected in 1969 there were 62 women or 13. 5 per cent of the total number of deputies while in the year 1938 there was only one among 208 members of the Sejm. There were three women justices in the Supreme Court of Romania in 1964 and 19 women deputies were elected to Romanian Parliament, whereas in 1975 there were 66 women present in Parliament. The well known Romanian writer Zacharia Stanku writes about the women's progress as under—

> "I can still remember the time when a women would not dare to raise her eyes from the stove and look directly at her husband. But look at her now — every where she holds her head high, affirming herself, speaking out publicly."[1]

Though the present election data in respect of Bulgaria, Hungary, Romania, Poland etc., is not available, it can certainly be expected participation of larger number of women in comparison to the past.

During the election before International women's year, in Mongolia, 99.9 per cent of all eligible women voters voted and a full quarter of those elected were women. Women comprised 21.9 per cent of the deputies in the people's Great Hural-the highest Legislative body in the country. In that period the prestigious post as member of the Presidium of the People's Great Hural, Chairman of the State Committee for Labour and Wages, Deputy ministers of the Health, Education, Foreign Trade, Finance and Communal services were held by women. The highest political post "Prime Minister" was held for a long time by women in India, Bangladesh and Pakistan. In Sri Lanka also the highest Political executive post "the President" was held by women for a longer time.

In the year 1964 ten women were elected deputies to the National Assembly of the Democratic Republic of Vietnam i.e. only 2.5 per cent of the total deputies, whereas in the year 1971 this number raised to 125, i.e., almost 30 per cent of the total. The women's political awareness and initiative was far greater in Vietnam in comparison to other countries during seventies of Twentieth Century. In the Communist Country the women occupied all fields and in all sphere of political life. The active participation of women in economic, social and political activity was accompanied by an increase in the number of those who belonged to trade unions.

In Hungary for example half of all elective posts in trade unions were held by women. Every year women play a greater role in the trade union movement in Cuba.

The women of Socialist countries carryout a tremendous amount of social and political work in mass organizations - the Father Land Front of Bulgaria, the National Front of the German Democratic Republic, the All Poland Committee of the National Unity Front of the Czechoslovak Socialist Republic, the Father Land Front of Vietnam and others.[2]

Legal Equality of Sex

Western Lawyers tend to think that much of the problem of sex discrimination lies in law. The distinctive history of sex inequality in the United States and elsewhere might well justify this view. When women have been subordinated, it has frequently been through law - not merely through old enactment depriving women of the power to vote, to hold property and to enter into contracts but also through current rules involving family law, welfare law and the criminal justice system. (These have been discussed in Becker's 'Politics', Differences and Economic Rights, University of Chicago Legal Forum (1989) 169, 172). But much of sex discrimination lies elsewhere than in law. Often no formal law is responsible for the sexual subordination of women. Sometimes subordination is the result of custom. The statement of Cass R. Sustien, the writer of the essay "Gender, Caste and Law" is noteworthy in this context. She states:—

> "I will not deal herewith the complex issue of what counts as law and what counts as custom. In many developing countries, the line between the two is extremely thin. I follow convention in understanding law, roughly, as the product of the will of some sovereign constituted with law-making power and custom as norms or practices that do not have this sort of authority". The last discussion of this is H. L. A. Hart, "The Concept of Law" (Oxford University Press 1961).[3]

Sometimes sexual subordination is partly the result of the physical power of men. In such cases, it is wrong to think that law is an important casual agent in women's subordination, as the Westerners understand that term. In India the women's atrocities like rape, and physical assaults are the result of men's physical power and law is no way involved. Moreover, there are limits to what can be done through law, even with a properly defined equality principle. Currently, we can find powerful legal guarantees of sex equality in such places as Albania, Czechoslovakia, Greece, Hungary, Portugal, Romania, China and Spain. Do in real sense the women of those countries have equality? Do they have equality in any of the form? Certainly not. Particularly in India legally equality for women with men are not sanctioned so far. Though there are frequent discussion and claims of women for equality with men, no judicial and legislative action has been taken to establish equality. The existing laws of marriage, inheritance and succession of property clearly shows the sex discrimination. Even the Muslim personal law does not sanction women's equality with men. Thus in India legal equality is also not granted to women.

Equality of Education for Women

Civilization of a nation considerably depends upon the development of status of its citizens. Thus it depends also upon the development of women population; because women are involved in shaping and maintenance of family the basic unit of a nation. Development of citizens' personality or status is mainly dependent on educational development. Therefore, women's development is also founded on their education. As a result of world wide women's struggle for equal rights with men Indian women were inspired to demand equal rights. Thus right to education has been provided to them in India also. Now we find Indian women in educational field equal to men. The brilliant doctors, engineers, educationists, writers, historians are in abundance in women population. Now the women enjoy equal opportunities to develop their educational career. The same faculty of education can be opted by women which the men alone opted earlier. This shows that Indian women have opportunities for equal education with men.

Equality of education granted to women has given ample opportunities to them to compete with men for the job and they have succeeded to secure job in the same category and skill with men. Now we find so many females on the top executive, technical and judicial posts. Equal opportunities of education for women have made the Indian women broad-minded, they are no more under viel and shy. Now-a-days Indian women are found in every field of social life. They have also become expert politicians, scientists, executive officers of the highest cadre. Even the police and military services, where were earlier the avenue for men only, are not beyond their reach. Women have proved their competancy with men in these services. Even some of the women in Police and Military services made remarkable record in the world. All these achievements by women were possible only due to the right to equality of education granted to them by law and legislation. Hence we find that Indian women enjoy right to equality of education and this right has raised their status from a hearth maintaining maid to a policy maker and administrator. Now the women throughout the world have understood the value of education in personality development and improving the civilization. Hence they are comparatively gaining lion's share of it than men. Position in India is also the same, women are keeping one step ahead from men in the field of education.

Despite the fact that women's education is indispensable for the national progress and progress of the society, there has been several forms of obstruction on the way of women's education in India. First among the obstructions is social obstruction influenced by the old religious belief and superstitions. Religious dicta of the past for several hundreds year made the women to be fit to household menial job, alert mother, a meek wife ready to work at the beck and call of her husband. The Hindu religious orders make a woman reduced to the position of better half of her husband, which means the wife has to carry out the order of her husband. The women's role in the family remains limited within four walls of the family parameter and does not allow public activity or going to public outside the boundary of home. This traditional edict obstructed women from acquiring education. Due to long run practices of the above traditions women themselves became submerged deep in the blind religious faith and superstitions which have forbidden them from acquiring education. There were all round oppression of women in the society which made the women of shrivel nature. Thus women themselves possessed resisting attitude towards education. Though women's organizations and the reformists were trying to inspire women to join educational institutions, girls and their parents hesitated to get their daughters admitted in schools. Most of the rural people have the belief that women's duties are within the house, outside the home their movement is restricted. One who keeps herself within the premises of the house round the clock and keeps herself under the veil in presence of outsider male is considered most dignified woman and she brings honour to the family. Joining school or stepping outside the premises of home lower their social dignity and brings bad name to the family.

Although the Indian literacy rate shows women's literacy is accelerating more than the men's yet in agrarian dwelling women are discouraged against acquiring education. The sex disparity is a greater resistance in society against the women's education. The males of the rural area are not yet ready to accept women's intellectuality. Thus in the family and society only males are encouraged towards education, on the contrary females are discouraged to this end. Sex based discrimination in society is so forceful that from the very birth of a female child she is deprived of the necessary care and nourishment. As a result the female child fails to develop her mental and physical health to such an extent that she cannot create inspiration and initiative in herself to acquire education. Thus she remains deficient of the potentiality conducive to acquire education. The practical social environment brings out that, even if the girls achieve education after having passed through many social oddities, they fail to receive higher education because of the attitude of male members of the family. I have met with so many instances of the above nature, where girls are debarred by the social trend and the parents, from higher education. There are documentary evidence of female students being much better in education could not pursue higher education, whereas the mediocre male got all sorts of opportunities and privileges to pursue higher education. Parents are found spending lavishly on the education of a boy whose performance is very poor whereas, the brilliant girl is discouraged and deprived of facilities for higher education. It is a clear discrimination of sex which became a part of the human thoughts of the society especially of the rural area. In urban area too the female students have to suffer humiliation and discouragement in family as well as educational institutions. While undergoing higher educational course female students are found to be the victims of oppression of the teachers and male colleagues. Male either students or the teaching staff always look down upon the female students, the former never fails to tease the later.

Due to all the above mentioned behaviour and attitudes female lag behind the male in the race of achieving higher education. Although now-a-days we find females shine in the field of education but the females had to tolerate uncountable opposition and humiliation at the hands of male and the male dominated society.

Economic Equality for Women

The National development is largely attributable to economic status of the citizens. So, the national all round development and potentials are affected adversely if the economic state of citizens is poor. Economic development of the country when attributable to its citizens' economic condition, then both male and female citizens are equally responsible for economic development of the country. Since responsibility is always sufficed with right, the citizens have the right to their economic development. Thus both male and female should have equal right to economic development.

At present in Indian society women have no equal right to economic prosperity. The works connected with economic gains are mostly gendered as male. Females have very limited scope in economic gains. Most of the rich monetary gainful job opportunities are beyond the reach of the females due to traditional way of life and religious injunctions. On the other hand patriarchal pattern of family also hinder the women to compete with men in economic field. But all these disparity and differences in job selection and absorption have adversely affected the national economy as well as the status of women. Since personality development in the modern world largely depends upon the economic improvement, the women can develop their personality and status only when they get equal opportunity for economic development. Thus women need economic equality in society with men.

Economic equality means the women should have the same rights and privilege to secure a job at par with men. The job classification, which so far been in vogue with major technical and skilled fields should cease forthwith, so that women can also enter those employment avenues which were earlier earmarked for male workers. Due to job restrictions females are also debarred from developing their mental faculty, i.e., skill in various fields. Whereas, it has been proved that women are not at all less skilled than men. Therefore, women should be given opportunity to earn money and shoulder the responsibility of economic development of the country by engaging themselves in highly skilled and productive work. As it has been accepted by experts that women engaged in mines, factories and jute mills have shown their excellence in maintenance works and works require prolong patience and constant attention, it will be conducive for the fast development of the country to engage women in all sorts of work. This will improve the economic condition of the woman herself and the family. Family being the foundation of a nation, its economic development will have direct impact upon the national economy. Therefore economic equality of women with men is inevitable in modern days. Until the right to economic equality is granted to women in Indian society all will be farce to say about the improvement of women's status and to make them equal to men. Political rights and special privilege will be a futile effort to improve the condition of women if they are not given the right to economic equality.

For establishment of economic equality in society one must understand what the phrase "economic equality" implies. In the context of improving the women's status and make them equal to men in every sphere of social activity, the phrase means — the women should be given the same job which a man can receive. The women should have the freedom to choose her job outside the four walls of household. They should have the right to claim same remuneration what a man can receive from same employment. They should have the right to receive same nature of 'on the job training' which men receive. Nature of control and supervision on the job should be equal and female should also have the right to exercise control over the employees in equal degree and scale as the male have. In the commercial venture women should have the equal right of decision making with the men. There should be no discrimination on sex in policy making and allocation of task.

Social Equality for Women

In Indian society from the time immemorable the sex disparity or discrimination prevails. Women suffer subordination of men in every sphere of life. In other words, it can be said the customary, traditional and religious cultures and belief have made women like the objects of men's lust and pleasure. Women have to dance to the tune of men's whims. They hardly can enjoy the human rights in male dominated society. The position of women will be very clear to the readers while reading the discussion in chapters 3 and 6 of this book. In the modern world, there is loud cry of women world-wide developed and developing countries for equality and the human rights commission of each country have upheld the women's demand. As such in India too the Government have to look after the interest of women. There is no more chance for the men of the democratic republican country like India to neglect and oppress women. Now the people of the country are morally bound to lookafter the interest of women and help them to lead a prestigious human life.

But there arises a question, when we talk about the women's human right and the right to lead a respectable life in society, that question is — whether woman can lead a respectable life without right to equality? The probable answer is no; women can not expect to lead a peaceful, secured and respectable life in male dominated society without right to equality, i.e., equal rights with men. And right to equality can be expected in society when women improve their status equal to men; for this they need special care and privilege for education employment and establishment of dignity. Social equality though brief in its composition in terms of language but it covers a vast space in social structure. Social equality implies equality in status of education, employment, customary rites religious and cultural performance and no discrimination on caste, sex and colour. But do all these exist in our society? What is the condition of women in our society? The answer is very complicated and hurting. At present our women do not enjoy the right to equality in any field.

Since the country's civilization and national development depend upon the status and morality of its citizens, Indian women should be given the right to social equality. Therefore, women should be given equal right to education, employment, personality development. Thus women's status should be improved to a great extent and it needs social, customary, traditional and religious discrimination on sex to be abolished. Women should be given equal right with men in every field of human activities. Sex-based atrocities should be eliminated from the society. Right to monetary gain and rights to property are very meaningful for the women for development of their status in society. Due to lack of right to property and want of freedom for gainfull employment in public outside the boundary of household made the women dependent on men. Thus the male dominated society has subordinated the female and made them slaves to men's whims in family life. This tendency of the male has adversely affected the civilization of the country.

In the context of International evaluation of the country's development and improvement of civilization women can help a lot. For, in the present state a majority population are left behind who could not contribute adequately to national development due to social-traditional set up and ancient faith on religious injunction. If women are treated equally with men and allowed to participate in public work for nation building and economic improvement of self and family, the country's development would have twice faster than the present condition. Therefore, it is conducive for betterment of the nation as a whole that women are granted right to social equality at par with men.

Sex-based Inequalities

According to Susan Muller Okin, inequalities in sex are as follows :—

In the justice literature, the neglect of women used to be observed by the purportedly generic use of male pronouns and other referents-'mankind' and so on, the rather more insidious practice. The public/domestic dichotomy has serious implications for women. It not only observes intra household inequalities. It also results in the failure to count a great deal of work done by women as work since all is considered "work", what is done for pay, in the public sphere. All the work women do in bearing and rearing children, cleaning and maintaining households, caring for old and sick and contributing in various ways to men's work does not count as work. This is clearly one of those instances in which situation of poor women in poor countries is not qualitatively different from that of most women in rich countries but rather similar or worse. Even in some cases for more of the work done by women in poor countries is rendered invisible not counted or subsumed under men's work. The work of subsistence farming, tending to animals, domestic crafts especially if not for the market and often arduous and extremely time-consuming fetching of water and fuel, are all added to the category of unrecognized work of women. As scholars of development have recently been making clear the multiple inequalities between the sexes in a number of poor countries have not only highly detrimental, but fatal consequence for millions of women. Amartya Sen has recently argued that because of severe sex-based deprivations of various kinds as many as 100 million fewer women exist in the world today, than might normally be expected on the basis of male/female mortality rates in societies.

Susan Muller further mentioned about the justice in family that the devaluation of women's work as well as their lesser physical strength and economic dependence upon men, in turn allows them to be subject to physical, sexual and psychological abuse by their husbands or other male partners. Thus, though most poor women in poor countries work long hours each day, they are often economically dependent on men. This too, is similar to but worse than the situation of many women in richer countries. In both rich and poor countries women who provide the sole economic support for the families often face particular hardship.

Discrimination against women in access to job, pay,

retention and promotion are common to most of the countries. The research on the cases of divorce has revealed various factors of women's socio-economic challenges. Studies conducted in a number of different states confirm the fact that there is indeed a significant difference in socio-economic outcome of divorce for men and women.[4]

References

1. N.A. Kovalsky and Y.P. Blinova "Women Today", p. 93.
2. *Ibid.*, p. 95.
3. Martha Nussbum and Jonathan Glover's "Women, Culture and Development", Clarendon Press: Oxford 1955. p. 355.
4. Martha Nussbum and Jonathan Glover's "Women, Culture and Development", pp. 286-287.

Three

Women's Position In India

General

We may look at the social picture of India in the context of women's position. Women are considered foundation of the human society from every angle. Without the active and significant role of women no family can be imagined. Thus they are the base stone of a nation, family being a unit of it.

The women who are first and foremost ingredient of society and work as the field of production of human race, what is happening with them in human society is a matter of great concern for all. Every body should draw their attention towards them. Here I am reflecting a picture of the society in relation to women depicted by the Family Planning Association of India in a seminar organized by them at Bhopal on 26-2-02. In this three-day workshop seminar his address to members of the field working NGOs the Director Health Services of Madhya Pradesh Dr. Yogiraj Sharma has accepted the report of the Family Planning Association about the death rates of women, (i.e., 100 women every third day) due to complexity of conception and want of maternity-home facilities in Madhya Pradesh. He assured to provide atleast one trained midwife to every village by next year. The Chief guest of the seminar, Justice Gulab Gupta, chairman of the Human Rights Commission emphasized upon education and awareness and said, it is not sufficient to be able to write the name, the women have to be aware in any social utility field". The report and the suggested measures clearly evince that women in Indian society are deprived of many essential amenities and services which they need as part of human rights but our society and administration are least worried about it.

The improvement in status of women depends upon many essential elements, among those most important are education, economic stability, social awareness, religious reform, cultural and customary change and the supermost is the common thoughts of the male population to treat women with equal dignity and respects and to consider them as the inescapable equal complement of men.

The opinion of many thinkers and philosophers have been attributed to the degradation of women in society. The imagination these social thinkers and philosophers reflected in their writings have portrayed the picture of women in human society at a very lower rank in comparison to men with the biological deficiencies and moral instincts. Jean Jacques Rousseau in his second Discourse stated:—

> "In men, the transition from physical to moral love is effected through the operation of the imagination. Imagination which causes so much havoc among us does not speak to savage hearts. Every one waits peaceably for the impulse of nature, yielding to it without choice—and needs satisfied, all desire is extinguished. But alas for this tranquil state gradually men develop the capacity to compare one woman to another and in doing so generate a fantasy of the ideal love object. Women or rather image of women, thereby incite in men amorous passions in excess of man's power of satisfying those passions — and it is in the gap between what may be gratified (the instinct demands of physical love) what is wanted (the idealized objects of moral love) that insatiable desire arises".[1]

The renowned philosopher by this statement wanted to depict the natural features of women to show that the physical passion which otherwise defined as love, in men is arisen by appearance of women. Women therefore is taken to be considered as an object of love, whose presence or even her image incite in men amorous passion which cannot be controlled and satisfied. The philosopher has identified or categorized women as means of satisfying the physical love and idealized object of moral love which create insatiable desires in men. The opinion about the significance of women in human society as drawn by the philosopher can be plainly interpreted or construed that, women is the fondling object for men. He further clarify the above opinion in his statement more deliberately as:—

> "It is through the operations of fantasy; then, that the eroticized self is created; the instinctual savage becomes the desiring subject yearning for ideal objects of love. Natural man gives way to social man, his sexuality shaped in a cultural psycho-drama".[2]

He further says in his book "Emile" (p. 324) "the male is only a male now and again, the female is always a female or at least all her youth; every thing remind her of her sex; the performance of her functions requires a special constitution." This statement contrive to place women in a segregated position in society with all the differences of her physical constitution and remain subjugated by men in all sphere of life. Thus we find many such instances where women are lowered in position in the society by our learned social thinkers generation after generation. The women were not given the opportunity of their development equal to men due to the pre-determination of men dominated society.

The political reservation and the status of women in Indian politics and social ambit can be examined from the statement made by former Sarpanch Kala Bai in a state level meeting of Women Panchayat Representatives held at Bhopal last year (2001). She expressed her experience and deep feelings during her speech. She said— "I do not know what does the "dalit" means? We are called by the name "Chamar" or

"Basode", misbehaved and treated as untouchable. If there happens to be a member from the "Mehtar" community then she is not allowed to enter the Panchayat office or attend meetings. She is not even heard by the Panchayat. How can she be expected of getting decision. Till to date women of her area are compelled to carry human excrements on their head". Ganga Bai of Gundroi village said that, in their village Raghuvanshi is in majority in Panchayat Harijans are supposed to sit separate. Women Sarpanch of Bhatsa Panchayat of Khategaon Tehsil in Dewas district of Madhya Pradesh said during her interview with reporters that male group is creating numerous obstacles in her working. The male panch of her village named Ramanand and Amar Singh demands bribe for share of the cost of any welfare programme to be sanctioned. There are several such story of plight of women Sarpanches and other women officials of the low caste. From all these statements it reveals that women of the lower castes have to face much more adversities in society than the women of higher castes. Higher castes women suffer subordination of men by way of religious dicta, customs, tradition and sexuality, whereas low caste women face first caste disparity in that they are maltreated by women and men both of higher castes then they further suffer the indignation from men of their own community. Thus sex disparity they suffer double in degree in comparison to their counterpart in higher caste. In addition they suffer caste disparity which is wide spread in Indian society. The political privileges given to them do not help them to establish their dignified identity in society, is proved from the statements made by various low caste women Sarpanches and members.

The status of women in Indian society can be examined in the context of treatment they get from male population either from their own kith and kins or from the common public. Quite often we are confronted with hienous acts of male in Indian society. It is a deplorable situation for women as the male treat them breaking all limits of dignity and affection. What a woman can expect from such society where animal like men live? In a recent report of Nav Bharat dated January 20, 2002, we find an underaged (teenager) girl was admitted in Kamla Nehru Hospital, Bhopal in raped and unconscious condition, who was found crying lying in a chair inside the Lakshmi Talkies. The accused of rape could not be tracted. Can a man of general prudence think of such act in civilized society? But we are compelled to see such misfortunate occurrence in India. Because in India women's position is suppressed in society.

What our society provide to our women folk can be imagined from a report the Madhya Pradesh Home Minister Mr. Mahendra Baudh gave in reply to a question in Assembly, as appeared in Dainik Jagaran Newspaper, Bhopal of August 22, 2001. He reported occurrence of 4154 rape cases, 13625 cases of harassment of women, 790 dowry death cases and 1382 cases of abduction during six month (from January 2001 to 30 June, 2001). Thus in Madhya Pradesh alone every day women population suffer 23 rape, 70 oppression, 5 death (dowry) and 76 abduction in the male dominated society of India. When the awful picture of our State is this, what a horrible scene of women population may be of the entire country.

There are numerous cases of sex scandal in women's shelter or hostel where not only the male can be blamed but women are also involved in such cases. In a case reported in Times of India, New Delhi dated April 15, 2001, five Ministers were implicated in a sex scandal at women's protection home in Varanasi. The Secretary General of Samajwadi Party indicated the Rajnath Singh government on this issue and said in a press conference, "a corrupt and useless administration like that of Rajnath Singh had never existed in the history of U.P." A case of "Nariniketan" of Varanasi's sex racket and murder of some inmates was revealed by CBI sources. It was revealed that, caretaker of Women Shelter Home at Shivpora along with six other persons entered into a conspiracy for supplying girls. It is said, the caretaker Shyama Singh used to entertain men frequenting the nari niketan. These men used to give her money while taking these girls to separate rooms. Inmates who protested were beaten up mercilessly by the caretaker.

Social Position of Women

The miserable and indignified state of women in Indian is evident from the fact that, in this country parents don't welcome a female child. For the last few years when the bio-science proved its experiment 100 percent success to forecast or foretell the sex of foetus, there were rapid foeticide. As a result imminent danger is foreseen in society to maintain balance between the two sexes. The census of 2001 has revealed the sadden state of male and female ratio. The disbalance in the proportion of male-female population and acute shortage of female population has become a matter of great concern for all, politicians, sociologists, biologists, anthropologists and so on. The analytical report published in Dainik Jagaran, Bhopal dated 5th September, 2001 revealed that, the shortage of female population especially in the lower age group is attributable to increased death rate of female children and mostly foeticide. Thus to improve the male-female ratio the government of India has enforced a law to deter foeticide and forecasting foetus' sex by doctors. The anthropologist, politicians and sociologists can very well examine and assist why the female foetus are spoilt or murdered? What are the reasons behind it? A prudent person will definitely be able to conclude why parents are not willing to cheerfully accept the new born female baby? The reasons are quite apparent in the traditional customs prevalent in Indian society. Had the Indian given equal respect and significance to female, there could never be such respiteful intention of the parents. Thus, it is proved that, the female population in India is under several subjection and oppressions. Equality or equal status of women with men in India is yet far from the imagination. Equality depends upon equal treatment in every sphere of life but in India first hindrance is of caste or varna. Even men of different castes are not equally treated then how women can be equal with men.

More glaring example of oppression of women in Indian society can be seen in a report of Danik Jagaran dated 4 April, 2001 (Deb Dashion Ka Dard). The report says, due to poverty who are compelled to prostitution, their number in India is almost 23 lakhs. In a report submitted to the Prime Minister by Bharatiya Patita Udhar Sabha, the problem of sex-slave is serious in Maharashtra, Gujarat, Rajasthan, Karnataka and West Bengal. These sex-slaves (prostitutes) are doing their business in Mumbai, Chennai, Delhi, Hyderabad, Ahmedabad and other cities and suburban market area. Every year almost 25000 new girls enter into prostitutions. The report also says that the number of prostitutes is highest in Mumbai, i.e., approximate 3 and half lakhs. In Rajasthan they are approximate 2 lakhs 80 thousand in number. In West Bengal their strength is about 2 lakhs 75 thousand and in Andhra Pradesh, Gujarat and Karnataka the strength of prostitutes is 2 lakhs 50 thousand each. The most degrading stigma on the Indian society today is that these prostitutes have approximate 50 lakhs children who do not know their fathers. What a terrific danger is created by the human in Indian society? Nobody is pained to look into the matter. The society will blame and disgust these innocent 50 lakhs children having no fault of their own. The prostitutes are blamed of polluting society but no one examine into the causes and pinpoint the responsibility of raising a huge population of prostitutes and bastards in the country. Had any body ever thought that, prostitute can not grow without the encouragement and support of the men of noble and aristocrat families. The first we have to find out, whether it is possible for a woman to practice prostitution if the male population are honest and pious to the core of morality? The answer is negative and it is universal truth that prostitute is created by men, women themselves can not become prostitutes if men do not support or entice them. The nobles and elites who disgust the illegitimate children should first find out who are responsible for creating prostitutes and bastards. The girls or young women become prostitutes being entraped by the lusty and greedy men of the civilized society. Had these victim women were given proper facilities to live a respectable life with full satisfaction of their daily needs for survival in human society, the picture would have been quite different.

The women's position in Indian society becomes more clear from an instance of very recent case. A 16 year old girl Kumari Bharati was abducted by three youths in the night of 22 August 2001 from the slum behind *Ram Mandir*, *Dhobi Ghat*, Sector 2 Piplani, Bhopal as reported in *Dainik Jagaran* dated 24 August 2001. Can any one of the nobles who boast in disgusting prostitutes or bastards, say what will happen to the above girl after she is released and survived? Will that girl be accepted in society? If not what will be the way opened to her for survival in this country? Answers to all these questions will lead us to conclude that one more girl will be compelled to add in the strength of prostitutes. Thus pollution of society by the prostitute is being done by the society itself. It is like the fact that people of a village damage the village road for a little gains and when the road is completely damaged then they blame the society of which they are also the members.

The women in India are usually subjected to man's atrocities are quite established tradition. It has lastly been accepted by the government also and due to the rising pressure of women's organization the government has agreed to bring a bill to the Parliament on Prevention of Women's Atrocities as reported in Dainik Jagaran, Bhopal dated 7 December, 2001.

Women are exploited in India, this cannot be denied. There

are still the force in society which compel women to adopt the path of whore/concubine or the day light prostitute. To free the women from this state of their social life the Indian Human Resources Development Minister Dr. Murli Manohar Joshi instructed Chief Ministers of all the states. Accordingly in Madhya Pradesh a Committee has been formed with its members being Principal Secretary Women and Children Development, Principal Secretary Home, Chairperson of Women Commission Dr. Sabita Inamdar, Sadhna Pathak of NGO Action Aid and Champa Bahen and Ram Snehi, social workers, as reported by Nav Bharat, Bhopal dated 11 October, 2001. Atrocities on women in India is a prevalent notion of Indian male dominated society. This was highlighted in a meeting of BJP Mahila Morcha held on 9-2-2000 at Bhopal. Thus it is clear that women in Indian society suffer men's domination.

Women's Position as Regard Health

The World Health Organization points out that about half of all women and two-thirds of the pregnant women in developing countries like India (excluding China) suffer from nutritional anemia. Anemia also common among poor women in relatively developed countries is caused by inadequate nutrition arising from poverty, and from food, allocation disparities. It is complicated by intestinal parasites and malaria. Malnutrition combined with frequent pregnancies can lead to maternal depletion syndrome that results in high rates of death in pregnancy and child birth. Death rates are exceptionally high for adolescents who are child bearing because of the physical and mental immaturity of young mothers combined with their lack of education.

The drug and alcohol abuse whether her own or partner is prevalent in poor and illiterate section of rural population, have the devastating effects on women. They are linked with almost three-fourths of sexual abuses including rape.[3]

The multiple responsibilities of rural women throughout the world only differ by degree. In most countries especially in India, they work long hours within home and community providing agricultural and maintenance services to their families without pay, ensuring that they will be the poorest of the poor. They lack access to resources which would enable them to be self reliant, quite often they have to work outside the home where they continue to be exploited. From Asian, African and Latin American nations speakers at the Forum-85 session on "Development Alternatives for Women of the New Era" (DAWN)" exposed the reality of women's universal economic condition. They emphasized a salient reality summarized by a Sri Lankan speaker:—

> "The more women work, the poorer they are. The white economy is the money economy, not the world economy."

The speakers said, women paid the cost of their countries' deficit. When husband migrate to urban areas and families cannot afford to hire agricultural labour, the women must compensate for losses by intensifying their unpaid labour. A Sudanes social worker reported:—

> "Women whose husband migrate to some other place, work around the clock. So do the others really. They have very little rest and are very stressed. No one helps them. They tend to garden, care for children, walk many miles twice a day for water, and gather fuel wood. They cook and clean and try to earn money. When they get depressed, people say it is the occult and ostracized them."

The situation in rural India is not at all different from the above. The practical observation of women of rural areas in India will give the vivid results as stated above.

Social Environment

Women are exploited in India; this cannot be denied. There is still the force in society which compel the women sometimes to adopt the path of a whore, concubine or the day light prostitute. To free the women from this state of their social life the Indian Human Resources Development Minister Mr. Murli Manohar Joshi instructed Chief Ministers of all the states. Accordingly in Madhya Pradesh a Committee has been formed with its members being Principal Secretary Women and Children's Development, Principal Secretary Home, Chairperson of Women Commission, Dr. Sabita Inamdar, Ms. Sadhna Pathak of NGO Action Aid and Champa Bahan and Ram Snehi, both social workers, as reported by Nav Bharat, Bhopal dated 11-10-2001. Atrocities on women in India is a prevalent notion of Indian male dominated society. This was highlighted in a meeting of BJP Mohila Morcha held at Bhopal on 9-2-2000. The meeting expressed concern at the increasing atrocities on women and backward classes during last five years. Dr. Sudha Malviya, who presided over the meeting emphasised full dedication of the Morcha to fight against the atrocities on women. Maya Singh, National President of the Mohila Morcha invited women to be more active in the field of politics to fight against atrocities on women and welcomed the proposal of NDA government for 33 per cent reservation for women (National Mail, Bhopal dated 10-12-2000).

The instances of atrocities like rape are frequent in India. Even the nearest relatives does not hesitate to do such heinous act with innocent destitute female. Dainik Jagaran of 5th April 2001 reflected a very unbelievable incident in which a tribal girl of sixteen has been raped by her uncle (maternal brother of her father). This is a burning example even in the family peremeter are always under direct or indirect pressure of male. The nearest relatives are often found to be oppressors of female. Some women's organization feel that political reservation will strengthen women. But does it fit to fight such type of heinous act of men by acquiring political rights. This sort of act is committed with the barbarous nature of male and it needs to be eliminated by reformation of human nature which can not be done with political power.

We find political power sometime also involved in atrocities on women. In the recent past a case of releasing nude photographs of nine girls of IIPS Indore on U. S. Website. When the investigation was started by the officials of the Devi Ahilya BH University they faced tremendous political pressure to go slow or stop the investigation against the five accused students (Times of India dated 19-4-2001). This colourful incident is a considerable proof that political power does not assist to improve condition of women and free them from men's atrocities.

The status of women in Indian society can be examined in the context of treatment they get from the male population either from their own kith and kins or from the common public. Quite often we are confronted with heinous acts of male in Indian society. It is a deplorable situation for women as the male treat them breaking all limit of dignity and affection. What a woman can expect from such society where animal like men live? In a recent report of Nav Bharat dated 20-1-2002, we find an underaged (teenage) girl was admitted in Kamla Nehru Hospital, Bhopal in raped and unconscious condition, who was found crying lying in a chair inside the Lakshmi Talkies. The accused of rape could not be traced. Can a man of prudence think of such act in civilized society? But we are compelled to hear such misfortunate event in India. Because in India women's position is suppressed in society.

What our society provide to our women folk can be imagined from a report the Madhya Pradesh Home Minister Mr. Mahendra Baudh gave in reply to a question in Vidhan Sabha as appeared in Dainik Jagaran, Bhopal dated 22 August 2001. He reported occurrence of 4154 rape cases, 13625 cases of harassment of women, 790 dowry death cases and 1382 cases of abduction during the period of six month. Thus we can conclude that in Madhya Pradesh everyday 23 women are raped, 70 women suffer oppression, 5 women die due to dowry and 76 women are abducted in the male dominated Indian society. It is noteworthy that this is the official statement of the Home Minister of a state; so the reality can be speculated for higher than that reported by the Home Minister. When the social picture of one state is like this what worsen condition may be indeed of the entire country. Thus we can conclude that the social environment of India is not at all conducive to bring esteem and human rights to women population of the country.

Caste Discrimination

The causes of atrocities on women in India include caste discrimination as a major issue. Caste based atrocities in India are evident every where. The glaring example of the caste discrimination is evident from the incident of Hoshangabad district of Madhya Pradesh reported in Dainik Jagaran, Bhopal dated 24-8-2001. The incident is of a Panchayat Chairperson Uma Arse, a scheduled caste woman who was being harassed by the Deputy Chairman of the Panchayat Shri Arjun Paliya, an upper caste, from the very day of her election to the chair. Even though the matter was reported to highest level of administration (Chief Minister) of the state but no action was taken against the culprit. This was reported by the Mahila Morcha organizer Vidya Pathak and she demanded action against the Collector and Chief Executive Officer of the District Panchayat for their negligence in taking action on the report of Uma Arse. The complaint made to the Chief Minister by Smt. Uma Arse says that the government accommodation and vehicle allotted to the Chairperson are occupied by the Deputy Chairman Palia. Even the chairperson was not allowed to possess office seal of her designation.

Worth of Women in Men's Consideration

Women's worth in the male dominated society of India can be assessed in the context of developed societies in other countries of the world especially U. K. and America. The condition prevailed in Britain as we find in the writings of Cynthia Cockburn that in the labour market, women comprise a special category distinguished from men and provide special scope to employer for exploitation. That is to say, that the women are prone to exploitation of the employer. Though some of the women in certain period of their lives may escape the exploitation and disparity in pay and condition of work, which are not much inferior to men. The nature of job, which the greater number of women are entrusted upon by the employers or superior officers, cooking, cleaning, washing, making and mending, caretaking and most of the menial and inferior, characteristically given to black and ethnic minority women. Here we find that, right to work and wages are given to women in an inferior grade in comparison to men on the other hand race discrimination has been implemented thereby the inequalities bred among the women also. In these developed countries also the "equal opportunities" has been construed as the equality in the base-line women workers and with all women of different races. More skilled and supervisory posts or training for skill improving have the traditional masculine character and women are kept away from such occupation. Most of the women are considered as worker with-domestic-ties, part-time low paid manual or office worker. To ignore women for managerial or professional career prospective, is mainly the needs and intention of employees as well as the men superior authority to keep them at the bottom of the organization finding this women super exploitable employees. Cockburn has mentioned that though the policy of equality of opportunity enable a few women to escape the women work ghetto and provide some generous provision to help them to cope with the domestic pressure but that is not enough to improve the condition and become equal to men. He suggested that real improvement can be made through the relevant policy for the majority women by changing the job structure itself, ending low pay, breaking job segregation or revaluating and upgrading their occupations and restructuring grade system to reduce differentials. But these systems are not going to be adopted by the employer easily. Voluntary changes in the traditional policy cannot be expected, even the sex segregation and tending disparity of men cannot be avoided. Only women's emancipation is possible when women are strong enough within them to overcome the resistance of male members.

Male disparity can be seen in the work field under-A study report published in 1982 showed the painful extent to which women in local Government employment were concentrated within the lower grades. Male manual workers characteristically occupy upper manual grade. But in 1985 a nation-wide revaluation and regarding affecting one million local authority manual occupations achieved something better for future. The labour authorities and manual workers union had been influenced in this exercise and a new job evaluation scheme had been introduced to remove the sex bias on job.[4]

As regards improvement in the condition of Women's work, a study by a London shop Stewards' combined argued – All manual workers are low paid and their work as a whole should be revaluated and its conditions "harmonized" with those pertaining to white collar work. This would certainly benefit a large group of working class women and is a strategy often legitimated by an appeal to sex and race equality. The manual unions argued that while revaluation and regarding the work will help women in the lower grade it is at least a redistribution of resources among the poors.[5]

The author of "In the Way of Women" while examining the position of women working in companies met many traditionalist men and found that several men of this kind asserted and felt women's place was in the kitchen. Some saw women kind frankly as sexual material for men's pleasure and comfort. One said, "I actually believe women are feminine creatures who are there to be administered".[6]

However men of the new age and modern world specially

after starting the computer regime are or different view. Since the computer department of service is generating iconoclastic fast moving fun expanding zone the relations in both old fashioned and the new fast moving were competitive and the competition centered on expertise and career pace. They thus thought, it was no coincidence that women's statistical position was inferior in the information technology divisions of both organizations compared with their position in the labour force of the organization as a whole. Cockburn has also observed that national scarcity of women with IT qualification is attributable partly to masculine appropriation of technology and its associated skills, a cultural exclusion of women prevailed in training and employment. The women had identified this new type of male not only in High Street Retail and Services but also in the Trade Union and the Local Authority. Now this masculinity does not share the "women's place is in the home" mentality of the old guard. These men expect to find women in the public sphere. These new men actually welcome women into this existing new world not because they consider women equal to them in every respect but because, their presence will add sexual spice to the working day. The equality with men cannot be actuated however they may be placed in a double bind by the men's sexual regime. They are expected to be sexually combative and amusing as men, yet their ability to be so is undermined by the asymmitry of heterosexuality. Even it is observed that when they ignore the sexualized culture they are in turn ignored and marginalized by their colleagues and when they resist the sexualized culture they are labelled as spoilsports, lacking in a sense of humour.[7] Thus 'equality for opportunity' or the equal status for women in male domination is not possible. Though in principle equality be granted but the practical course of interaction between men and women will uphold the view of old traditionalist men. The male power is not dying out with the retirement of the old traditionalist men. It is being reproduced in new, one might say it literally a "virulent" forms that are appropriate and effective for twentieth century and the present days.

There are complex question on improving the status and entity of women workforce because, the work they perform either manual or mental labour they are supposed to be dressed and presented for, according to the norms of the organization which may involve deliberate sexualizing or desexualising the body. Some employers desires the body and sexuality are to be sold. But all these exploitations are not always enforced. It depends upon one sense of identity and pleasure, how much it appeals to and enforcing upon. It is always an open question how much one presents herself and behaves as they want her to, how much she works to develop and expresses bodily and sexual identity are cherished. The tendency of young women for instance avoiding technical training that seems to diminish their feminity also perpetuate the inequality between men and women. The remarks of Rosemary Pringle is noteworthy to conclude how inequality breeds among men and women. Pringle says, "men control women not only through rape or through forcing them to do what they want (them) to do, but through definitions of pleasure and selfhood".[8]

The equality policy for women with men needs to :—

(1) Instil respect for women
(2) Effective banning sexuality from the workplace
(3) The above two principles should be a popular move with all women
(4) The new "liberated" management style coincident to the above principles.

The question of sexuality at every step of women's life discriminate them from men. Women have to act asexual if they are to avoid being seen as sexy. What needs to change is not the sexiness of women but the vulnerability of women for establishing equal identity. The women's movement in organizations should be to strengthen women's position and confidence in many different ways so that they can maintain and use themselves according to their liking and suitability.[9]

The above discussion reveals that the value of women in the eyes of men in human society in any country, especially in India depends upon the women's own conscience and behaviour. On the other hand, the equality in status can only be granted to women if the attitude of men is entirely changed from that of the old tradition and culture based on religious taboos and scriptural myths.

Position of Women in Medical Profession

There were sex-segregation norms in services, despite the educational development of women they were not given opportunities of services in institutions designed for men. Therefore women leaders demanded new institutions to be staffed by female professional. So the line of services were demarcated for women in the late nineteen century and medical profession was chosen as one of the career prospect for women. In the year 1885, Lady Dufferin, wife of the Viceroy established the National Association for supplying female medical aid to the women of India. This association provided financial assistance to women willing to be trained as doctors, hospital assistants, nurses and midwives; aided in establishing medical training programs for women and encouraged construction of hospitals, health centres and dispensaries. From 1888, the Government of India started supervising the work of the association and providing employment for women graduates.

The first Indian woman successful beneficiary of the Dufferin's National Association's scheme was Kadambini Basu, who graduated from Bethune College in 1883 and admitted in Medical College the same year and received a monthly scholarship of Rs. 20/- from government. Shortly after her admission in Medical College she was married to her long time mentor and friend Dwarkanath Ganguly, who was a staunch member of the Sadharan Brahmo Samaj and an advocate of male-female equality. Though Kadambini could not secure the MB (Bachelor of Medicine) degree having failed in one paper of her final practical examination, she was awarded the GBMC (Graduate of Bengal Medical College) in 1886 and became the first Indian Women doctor. Another first Indian Hindu Women who studied medicine abroad was Anandibai Joshi a Marathi woman. She graduated from Women's Medical College in Philadelphia in 1886.

Kadambini Basu and Anandibai Joshi's graduation in Medicines encouraged many fellow women students to opt for medical profession and their number went on increasing year after year. Later in 1929 men's medical college started admitting women students. By that time a women medical college and four medical schools were already established.[10]

Despite the liberty in education and encouragement for women in medical profession the general attitude of male professors were not very favourable for women in medical colleges. They had to suffer self depression caused by professor's behaviour and the tendency of their male colleagues. Geraldine Forbes states in her book "Women in Modern India" about the condition of women students in medical colleges as follows:—

> "These young women students had to guard their reputations. This meant avoiding unnecessary travel and missing the dramas, clubs and other entertainments available to their male colleagues. Attending classes presented yet other hurdles.

Muthulakshmi Reddy like other women of her generation was neither the lone female in her classes or in the company of one or two others. Professors usually placed women at the front of the room, off to one side or in some other way separated them from the male students. There were a few professors who did not allow female students in their classes and assigned junior assistants to lecture them.[11]

The position of women in medical profession during

British period was not good. First the women doctors faced tremendous hardship to meet the obligations of their families and the profession; moreover, society was not ready to tolerate women in public service.

Secondly they had to fight against the sexual harassment. In Ahmedabad in the early 1930, the case of Dr. (Mrs.) Ahalyabai Samant, the director of the municipal dispensary of Nadiad was reported in newspapers. Dr. Balabahi Harikishankar Bhatt, the municipal councillor abducted and assaulted Dr. Samant. The district Session Judge sentenced Bhatt to one year imprisonment hoping, this would make it clear that women doctors were to be treated with respect but the Chief Justice of High Court overturned the decision and simply fined Bhatt.[12]

Thirdly Indian women doctors worked under the domination of European and Anglo-Indian women. They had to fight racial prejudice: Gender discrimination was evident in salaries paid to Indian women doctors of Dufferin Fund. They received less than one-third of the salary of British or Indian men in the Indian Medical services. Even they suffered in disparity in salary with British women because Indian women without the knowledge of english could obtain the VLMS (Vernacular Licentiate in Medicine and Surgery) Certificate but not MB or MD degree and salary depended on credentials in which Indian women were treated inferior to British women who held MB or MD degree. Thus Indian women used to earn salary less than one-tenth of that earned by the British women.

Position of Women in Miscellaneous Fields

The similar position, as like the medical profession, of women was in the profession of teaching and lawyers' profession. They faced the similar problems as medical professional women faced.

First the women could not obtain required training for the professional certification. Sometimes they had to study privately for examinations. Even though they required requisite qualification and talent by attending proper institution and passing the required examinations but failed to enter the professional field because of gender discrimination. The employment in the institutions serving both sexes was more problematics. Unmarried women and widows found it difficult to find a place to live and a way to protect themselves from sexual harassment. The higher salaries and the more supportive families were helpful to establish women in service and profession and command respects but those having no sound economic condition and family support, complained bitterly about the hardship they endured.

The account of factory workers is also very surprising. The first, cotton and Jute Mills established in 1850s employed women but their records are found available only after 1911. In Bombay approximate 1,00,000 workers were in textile factories, out of which 25 per cent were women of whom ¼th were full timer in 1890s. The position of them in the factories were not above the labourers; they were deputed on cleaning cotton, winding and reeling thread but never entrusted with the job of weavers. There were about 14,000 women working in Jute Mills of Bengal at that time. They too performed unskilled tasks and were subjected to seasonal unemployment. During the last quarter of nineteenth century when British Parliament was drawing attention to factory condition in England, Major Moore wrote a report on the administration of the Bombay Cotton Department and Mr. J. A. Ballard, the Mint Master of Bombay reported hardships of women and children in the Indian factories.

However the local people, i.e., Indian, opposed any legislation to regulate the working condition of women and children. Yet the first Factory Act 1881 was enacted and the amendments were made in 1891 and 1911, which improved the condition of women.

As the regulation of factory works was being carried out

with greater attention towards the betterment of women, the factory owners gradually reduced the workers in different places. Male workers union was also responsible for reducing the women workers. There was discrimination in salary and employment of women based on domiciliary, religion and caste. In Calcutta 90 per cent of Jute Mill female workers were migrant from Bihar, Central Provinces, Madras and United Provinces and they had worked for three-times the wages of the Bengali women.

The poor condition of work, low wages and sexual harassment together compelled many workers in Calcutta to extend liaison with men or outright prostitution as most of them had migrated to Calcutta as single woman from other provinces.

Dominant gender ideology constructed women as dependent housewives but the reality was different. Thousands of women had to work to survive. Many women without any guardian from rural areas were attracted to urban area seeking jobs survival. Those poor and uneducated women found themselves helpless to work as maid servants, coolies and prostitutes.

A team of women as members of the Committee appointed by the AIWC visited mines and mills to examine the real condition of working women and the impact of the working condition on their family life. Mrs. A Chatterjee an Oxford educated, Mrs. Renuka Roy a graduate of London School of Economics and Iris Wingale, an active member of the YWCA in India visited seven mines in Bengal and Bihar and several mills. They observed the condition of women as very poor in health, worn out by double work. They were using opium to keep their children quiet. They worked in mines because they needed money to survive and preferred working with their husb ınd, to being left at their remote villages. They also observed that in the prevailing circumstances these women would not appreciate the efforts of AIWCA and AIWC would have to bear the responsibility for finding alternative work for them if the regulation debarring them to work underground is passed.

Later based on the recommendations of this three-member Committee of AIWCA, its branches were entrusted to adopt a village for model work of upliftment.

Despite the efforts made by the AIWC and other reformers to improve the condition of women, the real condition of women even after passing of the regulation to abolish women's work underground was not changed an inch.

Backwardness of Indian Women

Scholarly works on the backwardness of women's education in India suggest that female illiteracy would be seen as an important problem to 21st Century urban cities in India as it was in 19th and 20th Centuries. They also suggest if a women's movement emerged it would be vary small in size and would draw on a narrow segment of population as it was seen in 19th and 20th Centuries.[13] The position has not yet changed much. Summarised information of crucial importance about the women's movement as stated by Jana Matson Everett are—

> "The progress of female education in 19th Century India was very slow for several reasons, Indigenous schools for girls had ceased to function, Christian Missionaries opened girls schools (beginning in 1819) but high caste Hindus would not allow their daughters to attend, as they feared attempts at conversion.[14]

The British government encouragement of female education was minimal; no schools were supported before 1854 and after 1854 the method used was grant-in-aid, which required indigenous financial contributions often not forthcoming. There was a shortage of women teachers and opposition to the idea of men's teaching girls. The efforts of educated Indian elites were also fairly tentative. Parsis in

Bombay, Brahmo Samaj in Bengal and other reformist associations opened girls schools in the second half of the 19th century, but these efforts were small in scope".[15] Though now-a-days there are large number of girls schools but those are not adequate according to the strength of female population. Moreover the social attitude towards women in rural as well as urban areas has not changed. Also the traditional and cultural effects on female population are very strong which demoralize the female population on acquiring education. Even the government has no concrete plan on women's education to execute. Government controlled schools do not pay adequate attention towards women's education.

Account of female education in 19th century, cursory details of 1854 was estimated to 7000 girls (mostly native Christians) attended Christian schools, while in 1882 there were approximate 1,27,000 female students, less than 3 per cent of whom were above primary level.[16] The following table which conform to the Census Report of 1891 (Indian Census of 1891 Vol. I, p. 64) shows the state of literacy of women of that time:

LITERACY RATES IN INDIA 1891

Province/Religion	*Male Literacy*	*Female Literacy*
Bengal	0.108	0.004
Bombay	0.140	0.010
Madras	0.149	0.010
Punjab	0.074	0.003
Hindu	0.115	0.004
Parsi	0.777	0.501
Christian	0.343	0.136
India as a whole	0.110	0.006

In 1883 two Bengali Brahmo Samaj women became the first Indian Women College graduates, they had attended Bethune College in Calcutta.[17]

DETAILS OF COLLEGE GOING WOMEN IN INDIA DURING 1891 TO 1945

1891	45
1901	177
1921	881
1937	6782
1945	201304

LITERACY RATE IN HINDU AND MUSLIM RAISED 1901 TO 1921 AS UNDER

	1901	*1921*
Hindu	0.011	0.31
Muslim	—	0.02

Hindu women students during the period upto 1921 were mostly from the families active in social reform activities. The literacy percentage of women has raised to approximate 46 pr cent in 80 years duration after a rapid national efforts in modernization of the country. This shows a clear picture of women's very slow progress in the country despite all round endeavour of the administration and the social reformists.

Position of Women in Foreign Countries

While examining or assessing the women in Indian society, it becomes essential to look at the women's social picture of the foreign countries. So I have made an attempt to reflect the position of women in other major countries of the world. The position of women in foreign countries as I could find from various sources has been described in the succeeding paragraphs.

The research carried out by Cynthia Cockburn has been revealed in her book "In the Way of Women" (in an Essay-Men's Resistance to Sex Equality in Organization) which make us to understand that the women in many occasion struggle for equal opportunities with men in the works and sometimes they feel discriminated on works but that is not applicable in all cases. Quite often women accept their subordination as inevitable, who are stuck in women's work. They also experienced that men are not ready to let their power in the organizations be withdrawn easily, therefore, the equality initiative of women involve struggle, may it be in different forms. The work analysis has brought out the result to say that a woman earns less than three-quarters of what a man earns, because much of women's work is done at home and it is unpaid. Consequently men have more income and much leisure time at their disposal than women. Still in Britain a particular class (mainly middle class and mainly white) extract additional gains, who have wealth and power in organization.[18]

The women's subordination and men's domination in the sphere of private relationship have been highlighted by the European writer and held that even the Communists have accepted that men are usually placed in position senior to women. There is also the sign of partial treatment as the direct comparison between men and women is avoided to ensure that, women however talented cannot put men in the shade. On the other hand Paleman held, "the terms of the sexual contract ensure that all men and not just craftsmen form an aristocracy of labour.[19] Thus it can be construed that, while men subordinated as workers they are not mere wage slaves. In their own sphere of private society especially in sexual relationship they are master and women remain subordinated by them.

Even the capitalist countries encourage identical employment contract for male and female workers and the patriarchal notion in reality make the women to prefer employment in organizations different from men. It is practically observed and accepted by the capitalists also that, there is sharp segregation in occupation between male job and female job which indirectly diminish the scope of sex-equality. Sex-exploitation cannot be ignored in employment even in the developed countries which clearly shows that, women suffer in the hands of men. Although every body realize that, women play a major role in society by maintaining social relation of house wife, owing to duties to husband, children and home. Yet they suffer degradation by distinction in works, mostly it is found that, the employers segregate lowest paid and least secured to be gendered female. This way the main stream of society in every country discriminate female from that of male.

Women's struggle for engagement in work on identical terms with those of men is in reality obstructed by men. The radical view of men about women's equality is deterrent. Men opined that in reality women live in men's world and they should not surrogate men.

Carole Paleman held that, "women's equal standing must be accepted as an expression of the freedom of women as women, and not treated as an indication that women can be just like men.[20]

There is evidence of women's oppression by men in European countries also. Even though the women's struggle was strengthened the perception that women's specificity should not be buried or lost in the struggle for equality sameness- versus-difference has been a source of conflict. Much more was the experience of differences and oppressions of black women. The black women experienced oppression by white women as well as white men and black men. Thus the women's struggle for equality in European countries had the same effect as in India. The racial distinction between white and black remained the same despite several struggle. Like India the white women claim for equality with men but do not allow or grant equality to black women. In India the distinction although externally does not appear to be racial but in real perception and meaning, caste distinction prevailing in India is the racial distinction and oppression. All the lower castes are black. That is why equality in presence of racial/caste distinction is not the equality in real sense. Thus women of the black race in Europe, America and Africa and of low caste in India cannot expect equality even if their struggle for equality with men is granted without elimination of racial disparity.[21] Women at present of the black and low castes of India are suffering the oppression double of that of women in higher castes and white race.

More harmful is the sexist culture in work place created by men which adversely check the progress of women to achieve equality with men. Men have developed a culture hetero-sexual and in contrast of women's occupation of men's position in works field; thus marginalized and controlled women's participation. In foreign countries like America, Britain and other European countries even in this advanced world women are treated like the things for amusement or enjoyment. They are quite often used as the source of entertainment of the audience or the associates. Specially the newly developed system of education covers a faculty of management and this particular field has become prone to apply the above culture. To illustrate the presence of sex disparity and dominating role of men over women in the developed countries Cynthia Cockburn has mentioned the following instance.

"There was a weekend conference arranged in a hotel at the expense of the High Street Computer Division for its middle and senior staff. The aim of this programme was to review the work and build *esprit de corps*. The first morning's business was opened with a presentation by a senior manager. He prepared a 'visual aid' in the form of a life sized photograph of a bare-breasted model. In the photo the model appeared leaning against a rock with a hole in it. In this space the senior manager had superimposed a second photo of the Divisional Director's face and commenced his address — we are lucky to have director with us this morning. He's just risen from a sick bed. His secretary has flue. This drew a laugh not only from the audience but from the director and his secretary. There followed other sexual allusion and jokes from the speakers. Subsequently the same presentation was repeated back at the head office for the amusement of larger group including junior programmers and other division staff. Among them were some young women. This time these sexy jokes were not welcomed. Later some of these women complained to the director. But the director felt, the complainants had failed to understand the humour. He became annoyed that, the serious side of the weekend conference, the technical presentation into a good deal of preparation had been wasted on these women who saw nothing but a sexual suggestiveness. However, he agreed to avoid such material in future conferences. But the manager who had given talk wanted to justify his deed and argued that for the last many years nobody had objected on his proceedings in the same manner. He also asserted that if he were to be censored he might prefer not to do it all. Even the divisional personnel manager did not feel offensive though he was obliged to give equality climate. Though the women remained unreconciled but some of them became afraid of being spoilt their career.

Finally the director wanted to pacify the anger of women and appealed to adopt popular culture. He said that sexual jokes are the stock in trade of management training — you were taught to drop "ice-breakers" and "livener" into your delivery to get the audience relaxed keep them interested.[22]

Besides the above statement of director he said, his secretary had not been at all upset by the reference to her in the joke. Because she likes to be flattered constantly about her appearance. She likes to wear sexy clothes and parade around the department sticking her chest out and encourage sexism right......... so I don't know what the offence is.[23]

The statement or assertion of the director evince that the men dominated society or the organisation, industries or workshops where women demand their share have to compromise with their own dignity and self respects and appreciate the liking of the male strength. Even in the civilized and developed countries the women cannot place themselves equally respected with their male colleagues. Thus we can conclude that the right to education and employment does not protect and grant equality and respect to female with male. In this context the learned men, social reformers and revolutionary personalities have not been able to find a permanent effective solution to provide equal status to female with male. The only way to achieve this objective is to change the mentality of male population towards their female colleagues and associates.

Similarly the traditional culture and customs need to be changed. The most important aspect of improving the status and entity of women is creation awareness in women themselves of right and dignity. The energy of the female genus should be raised and experienced by them. Till they know the strength of their latent energy and its impact in forming a civilized society, female will be neglected by male. The political privileges and manoeuvre can least improve their position in society in any country of the world without due regards to the above mentioned aspect of social life.

Many scholars have also pointed out the role of radical feminism in identifying not only woman but womanhood as a source of strength. It is an important source of women's employment, which can be seen to be gender specific and the women's bodies are often involved in the deal between women workers and their employers, which directly indicates as a detrimental step towards women's dignity and status. It is also noticed by some scholars that women's sexuality her smile, her dress, her femaleness is often an implicit part of the bargain with the male employer. This natural characteristics of women can be altered or changed, even it can be exterminate in full if the women desire themselves. Similarly these can be raised to a hike by their initiative.[24] So, the position of women can be improved only if they themselves desire it and avail the opportunities for improvement of women's status can be originated practically by adopting the ways stated above.

Struggle for women's equality as workers in the paid workforce has to take the form of double resistance. On the one hand women have to struggle against the terms of engagement between employers and employed. Their struggle is against the tendency of exploitative pay and the conditions of work. That is in other words to be a socialist struggle alongside working men, using similar resources of organized labour in the work place in society. On the other hand, it has a feminist struggle against the imposition of male sex-right by both the employers and the male workforce (colleagues). It is evident even in the nineteen century when Marxist and Socialist thoughts were inspiring new forms of trade union and political party the women had with men to get membership of the organisation. They had to compete with men for skilled work. As a result women's organisation came into existence as Women's Protective and Provident League, later Women's Trade Union League and the National Federation of Women Workers.

Thus we find the gradual improvement in women's position in workforce and society in general was the results of women's own struggle and awareness and not of any special privilege granted by the male dominated society. What is the Marxists and Socialists view about women in the relations of production is noteworthy to find a means of women's struggle for emancipation.

"Engels and later Lenin, were of the opinion that women's emancipation from patriarchy would be achieved precisely by their entry into the productive labour force. Twentieth century experience showed however that, though many more women now had an independent wage, their oppression as a sex continued. Its persistence was clearly not merely a hang over from a pre-industrial stage or from pre-capitalist society, nor of sexist attitudes and prejudices but of fundamental economic, political and ideological importance to the capitalist mode of production.[25]

Position of Women in Hindu Society

Hindu society is one where Hindu Law applies and Hindu Law is a branch of Dharma as understood by the Hindus and it signifies duty. The sources of Hindu Dharma Veda, Shruti, Smriti, Upanishads, Commentaries and customs. In the scriptures of Hindus, based on the above sources the position of women has been painted as most virtuous but the real practice in Hindu society reduces a woman to the position of slave or a personal property of man. According to Hindu religious injunction women have been created to become mothers later.[26]

In Ramayana wife has been considered to be the soul of her husband and in Mahabharata she is stated to be half part of her husband and the best friend. Here we can charge the statement with the practical differences — in Ramayana Rama indicted Sita without considering her to be the soul of him and compelled her for fire-test (Agni Pariksha). Similarly the best friend and half part of King of the Principles (Dharma Raj) Yudhishthir used Draupadi as his property (pawn) in bate of dice (gambling). In Hindu Marriage the daughter is given away to a man — that signifies a daughter to be a matter of value to be gifted to a person. According to Manu once a daughter is given in marriage she remains as the wife of that man for ever, whatever may be the conditions thereafter, she cannot severe the marriage tie though later Narad and Parasar have accepted five conditions when wife can abandon the marriage. These conditions ofcourse do not relate to their mutual disliking and other disputes. Thus before the enactment of Hindu Marriage Act 1955 there was no way out to get rid off the atrocities committed by a Hindu husband on his wife. The more deplorable condition is of a Hindu widow who according to Manu after death of husband has to lead her whole life simply on vegetarian food and in abstinence emaciating herself to minimal—thus leading a life of celebacy and chastity. A widower husband has every liberty to remarry, take food according to his choice and to enjoy company of others (male and female) but woman has no right. In the ancient age the Hindu religion accepted the very heinous form of marriage in which the girl was kidnapped or ravaged. Even to day the Hindu law and religion approve the marriage in which the bridegroom pay money to the parents of the girl i.e. to say, the girl is bought. In Hindu society atrocities on married women is prone even after the enactment of Dowry Prohibition Act 1961, demanding of dowry from the parents or relations of the bride is in abundance. This shows how the Hindu society treats a girl.

The copercenary property devolve upon the surviving member according to section 6 of the Hindu Succession Act 1956 but when the surviving member is a female this law does not apply. That is to say, a woman cannot hold any interest on the copercenary property after the death of copercenar. The Hindu female can become a Mahant of Math but she is not authorized to perform the spiritual and religious rituals according to Hindu Law. In a Hindu joint family the widow cannot represent the joint family in any suit as per the verdict of Patna High Court in a case (AIR 1978 Pat. 258).

In Hindu society women is degraded or looked down upon the event of sexual relationship before marriage, at the same time men are not stained. Hindu law though impose condition of monogamy at the time of marriage but the Hindu society allows bigamous marriage to women. Society demands women's predominant chastity. Hindu society has drifted towards the women's beauty shows and artful performance to amuse the public. The beauty contest, fashion show and lively or rhythmical movement have now consummated commercially. Thus it is apparent that women in Hindu society is used as an object of amusement to a great extent. As women by biological ingredients is made amorous, her caress for splendour further adorn her to be fondling object for men.

In the family female child from the childhood as a general trend has to bear neglecting attitude of the parents and relations. There are frequent reports of family coercion upon the female children in India. Specially in rural areas even in these days of global advancement girls are deterred from educational development. If we look into the affairs of the family, we find the female are subjected to perform all the dismal work of the household. Indian society is men dominated. Here women are depressed or deterred. The general feelings of Indian society is that women are physically weak and mentally dull. They cannot shoulder responsibilities in the same manner as men can do.

In Hindu mythology women are considered as fields and a land, mother and goddess on the basis of fertility. As land produces grains or foods, similarly women in Hindu religion is regarded as the base of production, the main source of sustenance and increase for domain of lordship. On the other hand, the Shiva or Vishnu is considered the overlords of the universe through the lords of the earth Kshatriya (monarchs) and each of the master of his household is the lord whatever caste he may be. Thus in Indian society of Hindu religion lordship and overlordship have been established to a varying extent since post-vedic time. And this discourse of lordship is marked by gender—a lord is a male, he is called purusa, the commanding and encompassing in a cosmological as well as in a practical sense while his domain is represented as female who is termed as his prakriti, the dependent and confined.[27]

Thus we find the position of women in Hindu society of India not better than a prisoner and to a better position as the fellow being subject to be ruled by man, her lord. Her primary obligation is to help in increasing domains by way of procreation. In other words woman's role is limited to procreation and obeying her lord or master, the man. In the concept of religion it is widely accepted in ancient and medieval time illuminate the genealogy of female subjectivity, which in turn became extremely important for the consolidation of masculine sovereignty and patriarchal authority in family. Moreover, the conceptual domain of pleasure has persistent link with women. Vatsayana the author of the first courtly manual is asserting the rights of women to study science of pleasure argues that women in their every day practice already have predisposition towards the theoretical knowledge of pleasure. Thus religious concept about the position of women is varied and quite often contradictory. The courtly society deployed a new concept of aesthetic enjoyment that relied on the notions of artification and ornamentation. This new aesthetics was articulated under more embracing science of Kama or pleasure, which form one of the four goals of man but Kama is linked with women as stated earlier. Thus position or status of women in Hindu society either in medieval or ancient time is not clear.[28]

The practice of untouchability was supported by the Hindu religious mandates. In the practice of untouchability the disparity in dealing with men and women in society was shown not only between men and women but it was based on the caste irrespective of sex. Even the population of same sex were treated differently based on caste. Thus the women of the lower castes were suppressed first by untouchability and then by the domination of men of their own caste. In the Hindu Society special measures were taken with respect to untouchable persons in a large variety of activities, such as conversation, eating, business, rituals, occupations and so forth. The disparity based on untouchability in religion were concerning territory and kinship and are manifested in rules of segregation and sanctions against sexual relation. The untouchables were segregated from men and women and the sexual relation of untouchables with other categories of persons were prohibited in religious dicta of Hindu. How and why this short of disparity or distinction were implemented, the authors of "Invented Identities" have illustrated through two examples from Parasar Smriti and its medieval commentary "the Parasara Madhaviya. " The examples given by the Mr Mikael Aktor in his Article "Untouchable, Women and

Territories Rituals of Lordship in the Parasara Smriti". He says that:—

> "first, domains of lordship and untouchables are interrelated by the process of ritualization which establishes and preserves the domain and also by the development which extended a pre-existing paradigm of ritual avoidances within the domestic sphere to the wider sphere of village and city. Second, the images of the untouchables that we derive from texts are ambiguous—untouchables are seen some time protecting, sometime as a threat to these domains."

Mikael Aktor explicitly says that threat to the domains of untouchability is due to polarity being projected on to various marginalized categories which are treated differently under the process of untouchability. His opinion about the untouchables is in conformity with the practical observation of happenings in society. It is observed that when untouchables are controlled they serve the villagers and townsmen by their capacity to handle impurity and when they are free from this control of lord they become dangerous and potentially lethal.

Position of Women in Muslim Society

The degradation of women is prevalent not only in Hindu society but also in Muslim community. Muslim Law (Quran) depicts the picture of women in society in the following manner.

According to Quran muslim women's condition is like a chattel as regards marriage because muta Marriage is also permitted which is a temporary agreement for sexual relation permitted for the amount paid to a woman. The duration of such marriage may be fixed or may be uncertain. According to Muslim religious doctrine the husband can dissolve the marriage by pronouncing 'Talaq' three times. Even the pronouncement of talaq can be made in absence of the spouse (wife). Thus the women's married life last at the discretion of men. The procedure of 'Talaq' under Muslim Law signifies that man after enjoyment of conjugal happiness can get rid of a woman by paying some compensation agreed upon, at his sweet will. Purdah system prescribed in Islam makes a woman bound to remain within certain limit and curtail her freedom of movement, whereas, no such restrictions are imposed upon the males. Women are supposed to keep themselves under a viel which is unique and distinct from other religions. Muslim women even in the present advanced society are supposed to restrict their movement and public contact. This in fact is a punishment to women and to demoralise them to make them slaves to the command of men.

As regards religious performance the women's status is lowered discriminately by not allowing them to approach the Mosque. The sex discrimination in Muslim Law is like the Hindu Law in religious institutions. The law lays down that a woman cannot be appointed as sajjadanashin, a religious teacher, spiritual head, manager of the institution and administrator of the charities, but she can be appointed as manager Mutawalli, a secular head. The muslim law though permits a woman to hold the office of a Mutawalli but restraint the right to perform religious rituals. Here also the law curtails the rights of women in religious responsibilities. Men are spiritually placed in better position than women by law. In the family life woman as a tradition has to remain subjected to obey men. Their willingness has no meaning as they are supposed to do the house hold task. In these days of scientific development the muslim female children are rare seen to attend higher educational institutions. Women go for service outside the periphery of their habitation are considered a sin by Islam.

The position of women in Muslim society can be assessed on the right to contract marriage in which one of the conditions for valid marriage according to Sunni sect is that a male can marry a Muslim female of any sect or a Kitabia. Marriage with a Kitabia, i.e., a woman who believes in a religion possessing a divine book viz. Islam, Christianity and Judaism is valid under Sunni Law. But cannot marry any idolatress or a fire worshipper. The same law lays down that a Muslim woman cannot marry any man who is not a Muslim, whether he is Kitabi or non-Kitabi. According to Mulla, a marriage between Muslim woman and non-muslim man is irregular but according to Fyzee such a marriage is totally void.[29]

Here we find the sex discrimination and subordinate position of women. Women are debarred from contracting marriage with a non-Muslim. However, there is no such prohibition imposed on the male.

In another condition "Prohibitive incapacity" is disqualification for valid marriage. According to that disqualification polyandry is forbidden to Muslim women. Accordingly woman cannot have more than one husband living or alive at a time, whereas, a Muslim male is prohibited from marring fifth wife – thus keeping four living wives is permitted by Islam. That is to say that the muslim law curtails the right of women but enhance for the men. It is sheer sex discrimination.

We find instances of subordination of women in Muslim Law. As regards remarriage of male and female after divorce or death of spouse. There is restriction prescribed in law for the validity of marriage of women after divorce. The law lays down that, woman has to observe 'Iddat' after dissolution of marriage by divorcee or death of her husband. Iddat is a term, which means a period of seclusion and to abstain from marrying another husband. Only women are required to strictly observe this before her second marriage but no such prescription is made in Muslim Law for the Muslim male throughout the world. Thus we find that women are again lowered in status and rights by Muslim Law for.

The rights and duties prescribed for the spouses towards one another in Muslim Law also evince that women are made subordinate or inferior to men. Men have many discretion to play upon the women which the latter cannot resist due to legal sanctions and religious norms. Like all other communities, in Muslim community also the wife has to obey all commands and fulfil the whims of her husband.

Although there are some legal protection provided to women in Muslim Law but the reality is quite different from the statutory figure painted in Muslim Law. Ultimately the women's position in the eyes of law in muslim community is not at all better than all other communities. On the contrary the position is worse than Hindu as regards liberty.

In the case of guardianship of minors the law lays down the entitlement of father first then other paternal male relatives and the merit of mother stands at third and at the end before the legal guardian is nominated, maternal relations within the prohibited degree come. Thus we find, the female is not treated equally with male and the former are subordinate or inferior to latter in all respect in laws.

The females in Muslim community also suffer many disparity in the hands of males. The Muslim Law does not recognise rights of the women especially in property and life-estates, adoption and will. Although in principle, the women are given the above rights but in practice in India they are denied because the customs prevail 'Rewaj-i-am' has been given the force of law.

According to Muslim law the position of woman is like a property. To explain the concept of marriage in Islamic personal "Mohammedan Law—by B.R. Verma" the author states:—

> "....there are many conditions and presumptions of law although in a limited sense, it may be said that in a contract of marriage the wife corresponds to the property and dower to the price."[30]

However a female on attaining puberty can enter into the contract of marriage. Guardian cannot compel her to marry. There is no restriction on marriage of saibba (a woman who already had sexual intercourse). Both virgin and saibba have equal right as regards contract of marriage unlike Hindus.

As regards completion of formalities on a valid marriage there is prescription for proposal by a party and acceptance of the proposal by the other party in presence and hearing of two males or one male and two female witnesses. Here we find that the Muslim Law recognizes the position of female equal to half of a male. That is to say, the value of woman in muslim society is just the half of man. So there is no equality in status and rights of male and female in Muslim Law. Hence any prudent person can conclude from the above illustration that women's position in the eyes of Muslim Law is much inferior to that of men.

Position of Muslim women can further be examined in the context of dower (Mahar). The definition of Dower given by Wilson is noteworthy to assess the value of women according to Muslim Law and tradition. According to Wilson:—

> "Dower" is a consideration for the surrender of person by the wife. It is the technical Anglo-Mohammedan term for its equivalent "Mahr" in Arabic."[31]

In Saburannessa V Sabdu Sheikh[32] Calcutta High Court has observed that Muslim marriage is like a contract of sale in which the wife is the property and dower is the price. Both the above definitions of Dower clearly express that Muslim Law and the tradition consider women as the property and the marriage is a ceremonial surrender of women's person to a man for which a price is paid or fixed to be paid. Thus the entity of women before a man like a matter or object which man can possess by paying the price. Though some of the legal experts and the religious stalwarts advocate Dower to be "consideration" paid by the husband to his wife as a mark of respect but this view do not hold so sound with gravity because the general practice and behaviour of men towards their wives in Muslim community have gave ample scope to conclude that women are treated like an object. Women lack right to equality and dignified status.

The Kharchai-i-pandan guzara and mewa Khori in Muslim is an allowance given to wife by the husband. It is a personal allowance to the wife customary among Muslim families of rank. This allowance also reduce the status of women in a family since allowance given to anybody on any condition is the sympathetic consideration. Sympathetic consideration is paid to one who lives at the mercy. Mercyful allowance never can be a part of right. Thus one who receive allowance cannot claim rights. As such women in Muslim society have no equivalent rights in family with the men. That is to say the women are subordinated in Muslim society either according customs or tradition or law.

In the context of Guardianship rights again the women in Muslim community is placed at inferior position to men. The guardianship right gives recognition to male first. Father becomes the natural guardian, in his absence members of male parental ascendancy how highsoever (i.e., father's father and so in ascending order) becomes the guardian. Then come the full brother and other male relatives on the father's side in order of inheritance given under residuaries. Only in the absence of male members in the residuaries of lineal inheritance mother get the right of guardianship.[33] Here any one can find the position of women in Muslim society inferior to men. Women are even neglected in family in relation to their children. The mother is entitled in Hanafi law to the custody (hizanant) of her male child until he has completed the age seven years and of her female child until she has attained puberty and[33a] in Shia Law to the custody of her male child till the age of 2 years and to the custody of her female child till the age of 7 years. Whereas, father is entitled in Hanafi Law to the custody of a boy over 7 years of age and of an unmarried girl who has attained puberty and in Shia Law to the custody of a male child over 2 years and an unmarried girl of 7 years or more. Here also one can find that women are subjected to suffer all sorts of oddities and men are to enjoy the privilege and pleasure. They enjoy prestige and dignity whereas, women are made to suffer all pains and miseries.

In customary law of Muslim daughters are excluded from the right of inheritance. Thus we find that women cannot inherit the property of the deceased father.

Position of Women in Christian Society

The religious differences from Hindus and Muslims are of the spiritual ideology, in Christianity. There are differences of customs and tradition as regard spiritual and religious observance. But the social status created for women by the religious customs and tradition of Christianity is not far better than that of Hindu or Muslim. Christianity also lays down norms of distinction between male and female from the very childhood. The female children in Christian society are poised in adverse position of the male children in every domestic or social activity. Thus from the childhood the female child develops a sense of inferiority and insecurity in her and gradually in adolescence she becomes solely dependent on male for her self protection.

The practical life of women in Christian community if analytically examined, it would come to light that their status except in the context of education, is the same as in Hindu and Muslim communities. Christian religion has also not given them equal rights with men to perform religious acts and rituals. Thus it can be concluded that in Indian Christian Society the status of women is not far better than the women in Hindu and Muslim society. Only in matrimonial home Christian women enjoy greater liberty than Hindu and Muslim women as their marriage is considered as a social contract now.

The position of women in Christianity can be assessed by the implicit construction of the concept of marriage incorporated in Christians law (canon law of marriage). The canon law proclaimed and enjoined the absolute doctrine of indissolubility of marriage. It held that, by marriage man and wife were made of one flesh by the act of God-marriage being a holy tie, a sacrament. Thus it was proclaimed "what God hath joined together, no man put it asunder". This doctrine was proclaimed by St. Paul to consider marriage a sacramental and indissoluble union likened the relationship of man and his wife to that of Christ and His Church.[34] This doctrine of canon law signifies that women's position is not at all better than Indian Hindu women since the marriage is considered as a sacrament and indissoluble. Whatever the liking and disliking of women may be in a marriage tie, once the marriage is solemnized she cannot severe it. Again it is clarified that her position is like a Church and man is like Christ. That is to say the role of women in household is to make her man a godlike personality and to look after him a grandeur, do all sorts of works which make the man adorable and supreme the divine power for her. Thus she never can go against his will. The substance of the principle is to dedicate women's whole life in the service of her god like husband without considering herself as a human creature like her husband. Individual liberty and identity of women in society, without husband is not recognized and is unimaginable. A contractual union though valid in law yet not spiritually complete without the blessing of the church. There was no escape from the holy tie of marriage. Only death can put it asunder. Moreover, in the old days marriage in Christianity, could not be solemnized without the prior permission of the church — the Bishop, the priest or the deacon. Thus it appears that position of women is more or less the same as in the Hindu community in the context of sacramental value of marriage. However, at later stage separation of the parties from the marriage tie was permitted but right to remarry during life time was not granted.

In Christianity also prescribes chastity of woman, it argues marriage to be a religious sacramental institution designed to avoid loose living, sex immorality and concubinage. Here it indicates that Christian society also emphasise on woman's sexual purity but no where abominate the male's sexual immorality and admonishes any measure to control men's sexual infidelity. As such one can conclude that women's position is inferior to men like Hindu society.

However at the advent of modernization the reformists group of Christians, who had deviated from the ecclesiastic doctrine of marriage being a sacramental act ordained by God, was called Protestants considered the marriage as a man made contract. As in other human affairs so in marriage, people should have the opportunity to rectify their errors. Thus dissolubility of marriage was accepted as the individualistic philosophy — the pursuit of happiness. Each individual is entitled to live his life as cheerfully and happily as he or she chooses. He has the right to develop those conditions and situations which tend to help him to live happily and to develop his personality, talent, capacity and potentialities. Though the Protestants consider marriage as a bond, a civil contract, but it is not a bondage, a slavery in the grab of super-imposed sacramentality. Among the Indian Christian marriage is regarded as a civil contract, thereby improved the position of women in comparison to the views of Catholics. Now the marriage can be dissolved by the verdict of civil court. Now the Christian countries have adopted the principle of divorce by mutual consent to maintain happy married life and to reduce the unhappy marriage tie in society. In India also Christian are liberal in this respect. Yet the principles and norms of marriage alone cannot justify the position of women.

To assess the position of women in Indian Christian society we have to find the practical life of women in Christian families. Since majority of Indian Christians are convertees originated in Indian land, have the customary and traditional differences from the Christians of the European countries and America. Indian Christians have yet the mentality and cultures of the Indian past and they are at home in usage of the same in day to day affairs. Thus the value of women, as regards freedom, liberty, dignity and exercising will power in the management of family affairs, is not at all better than the women of Hindu community. In respect of guardianship right the position of Christian woman is same as a Hindu woman because the Child Marriage Restraint (Amendment) Act 1976 has abrogated the Christian Law of Guardianship provided under the Indian Christian Act 1872. Thus as regard guardianship right the entity of Christian women is almost neglected in marriage as well as in all other affairs.

The position of women in Indian Christian society, becomes more clear when we look into the condition of society in the eyes of law, when we examine the customs and procedures adopted by parties to marriage and the relative effect of dowry in marriage. The applicability of Dowry Prohibition Act 1961 on all communities alike evince that in Christian community also Dowry system prevails. The evils of the dowry prevailed in Christian society compelled the legislature and executive to impose Dowry Prohibition Act on Christian society also. So, we can conclude that women in Christian community suffer the evils of dowry. The social evil like dowry is prevalent in Indian Christian community, because most of the Indian Christian follow their pre-conversion customs specially in Kerala, Karnataka and adjacent states and the rate of dowry is very high with the high literacy rate. The more highly qualified bridegroom is, the more he deserves and demand higher rate of dowry.

From the above facts we find that women in Christian society even after achieving higher literacy rate are not accepted by men in their matrimonial home if sufficient dowry is not given by the parents of the bride. That is to say that the beginning of household with a life partner needs gratification. If the bride brings more dowry with her she is applaudingly welcomed but if she fails to bring with her valuables and cash in-laws sneer upon her and gradually her matrimonial home becomes ghastly den for her. The judicial proceedings in the matrimonial dispute cases reveal that women after marriage become victims of dowry deaths, dowry suicides, battering, harassment, humiliation or taunts on the ground that she did not bring enough at the time of marriage. This happens with the Christian women also in India. The implementation of dowry prohibition act also on Christian Community deduce that women's position in Christian Community of India is deplorable. They never have the equal status with men. Rights and privileges are served for men only and women are reduced to the position of slave to their male relations and husbands. Every where in every community in India women are treated as an object of fulfilling lustful desires of men. Despite several legislative measures to protect the dignity and respect of women, everyday they become the victims of men's oppression.

Even the anti-dowry act is not competent to protect the women against cruelty, coercion and battering by husbands and in-laws because lawyers and judges quite often create confusion in interpreting the language of the statute. For instance in the case of Inder Sain Vs. State of Bihar[35] and in Kashi Prasad Vs. State of Bihar[36] the Patna High Court expressed the view that mere demand for dowry would not constitute an offence under the section unless it was shown that the other party consented to pay it. Justice Luthra of the Delhi High Court after quoting the definition of dowry observed:—

> "Thus the definition of the word 'consideration' leads to the conclusion that property or valuable security should be demanded or given whether in the past, present or future for bringing out solemnization of marriage, giving a property or valuable security by the parents of the bride cannot constitute a 'consideration' for the marriage unless it was agreed at the time of or before the marriage that such property or valuable security would be given in future.[37]

The interpretation of law given as above by the Patna and Delhi High Courts encourage the offenders since demanding dowry will continue but no legal action will be initiated against them as per the judicial interpretation of statute given by Justice Luthra. Delhi High Court in another case (Madan Lal Vs Amar Nath)[38] also held:—

> "Wherein the court felt that property given by the bride's father subsequent to marriage with a view to saving the marriage from being rocked did not constitute dowry."

Thus we can conclude that Law of the country is also failed to safeguard the interest and rights of female in made dominated society of India either of Hindu or Muslim or the Christian community. We find the evidence of cruelty on Christian women in the case of Long Vs. Long in which the husband assaulted the wife, persistently abused her, forced intercourse on her in circumstances of calculated and revolving indiguity, yet he did not desire her to leave the matrimonial home. Such kind of behaviour of husband clearly shows where the women in Christian society find their position.

How to Examine the Position of Women

We can reach to substantial facts to establish the position of women in society in comparison to men by examining the following questions and their apparent replies from the practical life of women.

1. How is domestic work regarded in the society?
2. What are the conditions of work of rural women, women in factories and professional women?
3. What are the contributions of women in the economic activities in the society?
4. How much do the women benefit from the economic activities in Society?
5. Are there laws in the society that are discriminatory in the society?
6. What is the extent of political awareness of the women in society?
7. What religious and cultural practices in the society do you consider oppressive or discriminatory to women?

8. What form of trafficing of women exist in the society?
9. What is the status of women in the family and in society?
10. How are women treated in the acts of media?
11. Is there any cultural and traditional practice which hampers women's advancement in society?
12. Does religion or custom impose practices or beliefs that interfere with improving the status of women?
13. What role the women are expected to play in society and the family?
14. What measures have been taken to change social and cultural pattern that lead to stereotyping or reinforcing the idea of the inferiority of women?
15. Who is considered, by law or custom, to be the "head of the household"?
16. Are there specified works that are considered as 'men's work' or 'Women's work'? What is the percentage of men and women in these kinds of works?
17. What kinds of work are forbidden to do, either by law or customs?
18. Are girls and boys expected to do different tasks in the home or at schools?
19. Who is responsible for the care of children?
20. In divorce cases, who is typically given custody of the children and why?
21. What are the rights given to daughters in the property of their father?
22. Does the widow without children have any perpetual right on the property of her husband when the predeceased has brothers?
23. What degree and extent of guardianship right the mother possesses over her children in presence of her husband?
24. What the pecuniary rights an woman enjoy in her family?

25. What are customary ceremonial rights the women enjoy in society?
26. What is the attitude of a husband when the wife intends to participate in politics?

References

1. Mary Wollstonecraft's "A Vindication of Rights of Women (1992 Ed.).
2. Mary Wollstonecraft's "A Vindication of Rights of Women (1992 Ed.) (p. XXXI).
3. Janice Wood Wetzel's The World of Women—The Macmillan Press Ltd, London (1993 Ed).
4. 'In the Way of Women', p. 107, by Cynthia Cockburn, 1991 Ed.
5. 'In the Way of Women', p. 107, by Cynthia Cockburn, 1991 Ed.
6. 'In the Way of Women', p. 156, by Cynthia Cockburn, 1991 Ed.
7. 'In the Way of Women', p. 157, by Cynthia Cockburn, 1991 Ed.
8. 'In the Way of Women', p. 158, by Cynthia Cockburn, 1991 Ed.
9. 'In the Way of Women', p. 159, by Cynthia Cockburn, 1991 Ed.
10. Dr. Hilda Lazarus Sphere of Indian Women in Medical Work, p. 165, Geraldine Forbes' Women in Modern India.
11. Autobiography of Dr. (Mrs.) S. Muthulakshmi Reddy (Madras M. Reddy 1964).
12. Geraldine Forbes' Women in Modern India.
13. J.M. Everett's 'Women and Social Change in India 1979 Ed. (New Delhi), p. 31.
14. Jogesh Ch. Bagal-Women's Education in Eastern India (Calcutta) 1956, p. 62 and p. 31 of J.M. Everett's Women and Social Change in India.
15. J.M. Everett's 'Women and Social Change in India', 1979 Ed. (New Delhi) p. 31.
16. Lakshmi Misra's Education of Women in India (1921-1966) (Bombay 1966) pp. 33 and 34 (p. 32 of Women and Social Change in India).
17. Syed Narullah and J.P. Naik's A history of Education in India (Bombay 1951) (p. 32 of Women and Social Change in India).
18. Cynthia Cockburn's "In the way of Women" (Men's Resistance to Sex Equality) 1991 Ed. (p. 17).
19. Cynthia Cockburn's "In the Way of Women" (Men's Resistance to Sex Equality in Organisation) 1991 Ed. (p. 23 and 24).
20. Cynthia Cockburn's "In the Way of Women" 1991 Ed. (p. 27).

21. Cynthia Cockburn's "In the Way of Women" 1991 Ed. (p. 27).
22. Cynthia Cockburn's "In the Way of Women" p. 154 and 155.
23. *Ibid.*, p. 155.
24. Cynthia Cockburn's "In the Way of Women" 1991 (p. 27).
25. Cynthia Cockburn's "In the Way of Women" 1991 (p. 22).
26. UPD Kesari's "Modern Hindu Law", p. 29 and 30.
27. Julia Leslie and Mary McGee's "Invented Identities".
28. Julia Leslie and McGee's "Invented Identities" (p. 162).
29. Text Book of Mohammedan Law by Aqil Ahmad (p. 63)
30. The case of Suburannessa Vs. Sabdu Sheikh AIR 1934 Cal 693.
31. Text Book of Mohammedan Law by Aqil Ahmad 1993, Ed., p. 83.
32. P-83 Text Book of Mohammedan Law by Aqil Ahmad 1993, Ed., p. 83.
33. Text Book of Mohammedal Law by Aqil Ahamad, Ed., 1993, p. 130.
34. *Ibid.*
35. Dr. Paras Dewan's "Law of Marriage and Divorce", Universal Book Traders, Ed. 1997, (Delhi) (p. 21).
36. 1981 Cr. L. J. 1116.
37. 1980 BBCJ 612.
38. AIR 1984 Del 66 (p. 213 Law of Marriage and Divorce by Paras Dewan 1997 Ed.).

Four

Miserable Condition of Women in India

The opinion of the reformists of 20th century about the plight of women in India attracted the attention of the reformist. The reformist ideology particularly in its view of women which was retained throughout, much of the twentieth century tell us that, first and foremost, Indian women were to be pitied. It is worthy of mention the statement of Mahesh Chandra Deb to draw a clear picture of women in India especially in Hindu society. He states about the prevailing condition of women of that time as under—

> "Suffice it to say every man who has carefully examined the condition of Hindu women cannot help pitying the benighted and miserable situation in which they are faced. Notwithstanding all their kind attention, their pious and dutiful conducts, their submissive behaviour towards their husbands, they frequently meet with severe scolding and are even sometimes cruelly punished from ungrounded jealousy or a tyrannical whims."[1]

The above statement encouraged Western critics of Indian society to highlight it throughout the country. And it was necessary for the benevolent thinkers and elites of the world at that time on humanitarian ground to highlight the issue to bring change to improve their condition. In fact the Western critics had inspired and influenced the Indian reformers; however, they were also familiar with their own traditions which sometimes proved to be a limitation in their activities.

It was admitted by the famous social reformers of the time like Ram Mohan Roy, Pundit Vidya Sagar, Swami Dayananda Saraswati and many others that, India has recovering from darkness and also they aspired—there had been a "golden age" when women were valued and given high position in social status.[2]

The historical research on women in India during 20th century led the researchers to opine and state that during this golden age women were educated, married only after they had reached maturity, moved about freely and participated in social and political life of the time. This statement clearly indicates that the historians found the miserable state of women in the past which they have asserted indirectly in their present report of the research they carried out concerning the Indian women. An Indian historian and member of the Brahmin Community though commented adversely against the opinion given above but she accepted the truth of the aforesaid conclusion. She says: "that for contemporary women this perception of the past has led to a narrow and limiting circle in which the image of Indian Womanhood has become both a shackle and a rhetorical device that nevertheless functions as a historical truth."[3]

Again we find some evidence of women's declination during the time of Smritis, i.e., a period when vast series of law codes such as Manusmritis, commentaries and epics—most prominently the Mahabharata, Ramayana and Puranas or stories of the God were written. Many historians argued that the decline in women's status could be traced in these writings. Thus we cannot ignore with the present state of women in India that condition of women in the medieval time were pitiable in the vedic period than the period of muslim rule. But most of the reformers blamed Muslim rules. In reality Muslim rulers such as Akbar attempted to abolish Sati and Muslim Law accorded higher status to women than in Hindu Law. The very dark sight of the Hindu Law were that, the

Hindu law givers claimed child marriage, prohibition on widow re-marriage seclusion and most the restriction on female education were to Muslim threat to women's safety.

Whatever may be the cause behind the miserable condition of women in India, the famous historian Mahesh Chandra Deb, to persuade his audience to draw immediate attention on woman question and to develop an ideology of legitimate social reform he said:—

> "in whatever light then, we view the situation of Hindoo women—whether we look to their physical or mental condition—we shall find to our great mortification that it is truly deplorable."[4]

This statement of Mahesh Chandra Deb help us to conclude that conditions of women in vedic period were miserable.

A sketch of the condition of Hindoo women and needed reform to bring them to a developed state if not equal to men but at least to better human condition give us clear evidence of women suffering. It is quite improbable to think that such deplorable condition the women suffered and brought the human generation to the present state. The present generation may be doubtful about the role of religion to place the women in such deplorable condition. But the reality had been accepted by the former historians and social reformists. By the illustrations from the religious customs and rituals the Colonial officials were made to agree and believe that religion was central to Indian life, Indian people were slaves to religion and sati and many other customs were religious practices.

The miserable condition of women in India has been vividly shown in a speech of Vidyasagar to his audience:—

> "Countrymen! How long will you suffer yourselves to be led away by illusions! Open your eyes for once and see, that India, once the land of virtue, is being over flooded by the stream of adultery and foeticide. The degradation to which you have sunk is sadly low. Dip

> into the spirit of your Sastras, follow its dictates and you shall be able to remove the foul blot from the face of your country."[5]

The above speech refers to the social reform of Vidyasagar for widow remarriage. The readers should not be taken into aback that social reform has played such an important role in twentieth century to uplift the condition of women that cannot be expressed in words.

About the evils of customs Raja Rammohun Roy wrote of "women who were forced upon the pyre 'bound' with ropes so they would perish with their husbands and Vidya Sagar wrote of – customs which had hampered the evolution of her (woman's) facilities", and D. K. Karve wrote of a caste widow who fell victim to the passion of some brute. All these reformers opined that these customs were perverted, twisted, distorted practices born of ignorance and fear and followed without recourse to common sense. Thus the contemporary elite and common people can have an idea from the writings and opinions of the twentieth century reformist, what a state of women were in the past and how it has improved to the present and plan further reform for future to improve the status of women. The advocacy of the present BJP led govt. for political reservation for women at par I think and most of the socialists and historians will consider, is not the solution to solve the problems of raising women's status equal to men's in the prevailing condition. The numerous social aspects of women's declined position explained above warrant social and religious reforms than political privilege for women.

According to Vivekananda there should be no hesitation in applying the full panoply of Western analytical methods to the "science of religion". Similarly Swami Dayananda made it clear that he would not defend "the falsehood" of the Hindu religion but would unveil them just as he had expressed the errors of other religions. These statements of the eminent religious personalities also bring out the fact that religious evils were responsible for the declined position of women. Therefore, religious reforms need to be implemented first then the other aspects of social life can be considered in this context.

Many eminent writers on the position of women in India have asserted that whatever the historical evidence discovered and recorded before the reformers programme whatever the picture or life sketch of women can be drawn are tainted by polemics and refer only to lives of women from the highest ranking, land holding groups. Unfortunately there are no reference of the vast majority of women who must have been living and working outside the normal human society of Hindu. Indian women population comprised of larger portion from these categories of women, who were not even considered by women of the upper social strata of Hindu society. Thus we can imagine the miserable condition of a majority of Indian women from the assessment of higher castes women's condition made by Mrs. Forbes in her book.

Reasons for Subordinate Position of Women

In the preceding chapter 3 the position of women in India with reference to various aspects of life in human society has been discussed. I have tried to cover all aspects of life. However, only the major relative aspects could be discussed in short. Even then the position of women in Indian contemporary society has been clearly reflected in that.

Now in this chapter I am going to discuss about the causes attributed to the deplorable condition of women in India. These are poverty tradition, inclination, social customs, Kanya Dan, Dowry motivation, religion, ancient scriptures, culture, media, film industries, patriarchal system, employment, women's reaction to social movement, mentality of women, political interest. and social Environment which are described in brief in this chapter, remaining several reasons are not discussed in this chapter as the same have been relatively discussed in the chapters concerning atrocities and causes of atrocities, equality of rights and improvement of social status.

Poverty

It is worldwide known that women contribute generously to the gross national product as well as to the well-being of their families and their communities. Women are the main providers for one-third of all families in the world, and two-thirds of the poorest. If truth be known, more women than men are solely responsible for their families. Three-fourths of world's micro-entrepreneurs are women, and in low-income countries like India women contribute 60-70 per cent production of food for local consumption. Not only India but also in every part of the world women work longer hours than men and perform wider variety of tasks. Though the fiscal resources affect differently in the support services provided by women in most of the countries yet women who work outside the home regardless of class or ethnicity are likely to carry the dual burden of responsibility.

But what the women get out of their work? They are neglected everywhere. Their contribution in country's development is not counted or recognized. Because women's efforts have been continued to be invisible, unpaid, underpaid and limited to low skill and dead-end job. Two-thirds of the world's women population live in poverty.[6] Particularly in India position is worse, because 70 per cent population are in rural area having no employment except agricultural labour for a limited period on low payment. The women's poverty is a global problem and it is in reality a major problem in India and Bangladesh but the government has taken the matter so seriously in the development programme commensurate to the gravity. Women's poverty is also due to lack of labor organizing experience, low wages, toleration of frequent job turn over with no security. In patriarchal gender discrimination women are neglected in family; they are not given the opportunity of developing their skill or ability to perform the job of pecuniary benefits. Research of various scholars suggests that women are not even conscious of their exploitation despite the fact that they continue to live in poverty while working long hours in extreme conditions.[7] The international division of labor continues to be shaped by capitalist economies so that cash in on cheap raw materials and cheap labour, which considerably affect the Indian economy, further deteriorate the pecuniary condition of women. The poverty of Indian women is attributed by this factor to a great extent. Despite certain generous and benevolent consideration at government level the economic condition of women could not be improved.

Women's poor condition is also due to the labour exploitation by the industrialists, which perpetuate the wants of poor women; as a result they become submissive to their basses with a hope to suffice their economic need by doing extra work at home in a very low wages. The legal rights of these women and children are not only not being enforced now, but if legalized their employers will be given implicit sanction to continue to exploit them. Their problems are deeply rooted in patriarchal gender discrimination and racism that segregates women in undervalued and underpaid jobs. Caretaking and maintenance work, traditionally considered to be "women's work" are viewed as something to undervalue in the first place. The main tactic by which women are controlled and maintained is sexual division of labour of the patriarchal system which permits men to reap disproportionate benefits placing them in positions of authority. Racial discrimination further weaken the pecuniary condition of women of the backward section by ignoring them for a beneficial job. Class analysis without an examination of gender relations within and between (racial and ethnic groups) has only perpetuated the subordinate status of women. Irrespective of culture and political party, when women are included in the labour force, the majority of them are integrated in the lowest levels, thus remaining a secondary, poorly paid, expendable work force. From the above discussion we can conclude that the women's poverty is attributable to many aspects of social, religious life, political and social activities of the country and personal ignorance.

Tradition

For the miserable condition of women in India, first cause we find is the traditional behaviour in society. In Hindu society when a female child is born the customary ceremony performed by the family distinctly indicates the birth of a female or male because of the differences in observance and degree of amusement. Thereafter the mother inculcates all those servility in the day to day movement of the child which keeps her depreciated in society in comparison to a male. Parents administer upon her all those rules and procedures in the family life which arrest her physical robustness, mental fertility and courage. At the adolescence the girls are taught and guarded by the mother and other female relations. Thus a recoiling tendency develops in them in every walk of life. The parents and relatives very much encourage the female grown up children to make their bearing more beautiful and delicate. Thus they develop habit of meekness and allurement.

When a girl is married and transferred to family of her husband, the in-laws make her to perceive that she is only the humble servant of her husband and in-laws. Even the younger in-laws frequently cast a disgusted look on her slight deviation from their choice and liking, they expect from her. These sorts of activities at the beginning days of matrimonial home are nothing but the rotten tradition of which knowing fully well to be derogatory and inhuman, unpalatable in the present day world, still repeat as a traditional norm. Though now-a-days women are being imparted education in academic/technical fields but they are compelled to do other household work which the male children are not required to do. There are enormous practical instances in the surrounding where girls being more brilliant than the boys are not getting full support from parents for education and self improvement whereas, the dull and disobedient boy gets everything from parents at his whims. There are plenty of instances in different section of society which evince that tradition to a larger extent prejudice against the women. Women's identity is changed after marriage is also a traditional degradation.

Keeping long hair by the girls is also a traditional segregation of female from the male. Wearing sari and different patterns of cloths from that of the man's wear is a traditional mark of distinction. Moreover, the pattern of dress prescribed as a tradition for women undoubtedly create obstacles in the quick movement. Thus from the very early age the females are traditionally made physically weak. They are hindered to develop their physical power by arresting their fast movement. They are made slow movers and soft physique as a traditional mark of sex.

Using different styles of language for women from that of men is also a traditional mischieve of men to isolate female so that they could easily be identified. The transfer of female after marriage to her husband's house is a derogatory tradition by which the female children are deprived of love, affection and regular care of parents. This system not only degrade the female child but also the parents as they lose the authority over the child which has been brought up through many austerities.

The above statements suggest to conclude that tradition has played a drastic role to lower the position of women in human society.

Family's Inclination

The researches carried out on the process of personality development of boys and girls indicate that it is the family which lay the foundation of inequality of sexes from the very childhood in the social process as a result. Right from the childhood boys and girls are brought up with powerful notions that, certain qualities are masculine and others are feminine and those are strengthened in every possible way in the social process. Through language forms, dress, behaviour, household task, vocations, leisure-time occupation etc. the girls are made distinguished from boys and the former's position became subordinate to the latter. These are inextricably tied up with certain notions of superiority of men and deeply affect the personality development of women.

If these inequalities between men and women are to be reduced, the only way to change the attitude of the family especially of the parents in creating values equality between boys and girls. These will be basic and most lasting and effective measures. The first and foremost role to play to equalize men and women lies on parents especially mothers. They should radically change their attitude towards their daughters and bring them up exactly with same care as their sons. No other way will be befitting to equalize in status the men and women in society.

Taking into consideration the above description, the political power or special political privileges without changing the attitude of society, family and especially the parents towards their children's care, will be futile efforts. The women's equal status with men in society is possible only by changing the mentality of public in a radical manner to treat boys and girls equally.

The basic differences between men and women are created in a family and parents of the children are the first creator of differences. The society comprising the family as its ingredient the parents suffice the strength of the society. Thus the social differences in men and women are based on the inclination of parents towards the sexual and biological differences, which is further strengthened by the parents.

Social Customs

The social customs degenerate the position of women in society. We have historical evidence that even though Vidya Sagar (Iswarchandra) made a gigantic effort to change the fate of widows but the opponents were not less strong to place a bar on his movement; thousands of signatures were appended against Iswar Chandra's drive for widow remarriage. Although the government approved the request of Vidya Sagar and passed the Hindu Widow Remarriage Act in 1856, the value of this act to improve the condition of women was questioned. This Act did not change the status of widows. In higher castes widows were frequently blamed for husband's death. Their customs did not approve wearing of jewellery for widow and they required to subsist on simple vegetarian food. Young widows were preyed upon by men who would make them their mistress or carry them away to urban brothels.[8] As regards the victims of men's atrocities the widows we have a glaring historical evidence of anger, a Marathi housewife in the following statement:—

> "In 1881 the court at Surat in Western India tried Vijayalakshmi, a young brahmin widow, for killing her illegitimate child. At the first trial she was sentenced to hang but on appeal this was changed to transportation for life and later reduced to five years. This case so angered Tarabai Shinde (C 1850-1910) a young Marathi Housewife, that she wrote "Stri-purusha-Tulana" (A comparison between Women and Men).

Vijayalakshmi's case had triggered an intense public discussion about the misfortune of widows and the issue of widow remarriage. For Tarabai, it was clear that this issue was simply a metaphor for the general mistreatment of women. She wrote-"so is it true that only women's bodies are home to all the different kind of recklessness and vice? Or have men got just the same faults as we find in women?" As for widows:

> "Once a woman's husband has died, not even a dog would shallow what she's got to". Tarabai Shinde's cry for equality went unheeded in a world where reformers wanted to help women, not accord them equal status."[9]

Position of Indian women is clear from the above illustration and also we find the efficacy of reforms. Reformists advocated for social reforms to improve the status of women but they never had in mind to grant equal status with men. Now again a question in independent India has arisen of giving political reservation to women. It is not clear to common men what does the political reservation mean. Our politicians do not consider women equal to men but they advocates for special privilege to women in politics. The eminent historians, educationists, sociologists and anthropologists of the world have brought out that development of human society to a large extent depend on the development of women population and they have also pointed out the sufferings of women in male dominated society. The male domination has not yet been checked in society specially in India the picture is very dark.

The observation of Vidya Sagar the reformists of Bengal is a surprising phenomena of the society. He lives in such a world where the male among Kulin Brahmins (Highest ranking Brahmin), an aristocratic caste with rigid marriage rules, were highly sought after as bridegroom and able to marry as many women as they wished. As per collection of data by Vidya Sagar on this custom he became horrified to see the magnitude of this problem. His observation on 133 Kulin Brahmins of Hooghly District he revealed the abuses inherent in polygamy. He found a fifty-five years old Kulin Brahmin had married 107 times. Consequently he presented petition for legislative prohibition on polygamy. But government declined to act on social reform being cautious in the wake of the rebellion of 1857.

The present society is not far improved from that of British time. Despite enactment of Hindu Marriage Act 1955 and the Special Marriage Act 1954, the position of Indian women is not improved. Women still become prey to the men's carnal desires and suffer life long hell in Indian society. Our able politicians and bureaucrats are least bother about new devices to bring equality between men and women in social arena first.

Another aspect of social customs which still prevails and create discrimination or differences in status among women themselves are the caste distinction and customary differences inherent in it. The differences in social and religious customs based on caste have created a gulf between women of higher castes and the lower castes. This difference in status of women of different castes became the first cause of misery of women, second being the distinction between men and women. Until women of different castes are not granted equality in status, the question of equality between men and women will be a farce ideology. Grant of political privilege to women if considered as the means of bringing equality and amelioration of women's misery, it will be an idea of planting paddy in sand and then making every efforts to use good manure.

It is pointed out from the records of women workers in Jute Mills in Calcutta during 1920, that 66,000 women, about 20 per cent of the total workers mostly worked in spinning, carding and finishing the jutes but never found in the jute presses. Hindu and Muslim Bengali women among the jute workers were very less, i.e., to say not more than 10 per cent of the total women workers. The real cause of very less number of Bengali women in jute mills was the purdah, restrictions of Hindu and Muslim customs of Bengal. Thus customs hindered their performance in Jute Mills.

Kanya Dan

The traditional customs influenced by the religious belief as regard celebration of marriage of young match, the process of "Kanya Dan" has a pervasive adverse effect on the all round position of women. The term "Kanya Dan" itself confirm and poise the position of a grown up well educated and competent girl like a piece of property from the very beginning of her new household. Thus she is thrown into the ditch of slavery in a new family. Until and unless this rotten custom is abandoned the women will be reminded her insignificant position in a family and in society as a whole. The social reformists and the advocates of women's rights should take adequate steps to abandon forthwith this ignoble custom. If the girl or the boy finds a suitable match for marriage, they should also be ready economically and otherwise fit to set up a new household without any fetters from the in-laws of either side. To raise the status of women, they should not be treated like men's property. Therefore, the very first step of making a woman a man's property by donating her to that man should be prohibited and this is possible only by radically changing the attitudes of parents and abandoning the despicable custom of 'Kanya Dan'. The entire society should have deliberate thought on this custom. The society and the social thinkers should analyse the term and its practical implications upon the population. This custom's implicit meaning and influence upon women should be the main object of analytical examination. The practical behaviour relating to this custom, of parents and relations, upon the girl and the consequential treatment met to her in the house of in-laws should be taken into consideration in analytical examination of the adaptability of this custom. What the general notion from the ancient past till to date prevails in the society, give us an understanding that the continuation of this process of marriage ceremony makes the women morally weak and their position remains subordinated in society leaving men to use them as property according to their sweet will.

Dowry

The custom of dowry is also the creation of religious sanctions. If Sati is a bizarre—culmination of cultural value ramified by scriptures, religious beliefs and superstitions, dowry is curious but terrible products of their inter-action with rigid social structure based on caste and sub caste groups integrated through joint family and kinship groups when the scriptures propound that a woman is man's property, it becomes axiomatic that women has less value than men in human society. Therefore to compensate the position of woman to enter into couple life with a man she brings some valuable things with herself for her husband and in-laws who took the trouble of marrying her.

The system of dowry clearly demean not only the position of woman but also the position of her parents in society. The practice of dowry compel the parents of the girl to give away their grown up daughter, who was nourished with great care and docility, into a slavery to another family to work as a servant to sweep, to cook, to serve and what not. Even in modern days the educated employed girls are also made to carryout the work of slave in their marital home not by their own will but due to their in-laws and husband's demands.

The advanced elite society is also not free from this vicious culture. It is found that even after the marriage of boy and girl selected each as the mutual approach and attraction met with the same fate in the house of in-laws. Even the highly qualified and employed in the highest cadre of administrative machinery are not free from the clutches of this evil. In the recent past it was reported in newspaper that an IAS officer in Madhya Pradesh has murdered his wife by joint plotting with his family members for not getting the dowry demanded by them. This incident shows at what extent the evils of dowry custom is deep rooted in Indian society. The position of a woman came from another family to make room for her in the new family is quite harsh, she has to tolerate all sorts of insults by the in-laws and husband, especially when her parents fail to give dowry more than the demand of the husband and party. The educated youths make farce propaganda and arguments against the dowry. In reality no one of the bridegrooms either in high castes or in low castes can control the greediness of getting something valuable from the bride he marries. The parents in the hope of providing their daughter a peaceful comfortable life in new family give money, valuables and ornaments even without demand. But this custom has become so counter productive that, young girls are harassed in their in-laws houses for more dowry and if more is not forthcoming from the parents of the girl, she is burnt alive or compelled to commit suicide. These sorts of dowry death incidents have created a feverish effect in the minds of parents. As a result foeticide has increased manifold, even if the mother gives birth of a female child she becomes casual towards taking care of nursing the child. On the other hand the husband losses his attention towards the wife. Ultimately the society degenerate into a place of female's indignation.

Such type of scripture based cultural and customary tradition should be abolished immediately. However, it is not easy to abolish or eliminate the long trend by legal injunction or giving political power to women. To eliminate this social evil mentality of male population towards the females should be changed. If the males come forward to accept women as their equal complement in every walk of human life and consider them equally important in every sphere of activity. Superstitions and spiritual blind faith cannot be wipe out by exterior admonition but by the feelings and dictates of inner heart. Many reformists and politicians vehemently advocates for abolition of dowry but practically it is seen that they themselves encourage the same in their own action. Politicians often are found to the staunch supporters of this custom and in their individual cases gravely demand and extract dowry from the parents of girls applying several tricks and games.

These are all due to the deep rooted traditional belief and greedy blend thought of the society. Only the way to overcome this evil is to form firm will of the male population against it.

Motivation

Every society in the world provides powerful motivation for rapid progress of human beings, in the form of competition or recognition and honour for certain pattern of activity and behaviour. But Indian society provided no such opportunity for recognition and honour for women's works. In India whatever the motivational patters exist in rural as well as urban communities, are all to recognize and honour the men only. In villages some men are taken to the pinnacle of heroic deed like fighting the snake or the tiger or defending the village against the plunder of robbers or fighting battle against the enemies.

In some cases of recognition and rewards of men's heroic deed their monuments were erected on the village boundaries and the songs in their praise were recited by village bards. But nowhere such recognition or honour did exist for the deeds of women. Though every human heart craves for such honour or great recognition. Cultural motivation has been a great source of inhuman treatment with women in Hindu society. The Sati pratha (custom) is not only the deceit played on women, there are several other forms of indignation which are committed upon women in society on the pretext of spiritual value or the religious sanctity. There are several legendary facts described in scriptures to inculcate blind faith and superstitions in women which indirectly perpetuated slavery of women in Indian Society and the men are depicted as the lord of the women. According to the religious precept, position of women is insecure as she is said to be dependent on her father before marriage, husband after marriage and on son at the old age, for her protection. Women themselves also accept the same maxim.

As such equality of status with men cannot be achieved by women despite their struggle until they change their mentality and abandone the value of scriptural precept and cultural practices. The Indian society never sung in the praise and honour of women. The cases of recognition and honour of women could be found where the woman herself tolerated cruelty, barbarism and all other sorts of men's atrocities and finally sacrificed her life. Even the transitional society of the present scientific age witness many splendid accomplishment of women but fails to give due recognition. The women's participation in the highest cadre of administrative service, science and anthropological research have proved that women's capacity is no less than men's yet they don't find the equal place with men in Indian society. Satis are recognized and honoured not because they have done any heroic or glorious deeds, in fact they are admired and extolled to enhance the lordship of men in society and to encourage women to suffer self immolation and cruelty in the hands of men mutely. It is worthy of mentioning the statement of Dr. Sushila Mehta in her book "Revolution and Status of Women in India." It runs as:—

> "The recognition sought by Om Kanwar and Jaivitri and her kind is validated by the village people who admired Om Kanwar and Jaivitri for the heroic deed of self immolation in a noble cause. Investigation in these villages reveal that many village people felt that Om Kanwar and Jaivitri attained highest salvation through their sacrifice! Said Ram Murat Singh a well to do farmer of neighbouring village Jauhari; Jaivitri had done work befitting a Devi (Goddess)". Thakur Singh added "She has lived upto the ideals laid down in the scriptures".

The above statement gives sufficient knowledge of men's mentality about the women's position in society even at this advanced stage of science. Not a single man had any repentance for such superstitions culture and spiritual faith. Even the women had no negation or protest against this sort of custom. How women can expect equal status in society with men when they themselves accept and admire the old superstitions and blind faiths established by the men's domination. The political movements or the women's movement for political rights will never be any help to achieve equality in every walk of life with men even if they acquire equality or more in politics.

The question of equal status depend upon the men's view about women. Until and unless the male population change their look on women no equality either by legal provisions or political right can be achieved by women in Indian Society which is male dominated from the time immemorial.

Religion and its Role

Religion in the Indian soil has also a great impact on atrocities committed on women. In Hindu religion women is called Vaama (left). This word in other sense denotes what is rejected or refused or useless. That is to say, the neglected one in the human society. In Hindu Dharmashastra like Veda, Vedanga and Smriti woman is called Sudrani which means the maid servant (female slave or wife of a slave). Word 'Sudra' in Hindu religion derived from the name of a Varna which is the lowest in social strata and the classification enjoins upon women of this varna all sorts of service to men of upper strata. Hindu religion directs the women to be obedient to the command of their husbands and remain under shelter and protection of the husband. None of religions Hindu, Muslim or Christian has allowed women to take part in religious rituals and worship though a slight difference is noticed in Christianity and Sikhism. Nuns have some rights to participate in religious propagation, preaching and performance of rites. Here I quote a verse from Al-Quran in which Holy Mother Mary (Sura

Mariyum) is addressed with an honour which is not to be found given to Mary in Christian Bible-

"O 'Mary'
God Hath Chosen thee
And purified thee
Above the women
of all Nations" (Al-Quran 3:42)

But I ask my Muslim brethren, can they show me the practical use or adherence of the above verse in their daily family or social life? So far my practical experience and observation direct me to state that, though in Quranic verses women have been treated with honour and utmost dignity but in natural leading life in Muslim community, women are comparatively degraded more than the Hindu and Christian communities. As far as the religious status of women is concerned, the Sikh only in India has raised the status of women equal to men. A lady became the chairperson of the Shiromani Gurdwara Prabandha Committee in the recent past, signifies my above statement. Another Quranic verse very lucidly states, the male should not forget all important roles which a female performs. It says, the mother who bore us must have our reverence. The wife through whom we enter parentage have our reverence.

"You demand your mutual rights and (Reverence)
the wombs (That bore you)" (Al-Quran 4:1)

Almost all the Muslim disobey this verse of Quran in practice.

Similarly there are numerous prose and verse in Hindu religious scriptures but the real practices entirely give opposite results.

The worsen state of women in India is due to the religious customs, has been the opinion of colonial officials. There is evidence of the same in the statement made by Geraldine Forbes in her book "Women in Modern India". To quote, she writes:—

> "Colonial officials agreed that religion was central to Indian life. Indian people were slaves to religion, and Sati (and many other customs) were religious practices".

The statement clearly evinces that the custom like 'Sati' had the assent of the religion and thus the life of women was made a matter to be treated at the sweet will of the religious authorities or to service on their mercy. That is to say, the law of Hindu religion lowered the position of women in society; in every respect women were under some bondage as regards their daily life and inter-action with other fellow beings. The Hindu religious customs and traditions make a man God and a woman the slave of man. As it appears in Hindu Shastras Geraldine Forbes mentions—"Her husband was to be regarded as Supreme God among all the Gods and served him accordingly". Here as a human can very well gather the mischievous ideas the Hindu scriptures uphold and command on women. A layman of the present day can easily find that a man who survived in this world have no better biological elements present in him than a woman; both have to feed and nourish themselves with same foodgrains, need air, water and shelter, no one can live without food. Moreover, neither a male can live a perfect life without female companion nor a female can live without a male and the procreation of future generation is not possible by one independently. Yet the male is considered to be the Supreme God for women. Here it is a sheer discrimination and wilful preplanned subjugation of women by men established by religion. Most unfortunate is the attitude of women who happily enjoy their slavery and subjugation without any complaint. However, in the last interests of mankind, this discrimination needs to be removed immediately.

The common attitude of the society about women as regards procreation is such an illogical and indignant that women are considered fortunate who give birth of sons and those without issue or give birth only of female children are despised in society, whereas this is neither within the control of human beings nor it is due to any discrepancy in women alone. Such kind of religious faith and customs prevailing in society made the life of women miserable. Therefore Raja Rammohan Roy, Debendra Nath Tagore, Ishwar Chandra Vidya Sagar, Keshav Chandra Sen, Swami Vivekananda (all from the higher castes) and Guruchand Thakur (of the untouchable Namasudra caste) of Bengal gave deep thought of reformation in Hindu religious customs and practices and made endeavour to bring equality for women. Iswar Chandra advocated for female education and led a campaign to legalize widow remarriage. Raja Rammohun Roy, Keshav Chandra Sen and Debendra Nath Tagore shaped a separate religious society, Brahmo Sabha which later on was recognized us a separate Brahmo religion and called Brahmo Samaj. Guruchand Thakur in East Bengal advocated for equality by giving equal role in every social activity by propagating Matua Religion. Vivekananda emphasized on reformation of religious order of Hindu to revive women to powerful regenerative force. In the north India Swami Dayanand Saraswati founded Arya Samaj to champion female education and condemned Hindu customs to raise the status of women. Rai Saheb Salig Ram (alias Huzur Maharaj) a follower of the Radhaswami faith advocated female emancipation through his writings titled "Prem Patra". Among the Muslims of North India Kwaja Altaf Hussain Ali and Sheikh Muhammad Abdullah are not less prominent reformist in Muslim society. They introduced and held the importance of education for girls.

Instances of social reform and upliftment of women in western part of India are not scarce. We have famous personality of Indian politics Mahadev Govind Ranade, who founded the National Conference to high light social reforms and attract attention of public. Dhondo Keshav Karve of Poona made dynamic efforts to ameliorate the miseries of widow by educating young widows through his institution at Poona to become teachers in girls school.

In the south the prominent figure in social reform and emancipation of women is R. Venkata Ratnam Naidu, who vehemently opposed "devdasi system" of Hindu religion. The other champion of women cause was Verasalingam Pantulu who worked for marriage reform. Both of them emphasized on education.[10]

The activities of the above reformists give us an account of Indian society and the position of women. Which shows irrespective of religion and caste women in India were leading miserable life and they were either by religious customs, caste system or the male tendency in general, under bondage. Their upliftment as the reformists endeavored, though has been to a considerable extent achieved yet in Indian society they are not equal to men.

Thus, yet special drive should be given for their social upliftment. Political liberty can be availed by women only when they are socially liberate. Social liberty is possible when the religious reform is done. Social liberty on the other hand is not limited to education alone. The domestic responsibilities, social inter-action and behaviour of men towards female should first be changed into the line of equality then only the political privilege can be availed by women.

The religious degradation of women can be observed in the medieval time, also in the Gupta period. The disintegration of the Gupta empire which at its height held most of India in its sway and attained a high platue of social, political and economic stability, initiated a period of turmoil from ninth century until the Mughal conquest of India in the fifteenth. In the intervening centuries, waves of invaders from the north-Scythians, Huns, the Mangols and the Afghan broke the cultural unity of India achieved under the Gupta Empire. The dissolution of cultural authority forced the Hindu social ethos to seek survival regionally which led to the growth of different powerful traditions in religion. Due to the weakening of the state power which patronized Brahminical religion, folk religions became firmly established often by amalgamating with the Brahminical principles and practices. The religious developments were to affect the lives of people of India including their social customs and tradition.

On the other hand religious ideology had affected much the lives of women. Women were expected to follow the dictates of religion as laid down by paternalistic establishment in the community, home or in the temple. This was the time when the subordination of female to male rule was implemented inconsistently with the contention of glorification of goddess as forms of Shakti with women. The essay of Ms. Madhu Khanna titled "The Goddess—Women Equation in Sakta Tantra" published in the book "Faces of the Feminine in Ancient, Medieval and Modern India edited by Mandakranta Bose clearly depicts the picture of women's subordination through religion in India. The more surprising and ridiculous arguments appear in scripture to idealize the character of women with heroine and goddess. In disguise of religious reverence and worshipping, women are placed perpetually at a despiced position in the human society. As Ms. Khanna mentioned, we find several myths and legends illustrated in the scriptures, to idealize women. The two epic heroines and goddesses Sita and Parvati's characterization provides exemplary role models of women. The role played by Sita and Parvati will make a simple women a goddess, if she plays. Such is the instruction and dicta the religion gives. Thus, the religious instructions to follow the characteristics of Sita and Parvati encourage women to forego all sorts of human rights and lead the life of a slave on the mercy of men. As Sita in the Ramayana embodies the ideal Hindu wife who forsakes the luxuries of life to live with her husband in exile for fourteen years and when she is abducted by Ravana and held captive in a grove, she spends her days worshipping and waiting for

Rama to rescue her. Finally after being rescued she is made to undergo Agni Pariksha (fire ordeal), a test to prove her fidelity. Another central character is the goddess Parvati whose only aim in life was to win Shiva as her husband. To achieve this end she performs fierce austerities for sixty thousands years. Next she desires sons, lives happily with her husband and spends a life of devotion and self sacrifice.

Through the above legendary stories characterizing divine women, the Hindu religion dictates women to suffer all sorts of humiliation, violence and subjugation to men as the religion prescribes ideal women to be selfless and without any desire of her own. She should be a passive instrument of other's pleasure, should live a life of devotion and self sacrifice. That is to say, an ideal Hindu woman should worship her husband like God and abide by all his instructions. She should always be in service to provide him desired pleasure and comforts and never should resist his power or question his authority. The suffering heroines of Hindu epics are celebrated for their wifely self-effacing virtues and young girls are traditionally taught to emulate the exemplary traits of the epic heroines. Thereby women's subordination and sufferings are caused by religious sanctions and dicta.

What a ridiculous philosophy the Hindu religion inherit! On the one hand it treats women as the Sakti (Goddess) simultaneously treat them as the object of pleasure of men and prescribe their roles as a simple bounded labour who is supposed to serve the man during her whole life and never care for her own comforts. The portrayals of Sita and Parvati are supported by the theology of subordination of the feminine, which expounds the notion of male superiority over the female. But again we are confronted with the negative view of women themselves about their freedom from the male domination. We find that all sorts of religious superstitions and myths are vehemently supported by the women only.

If the women still want to become Sita and Parvati or any

other imaginary deity who can help them in acquiring equal rights with men? If they want to be deity only but not to lead human life, they should be left at the mercy of the theologians. What a surprising state of Hindu mythology, people believe that Parvati undergone severe austerity for sixty thousand years to achieve Shiva as her husband! Can a man of general prudence believe this? Was it a fact ever happened or is just a fabricated story to motivate people to be fool and practice what the religious teachers or the preachers state. Nobody knows how, when and who narrated this story, when the Hindu religion itself had no existence in this world before four thousand years.

If Indian women enjoy worshipping Sita and Parvati then women's movement for equal rights seems to be useless because, there are role-model legends, which comprise a vast body of literature dealing with *Stri-dharma* or *normative dharma*, outlining the conduct and postures of good and evil to be followed by Hindu women reinforced in *dharma-shastras* and the *smriti* literature they should follow. I would like to inform the Indian women who uphold the value of religious scripture and the laws incorporated therein, that the law of Manu laid the foundation of social, legal and moral code concerning women. The same law of the Manu (*Manusmriti*) eulogized the eternal nature of *dharmic* marriage and introduced a husband-deifying ideology, according to which the husband must be worshipped as God by a faithful wife. The women should note that the Manusmriti was compiled during second century Christian Era (CE) and only during that period the women have been made slave and the men their lords. Before the compilation of Manusmriti the women and men enjoyed the same status and rights except the distinction of physical structure and strength but the Manusmriti became the means of abolishing female property rights and prohibiting widow remarriage. Girls were disqualified from performing *Sraddh* rituals in favour of their parents. Marital restriction placed on women by the Manusmriti decreased their authority considerably and introduced an era of sexual double standards that perpetuated the theology of subordination and weakened the autonomy of women.

Besides the myths linked with Sita and Parvati which give us the paradigm of goddess—women equation, there is another view point on the ideal feminine and the corresponding images of women came from the *Sakta Tantra* which edifies women to be reverential. However, in the Hindu context there is no such category as an absolute dharma. Sakta Tantras addresses the relationship between the idealized image of the feminine the great Goddess of the Saktas conceived to be the primal energy of the cosmos, and secular women on the human plane. One of the most interesting features of Sakta Tantra is that, women share with the goddess a continuity of being. All women irrespective of their caste, creed, age, status; or personal accomplishment are regarded as the physical incarnation of *Shakti,* the divine cosmic energy, the great Goddess. All women at birth are the bearers of an intrinsic *Sakti.*[11] Saktihood is not extrinsic to their female experience as something to be acquired from the outside of their own selfhood, but a spark that inhere naturally as a part of their being at birth.

Here it becomes some futile thoughts when the Sakta Tantra talk about the feminine Sakti that, they need not acquire any energy from outside and the incarnation of Sakti personified as women have the divine cosmic energy. On the one hand the Tantra compares women with goddess at the same time says that the Sakti "is not extrinsic to their female experience" that is to say that women become devi (goddess) a Sakti only when they perform the feminine obligations. That means if any woman wants to exhibit her Sakti she has to serve as a slave to man's wishes.

One of the most interesting features of Sakta Tantra is that women share with the goddesses a continuity of being. All women irrespective of their caste, creed, age, status or personal accomplishment are regarded as the physical incarnation of Sakti. The women—goddess equation is echoed throughout the Sakta texts.[12]

> Every woman in this world is my (human) form[13]
> All women are Thee, and all men are Myself O beloved.[14]
> Merely by knowing this, the devotee attains Spiritual powers
> Every woman is born into the family (Kula) of the Great Mother.[15]

The above textual stanzas depict women as the human form of goddess again says that all women are the beloved of men. The object of lust of men. At the same time women are personified as the honoured mother. This sort of religious concept dupes the women and makes degraded in position than men in human society. Further more interesting precept of religions we find in *Tripurarnava Tantra* which says,"Even outside the sacred circle, all women are born of thy parts"[16] because it is the great goddess alone who having assumed the form of the physical women created this world". Due to this assumption, volume of hyms in praise of nature and attributes of women having been composed in *Sakti Samagama Tantra*[17] like—

> "Woman is the creator of the universe
> The universe is her form;
> Woman is the foundation of the world,
> She is the true form of body.
> Whatever form she takes is the superior form.
> In woman is the form of all things of all that lives and moves in the world.
> There is no jewel rare than woman,
> There is not, nor has been, nor will be;
> There is no kingdom, no wealth, to be compared with woman;
> There is not, nor has been, nor will be any holy

> place like unto a woman.
>
> There is not, nor has been, nor will be, any holy yoga to compare with woman, no mystical formula nor asceticism to match a woman.
>
> There are not, nor has been, nor will be any riches more valuable than her.[18]

From the above eulogies it appears that Tantra in a unique manner praises exalting women. It has made genuine and sincere attempt to develop code of ethics and rules of conduct which are entirely in favour of women. Thus the true Sakta devotees has to honour all women and look upon them with great reverence. In Sakta circles, all women—be they young maidens or mature women—are addressed as Maa, or Devi or Vira. This title in principle protects women from being looked on in sexual terms. What is noteworthy in these texts is that, for the first time in Hindu religious history, an attempt is made to actuate the divinity of women on the social plane and thus introduces an ethos of equality and reverence for them. Unfortunately we observe the condition of women a farce exalting effigy. In reality by imposing the religious title their human rights have been taken away by men. Religious impostering of women has been resulted in subordination and depriving the rights of women. They have made goddess but not allowed to avail the human status equal to men. It is in fact a religious delusion played on women to make them dependent on men.

As regards position, women in Sikh religion there is general belief that men and women are inherently equal in the Sikh world view but in reality, historical writings say virtually nothing about women apparent from occasional exceptional woman who has been deemed worthy enough to have made pages of history. With regard to the status of Sikh men and women one writer asserts—

> "The Sikh woman has enjoyed superior status compared to her counterpart in other communities.

> She has earned this by showing her ability to stand by the side of her husband in difficult times.[19]

Yet if men and women are inherently equal in tradition in term of role and status, why are they not given similar representation in the pages of Sikh history? It is a question perhaps best explained in the light of McMillan's differentiation namely, what is officially touted as normative with regard to gender in history is not necessarily the same as the actual and operative aspects of same Sikh history. That is to say, whatever the religious exaggeration about the women's status we came across, reality is far from the theoretical perception. In fact the women of Sikh community also do not enjoy better status than women of other communities. Harjote Oberoi has noted that the principles of "silence" and negation are paramount in addressing issues that could be conceived as ambiguous within the tradition. The guiding principle of Sikh history is silent with regard to the role of women. The overwhelming impression we receive from reading the text of Sikh history is that women do not have a history. Thus we can conclude that the position of women in Sikh religion is more or less the same as in other religious communities of India.

Ancient Scriptures

The scriptures like Upanishads, Ramayan and Mahabharata are full of instances of women's subordination, immolations, rape etc. A very well known story of Draupadi's instance is nothing but a classical example of rape before the august public. The great heroine of the epic Mahabharata was raped in the midst of an august assembly of nobles. The act was committed before the very eyes of all the respectable and powerful men of the society. Surprisingly enough none of the greatmen and elders including mighty kings and the eldest noble of the clan uttered a single word of condemnation of Duryodhan, nor did they try to help her to save the honour of Draupadi! Thus it is obvious to think that, perhaps the august audience of nobles enjoyed some perverse pleasure in seeing a woman made naked against her will! It is strange to note that Indian society has not progressed much since the ancient Mahabharata when we read incidences of numerous rape in newspapеr every day. Since time immemorial women were never treated as equals though they were called "ardhangini" in Hindu scriptures. Hindu scriptures prescribe the role of a woman as a slave of her man. The wife is laid to a position of slave and called "Dasi". Man (husband) is defined as the "Master", Lord, Swami or 'Devata' and the woman (wife) is made his "Mistress, Vanita or Daasi". Is it not sufficient proof of women's degradation? The respectable men like Yudhishthira, who was considered to be model of truth and honesty did not hesitate to use his wife Draupadi as pawn in the game of gambling. This instance unequivocally proves that, in the Hindu scripture women's position is not better than a chattel and men are given the supreme authority to use woman as a piece of property according to their sweet will!

Take the instance from Ramayana, Rama who was a model of a king did not hesitate to abandon his virtuous wife Sita in the forest in order to secure his power and prestige! Is not this a case of sheer insult on women? And that the society accepted and yet extol it as a pious deed of the king, a purushottam. On the other hand Ravana who is also highly glorified in some parts of the country, raped his own daughter-in-law Rambha! Another instance in the Hindu scripture is, the model truthful king Harishchandra sold his wife Taramati for a trifle sum of money! An analytical study and examination of these instances which are described in details in the ancient scriptures bring out the fact that, women were not treated as human beings but as property and in every step they are despised by men. Our society still possesses the highest degree of respect for these scriptures. Thus they also repeat the same incidence in their life everyday.

More disgusting instance appears in Upanishada of women's degradation which a prudent person of civilized society cannot believe. One of the sections of Brihad Aranyaka Upanishada which is often left untranslated by scholars is fourth Brahmana of sixth chapter. The two slokas of which sanction use of force to fulfil man's lusty desires for sex, which may be translated as under—

> "Thus verily indeed, is loveliness among women, when a woman has removed the soiled clothes of her impurity! and is beautiful, one should approach and invite her."
>
> "If she should not grant him his desire he should bribe her. If she still does not grant him his desire he should hit her with a stick or with his hand and overcome her, with power, with glory, I take away thy glory, thus she becomes inglorious!"

This old traditional scriptures clearly encourage men in their use of force against women to fulfil their own lusty desires for sex, thus encourages man's pride of superiority and chauvinsm towards women in Indian Society. The stories in scriptures leave no doubt that, they depict men as lords and the masters and they can use or abuse the women according to their sweet will for their own pleasure without considering their liking or disliking.

Thus it is clear that, the women's subordinate position and their incessant indignation are attributable to the scriptures. When women will be full aware of the facts their faith on Hindu scriptures will be shattered. The women's movement for equal rights or equal status with men cannot be successful until the mentality or tendency of the human beings is changed, which is possible only when they abandon blind faith on scriptural tradition.

Indian Culture and Women

There have been numerous research and scholarly studies on the feminist characters in various universities in Britain and USA. Most of the scholars have tried to find out the extent and importance of gender in human society. Moreover, many researchers emphasized on their research work to find out the position of women in Indian culture and Hindu religion. There is evidence in the book "Invented Identities (Interplay of Gender, Religion and Politics in India) "edited by Julia Lesli and Mary McGee, that in India women suffer from the gender disparity in society, especially in Hindu religion their position though different from that of other religion in principle but in real practice not better than Muslim as far as the dignity and self respect is concerned. As regards equality with men, none of the Indian communities has yet considered women equal to men, how intelligent, capable and robust the women may be in their field of work or profession. The learned authors of the aforesaid book, which is very much the research document of the scholars, have mentioned:—

> "This is not surprising as many scholars continue to be captivated by the seeming paradox within (Hindu) Indian culture that reveres and values the feminine (represented in the form of the goddess) while simultaneously subordinating and devaluing the female (in the form of women)"

Now-a-days women's problems and their deserving human rights in society have become the significant questions before the world to be considered to shape the world's civilization. Therefore there are series of research carried out and being carried out in various famous universities of the world. Most of the scholars have been concerned with the causes of disparity on the sex in society, and the scholars have pointed out the fatal causes of women's degradation and suggested ways of improvement. However, almost all of them have concluded that women's degradation in society attributed to feminist attitude not only of the female herself but entire community, religious sanctions and the developed cultures in which from the very day of the birth of a female child the social cultural treatment of parents and the religious observance create a sense of segregation and sex sensitivity. Thus at the age before attaining puberty the female child keeps herself distinct and sensitive from the male. While carrying out the research work on the position of women almost all the scholars concentrate their studies on local environment, religion, customs and tradition and the present day industrial revolution (working condition and allied matters). Though political field and environment are examined in the context of human rights and the effect of governing principles of the country but there is seldom any recommendation or emphasis on special political right for them to give them equality or equal status in society. The research works of scholars have had investigation of a myriad sources, principal among them are mythology, religious practices, folktales and the experience of women and for better understanding the problems of women many a scholars have further suggested studies of texts, sexualities, ideologies, classes, paradigms but there is rare a suggestion for political studies to improve the women's status. Thus political rights or reservation in politics is not the solution of women's problems in the context of equality with men.

Most of the scholars at the SOAS conference interpreted the emphasis on "gender" as a focus on women and feminism. They used the opportunity to examine closely the notions of masculinity or to scrutinize ideas about gender in a less dominant Indian cultural domains. The result of research work and documentation have revealed that World Bank had documented the gender disparity, it is manifest in child mortality rates which are higher in South Asia and particularly in northern India and Pakistan for female children than any where else in the world. The World Bank records of studies also reveal disparity in children's treatment of illness, the girls receive less medical treatment and in the field of education girls between the age group of eleven to fifteen years are more disadvantageous than boys.[20]

Two eminent scholars Vasanth Kannabiran and Kalpana Kamabiran have opined that:—

"The viel is social practice discriminatory inheritance laws are enshrined in religion, the restitution of conjugal rights as a male prerogative is social practice; caste based oppression is codified in Hindu religion; female infanticide and female foeticide are social practices; strict code of dress and mobility for women are social practices; marital violence is social practice; rape is social practice ....everyone of these social practice is welded to the question of identity and gender."[21]

The above opinion clearly indicates that in human society the identity of women is lowered by the social domination of men. Hence to establish equal status and entity of women, political prerogatives will not be helpful, only the social reform can improve the status of women. Social practices mentioned above which are directly responsible for degradation of women's status cannot be eradicated by the political rights or forces; it is evident from the fact that during the rule of a woman Prime Minister the women of the country could not find a little change in their status and social value. The social practices become the indispensable part of culture and to change the culture women's personality development is necessary.

The cultural norms accumulated in the society due to influence of scriptural events have brought about perpetual physical, mental, intellectual and even spiritual slavery of women in Indian society. Even the women themselves have grown in them the concept derogatory to their position in human society. These being despicable and dependent brought about downfall of women to slavery and resulted in fantastic and bizar idea like terrible inhuman customs of 'Sati'. The clicke of sati dramatically demonstrated the belief that a woman's life is worth nothing without her man! Such was the degeneration of the role and status of a woman in Indian society that, an ideal woman is called 'sati', who can tolerate infinite insult, like any amount of beating by her man and live a beastly life of drugery and subordination without uttering a single word of resistance. The cultural values in the society have created the environment that a word like "Resistance" should not be found in an Indian Woman's dictionary.[22] It is this absence of resistance to abuse, cruelty and slavery gives further impetus to more cruelty and abuse till the poor woman dies the death of a beast.

Indian culture has often been characterized as having an hierarchical world view, in contrast to the egalitarian world view of the modern Western Societies. The hierarchical world view is grounded in the caste system under Hinduism, it operates at the level of social relationships and at that ideas and values. There are several implications which may flow the hierarchical world view of Indian culture which have relevance for the development of Indian women's movement. In this context Louies Dumont points out that, in an hierarchical system there is a high level of tolerance groups with widely different practices live side by side, for there is general agreement on norms which rank and divide them. The high levels of tolerance and segmentation in Indian society make it likely that opposition to the involvement of high status women in public affair would be confirmed to high status groups, in contrast to the wide spread opposition to the involvement of British and American women in public affairs.[23]

Indian culture is influenced by Casteism, has been noted by some scholars they say that, another aspect of Indian culture is the tendency of caste groups to imitate both the Brahmin and the Kshatriyas as a means of improving their ritual status or political power. British occupied analogous position to Kshatriya in India. In the name of cultural reform the process adopted for sanskritization and modernization can be termed as the tendencies to imitate priest and king. The process provide means of social mobility. This indirectly guides us to conclude that caste discrimination and supremacy of particular classes also influenced the culture of India. Though the culture affected women alike but the rank or status of different castes were not same. Thus women of different status suffered differently concerning Indian culture. Similarly they had never similar role to play in social reform.

Before the Indian elites go for reservation for women in politics they should look into the past and present cultural heritage of Indian society irrespective of religion castes and heredity. Some of the instances, which we happen to see in ancient literatures and the modern literatures on history, sociology and politics are relevantly stated below to bring into the notice of readers, to enable them to arrive at any decision to grant reservation to whom and in which field.

Indian social culture and belief compel the women to believe its their pious duty to perform the role of housewife duly married to a bridegroom at an appropriate age as per the wishes of their parents or guardians and the society they belong. Practically even at this modern age it has been observed in female adolescent population that, to be married on attaining puberty is their moral duty, is seated in their mind. But there is little who deeply thinks over the purport of marriage. What they can earn or lose after marriage? Indian Hindu society teaches their female to regard her husband as lord (swami) and she should serve him like a slave (dasi). After marriage she is transferred to the family of her husband and all rights including surname are changed to identify her in the new family with all relationship a new. To a greater extent we find her as in a second birth. Female cannot use their parental identity after marriage irrespective of religion. All the religions in India only accept the name of her husband after marriage to identify a female. The marriage being an essential social obligation a woman lose her independence in family, society and nations as a whole. The Hindu and Muslim religious edicts govern a female by male and depict the features of female to be protected and maintained by male. In Indian society though Hindu Law does not permit polygamy yet men are freely keeping more than one living wives but administration fails to eliminate this tendency of men; as a result women have to suffer all sorts of humiliation in their married life. Even if we forget the past instances of Indian social tradition yet there are glaring numerous examples of atrocities on women of the present age arisen out of this traditional marriage tie.

What kind of equality our society allows and our administration grants to women as they advocates? Daily news papers are flooded with reports of female murders, suicide, dowry deaths and humiliation bred out of marriage tie. Although the modern scientific advancement and industrial worldwide revolution have proved that women can survive without being dependent upon men, yet the Indian culture and tradition vehemently oppose the advanced way of independence of women. It is very joyous to see that educated skilled women have started leading life with pride and self respect in family but it is a matter of regret that, what amount of independence and comfort they enjoy in family life is scanty and that to at the cost of their hard labour and alertness. The responsibility of looking after the children remains with the mother and usual work for hearth as well can not be set aside. Here again they are placed at adverse and inferior position to men's.

Despite all the above discrepancies of married life, human society cannot turn back because it has also supported by natural law. Men and women as a general rule cannot be a perfect alone in themselves and also cannot challenge the natural instinct in them for union with each other. Thus to maintain peace and harmony in society what is needed much is not the political reservation for women to improve their status equal to that of men but to change look and attitude of men dominated Indian society for which special efforts should be made to formulate law and implement it meticulously.

Here it is noteworthy that the statement of Mr. S. R. Biswas, author of Edesher Sanrakshan Vyvastha Bahujan Samaj, on page 130— "It is doubtful, how long social customs of marriage will last, if the males do concede to give equal rights to women in leading family life?"

From the time immemorial, Hindu society in India very much inclined to justify and uphold the possession of chastity of women. Every man expect his wife to be faithful and chaste, although he himself fiddle with or enamoured upon other women. The socially reputed persons quite often are found to be disloyal to their wives, lead lustful life according to their sweet will but tend to administer stern discipline and sexual austerity on their wives. The most distinguished and dominating custom is that, a married woman is supposed to put Bindi or besmear vermion on forehead, wear specific bangles and rings on toes to identify her as married to some one but the men don't have any sign of marriage or having entered into couple life with a woman. Here we find that the society has adopted several such cultures which dominate women by men and even lower the status of women before men.

More discriminating event occurs in Hindu culture. According to Manu's account of domestic rules, which are predominant even in the present days, the upper castes male children had to undergo initiation (Upanayana) ceremony. On that occasion the boy is invested with a holy thread. But there is no such ceremony is performed upon a girl. Just like caste discrimination the Hindu social culture has sex discrimination also. As lower castes have been given very limited rights in society similar is the position of women in comparison to men. One more grave discrimination we find with women in Hindu culture that, although by now the modern democratic government with the spirit of laws laid down by Britishers in India, the widow remarriage has come to be an usual social customs and culture, yet we should remember the following authentic statement of renowned historian R. C. Dutt incorporated in his book, "A history of civilization in Ancient India" (p. 96).

> ".......Manu is indignant against widow-marriage, which ancient was becoming unpalatable to the later Hindu; ......We are told in that a widow must never even mention the name of another man after her husband has died, and again that a second husband is nowhere prescribed for virtuous women."

The above statement help us to comment that the Hindu social customs had curtailed the rights of women as regards remarriage but at the same time men have full liberty. This is a clear instance of male domination in society, which has placed women at inferior position. Thus political reservation without changing the socio-religious customs, will fail to improve the status of women.

Taking into consideration the Hindu religious edicts and the past history of social reforms advocated by personalities like M. G. Ranade, Dayanand Saraswati, Vivekananda, Raja Ram Mohan Roy etc. and the upper castes people's reaction on that, a spontaneous question arise—the ruling class of the present day, who during the British Raj did not concede to bring reform in society to uplift the position of women, why they after 54 years of independence are so eager to give special privilege in politics to women? And why not this special facility is provided for them in proportion to caste-wise population?

Role of Media

It is evident from the world history of renaissance that media plays an unequivocally important role to change the social environment and history of human race. This media when plays a partisan role the history changes unnoticed to the artificial state. This is the theory, the Indian media adopted in the case of depicting picture of Indian women. Media over-emphasise in highlighting the weakness of women whenever a case of women's depression or derogation comes to the notice of media, it sarcastically gives colour to the story in such a way that the public amuse on the indignified impulses of the women displayed in the media report. Our Indian mentality is so poor that nobody takes pains to reach the truth either in imagination or physical verification of the incident. Media is very perfect to articulate the instances to hide the truth and vindicate the falsified aspect of it. In this way woman character is blemished before the public so that a rational view of public goes against the reputation of women thereby making them always subjugated before the men. The media report sometimes reflects the character of women in ridiculous way so that common intention goes against women's character. Thus when any atrocity is committed upon a woman by a man the woman stands on the discredited state. Media also fabricates amusing stories at the cost of women's dignity. The general picturesque of women by media allure the male to commit ravaging act against women whereby, women remain as the puppet in the hands of reputed and notorious men with the hope of escaping with reputation unstained. But such an act on the part of woman derogates her future. In this context it will not be exaggeration to say that media to a great extent distort the image and reputation of women in Indian environment. Most of the disgruntled women are prey in the hands of media. Good quality and genius of women are not properly highlighted to enable them to earn reputation but easily goes against it. This is because the media personnel are the tools in the hands of corrupt aristocrats and politicians. White collar crimes, which are indirectly linked and responsible for women's miserable condition in the society, are sheltered under the artful and tactical projection by the media. Media also is responsible for the degradation of women by publicizing the films which reflect the obscene pictures of women's character to create impulses and amusement in male population. It indirectly encourage women to be object of men's lust by advertising different products of business group which suggest improving the physical beauty and feminine styles. Regular advertisement of cosmetics products emphasizing beautification and delicacy of women's physique by media makes the women attracted towards eroticism.

All the above elements related to the role of media make us to understand that women's degradation is caused by media to a considerable extent.

Role of Film Industries

Film industries and advertising agencies' role to lower the dignity of women in Indian society is not a less. The fashion show, beauty contest and other physical features display in India are inadvertently overemphasized by business magnates with the help of media. To attract public demands the film industries create obscure scenes on woman character. Repeated display of sexy pose of women by the film industry in cinema not only lower the dignity of women but also encourage men to commit offences against women. Thereby the young women are misguided to be attractive towards modelling and dancing in the aspiration to be promoted to Heroine. Modelling is though an artful performance and a talented work but it creates feminish and servile attitude in women. The women develop in themselves a sense of self beautification and lose other talents capable of rebutting the superiority of manhood. The present trend of women participating in beauty contest, modelling and acting in cinema have made them more or less to feel that they are creature of God on the earth to appease men. They being a matter of fondling consider them to be an amorous object for men. They never compare them with men to earn reputation. On the contrary they become more and more concerned about the tactic they can employ to draw attention of men. Film industries are exploiting women to be a commercial object out of which millioners earn profits for their own betterment. There are many obscene pictures of women in advertising material which diminish the prestige of women in society. I don't know what impresses the public when a sample item of new products is advertised for sale by a woman, whether the product or the beauty or the artful movement of the lady? It is observed that majority of spectators draw their attention towards the impulsive artful appearance of the lady. Thus we can more or less form an opinion that beauty of the model appeals to the public and not the quality of product. That is why almost all the advertising agencies prefer to employ beautiful young ladies in advertisement programme. This directly creates a sense among people to adore women as the source of amusement. Naturally the women do not care to develop their personality in other fields but to become beauty conscious. As a result it becomes an inherent character to allure male in every action of a woman. Regarding the question of equal status and rights in society for the women, it needs competitive attitude which is rare in women's character in India till now. Equality therefore cannot be earned by women with men until they themselves strive for the same.

Men's Mentality

Though there is increasing hue and cry for the grant of equal opportunities to women in the developed countries in Europe and America but the reality is quite different from that of the principles and records apparent. The question of equality for women in social status with that of men in country like India, where orthodox views prevails and the religious superstitions are enliven, is beyond imagination. The country like Britain where education, culture and industrial revolution have brought a sharp change in social strata, have not yet been able to practically grant equal opportunities to women in job profile and other social institutions because the policy they lay down to this effect is not practically implemented. The impediment at large is from the men who vehemently advocates for equal opportunity to women. To clarify this aspect further more, Cynthia Cockburn has stated in her book "In the way of Women" as under—

> "The senior officers were using women's issues like the rungs on their ladder of personal advancement. It's popular. It's the flavour. So you do it. The men have learned how to swing in women's organization. They know what sort of language you can use and what can't. It does not change the feelings. Even the most supportive men could not imagine a union in which would actually step down from power. A man said I can't see men sitting back and letting women go forward and run the whole thing themselves...... I do not think any man would say; will be in the background."

Cynthia Cockburn further illustrated the men's ego and superiority over women by stating that—

> "Women do observe that sometimes deals are done over jobs within the leading group of senior men. People's feelings are saved. Failure to get one post is compensated by appointment to another. That is how women's interests are sold out to save a men's ego.[24]

In the Indian scenario, it is almost same or even worse. Recently after decentralization of power through the Panchayati Raj set up, many women have been inducted in politics at village, block and district level through the privilege policy for women either in reserved categories or otherwise. The resultant feedback by media or the practical observation reveals that women even after being theoretically accepted according to political norms but the defacto power is held by the male colleagues or associates. In some instances it was found that the women Sarpanch's were not at all allowed to attend the meetings or take decision judiciously.

Even in the services though now-a-days women are given equal opportunities but usual treatment and feelings of male employees make the women feel alienated or undermined by their co-workers in the organizations/institutions.

Cockburn has rightly painted the picture of women in Britain which help us to justify the injustice met to Indian women in getting equality. She says—Women end by feeling that equality is a frail plant grafted on to sturdy old stock. Were they stop cultivating the men they would immediately revert to kind. And men indeed admitted that much does depend on women pressure.[25]

Though the elite group of men talk about and concede to the principle "equality of opportunity" for women with men but the practical scenario is quite different. The Indian society is far remote in the liberalization than that of the European Countries. We have some glaring examples of sex disparity in Britain as under—

> "Women who had been rash enough to take a role of full time officer reported being systematically undermined by male colleagues, employers, lay representatives and members. Senior men had many ways of holding a woman back. They intimidate you by contradicting things you say. Men can push you back quite gently. They are extremely clever at keeping you in the background."

One described how her male colleagues would be scrupulously polite, treat you like a queen, then undermine you behind your back. Many men show you scant respect, will not hear you out, shout you down. Sometimes even the women discriminate the woman officer—A group of manual workers had told one of the female officers, "we don't want any more women at our meeting". Another example of women discrimination in the workforce is—"a woman officer obtained her position in direct competition with a male branch secretary in her division. He was so angered by being passed over for a woman, he threatened to leave the Union, taking his entire branch of 3000 members with him. In Indian society the mentality of men towards the women is same, even at this advanced age it has not changed an inch from its past state. Thus we find the position of women in society is degraded due to anti-women mentality of male population in all sphere of activities.

Patriarchal System of Family

In the patriarchal and patrilineal joint family system boys assume adult status and role within the same family where they are born and brought up, they are permanent member of the family. A girl on the other hand, is looked upon as a transient member of the family because on marriage she has to be transferred to her husband's family. Whatever rights and duties she has are in the family she marries into and not for or in the family she born and brought up.[26]

The socialization process and the personality development in the family emphasize differential in boys and girls in their future adult role.[27] The illiteracy among the women in rural area is increased due to the male domination and patriarchal system of family. The patriarchal system inculcated in the minds of parents the more significant role of boys in their family and made the girls a temporary indemnified property of others. The rituals in Hindu scriptures prescribe over all familial and ancestry rights for the boys and deprive the girls from their equal birth rights and duties towards their parents. The parents gradually concentrate on boys' development and inheritance of ancestral property and social rights of the family. On the contrary on reaching the age of puberty the girls feel them to be time bound temporary member of the family. They, despite their kin interest in the betterment of family as a whole, lose their rights and interests on the family they born. They clearly observe that, their parents feel themselves to be under a heavy burden until they are married and sent off to another family. In every step patriarchal pattern of family reminds the girls to be a casual member of the family they born. On the other hand parents lose interest on their personality development in comparison to boys. Even in these modern days when it has been proved worldwide that women are in no way less capable and competent than men, many parents are found to be cursing themselves for having female child, especially in rural area the female children are neglected most by their parents. As regards literacy, the rural parents still avoid sending their girls to schools and obstruct them from taking part in any activities outside the home. They are forbidden to surpass the boundary of home without male attendant or female adult relatives or family member. That is to say where boys are allowed to go girls are forbidden. The parents do every thing to educate their boys and avoid girls' education despite better academic performance of girls than the boys.

The increase in population, i.e., having more children is caused due to patriarchal system. Everybody wants male child, thus who have no male child they go on procreating children till a male child is born. Male domination which is the end of patriarchal system of family, discourages women's education resulting in women's nourishing superstitions and blind faiths and fail to plan a happy family by adopting birth control. Illiterate women believe the child is blessed by the God to parents according to their deeds of the past life and they should not do anything against the will of the Almighty God. It does not matter to them how many children they produce, whether they are able to manage their maintenance or not, what will be the impact upon the national economy on over increase of population? Nothing troubles them. They are least worried about the economic state, health and happiness of the family. Even they are not aware that, frequent pregnancy tells upon their health and they are mainly responsible for care and bringing up of the children, no other man.

All families display beliefs and values relating to children common in the traditional Indian family and society which is patriarchal and male dominated. The society and family believe a son is necessary because it was only on him that they could depend as a matter of right, particularly in their old age.

In patriarchal system families show far less concern about the education of girls compared to boys because the parents think that education is meant for achieving source of earning, an employment so that the boy can bear the burden of family in future whereas, the girl has to leave for another family. The parents encourage girls for beautification to be looking attractive instead of gaining knowledge and becoming intelligent. They think the girls should be beautiful so that man should like her and marry; since the women's role in patriarchal family is limited to lookafter the hearth of the family and procreation intelligentia has no importance. Thus girls become very careful to maintain their beauty and shine further in their physical appearance. Though sometimes girls are found to be interested in gaining knowledge and negligent in their physical care but their parents discourage it and scoff at them. The goal of girls education was limited to functional literacy. The family or parents want them to be able to read and write. A girl's education is thus narrowly conceived. It does not include her personal development or social nobility or acquisition of vocational skill.

Male domination in Indian society is so deep that parents when arrange the marriage of their sons they prefer illiterate or less educated daughter-in-law, who would be obedient to them and serve the family, though there is little change in urban cities and towns now-a-days.

Mother all the times hammers onto the girls that they should be good housewives and daughters-in-law and discourage them from giving more importance to education. They emphatically say that more education would make it difficult to arrange the marriage of their girls. Girls as they believe, after all has to be given away in marriage and they have to work in the domestic sphere; this does not require any high level education.

The patriarchal pattern of family cultivates braveness and many qualities in boys while encourage girls to be within four walls and cultivate feminine qualities of meekness, docility, servitude, obedience and adaptability and to be efficient housewives and daughters-in-law. Thus we find from the above discussion that women's degradation in society is mainly caused due to the patriarchal system in family which makes the girls like slaves to obey and carry out the orders of men. The entire society become male dominated and women's subordination in every sphere of social life.

Employment Tradition for Women

As regards women's working in Mines before enactment of Mines Act 1923 to restrict women's employment in mines as underground workers, the government asked the opinion of Mining Board, Mining Federation and local government. Most of the respondents restrictions arguing the tribal people preferred to work as families. They said, "men cut the coal; their wives and children carried it away and loaded it." These informants argued "men cannot carry coals and families needed the earnings of both men and women to survive." On the other hand Mr. Swan the Chairman of the Mining Board of Bengal admitted that if only men (i.e. no woman) worked underground, coal price would be higher. The Secretary of the Mining Federation upheld the evidence of child-bearing as the proof that underground work was not harmful to women. Almost all the respondents opposed the regularization of mine condition on one plea or the other keeping in view the business profit involved.

Most of the mining official did not look into the social and political rights of people and all those factors responsible for modernization of the world. The workers being poor and helpless could not think of humanity, society, nation and the rights and obligations of human society.

A helpless hungry person first needs something to satisfy

his hunger then comes anything else in mind. To emancipate people from this state of depredation and miserable condition, political privilege or formulation of rules and regulations for job in particular field will not be adequate. The difference in status between a mine working woman and a woman of Brahmin aristocrat family in India in reality is not of individual case of intelligentia and efforts making difference. The difference crept under castes distinction and the most under racial discrimination prevailed in India. The reformists efforts to improve the condition of working women or the women in general will not be effective until the people accept social equality by birth. Till such time Indian society will accept and follow the distinction by birth in society, the question of equality will be a futile issue. The land where men are not equal among themselves, how can any one expect women to be equal to men? The working tradition and the salary systems, even the hours of work in mines and factories are distinctive for men and women, which neither the employers nor the men working force want to abandon. Thus the condition of women in work in the mines and factories suffer degradation not only in allotment of work but the salary, working hours, nature and condition.

The reformists talk about improvement but they did not search for the real cause of their depression. The women of low castes poor families were compelled to work for their survival; this was not with the higher castes families. Nobody ever can deny that, a child comes to this world with the same biological ingredients, the world is for all and nobody has created it under his absolute authority, then how one can claim him the owner and make others disown it? This question if tried by any one to reply, he will find the correct reply and way for emancipation of all the exploited and oppressed people irrespective of sex.

Before we claim equality of women with men we must make efforts to bring equality among women themselves. In

Indian society women do not enjoy the same rights and privileges. The higher castes women are on the top of the social strata, whereas the lowest castes or untouchables are at the lowest rung of the ladder of social strata. Therefore, until all women are made equal by providing special privilege to the poor and low castes women, equality between men and women will be a nightmare. Without making all women equal in every respect, any attempt to equalize men and women is a befooling device for common public for the benefits to politicians.

Mechanization of Employment

Due to the British domination the traditional economic system and the process fundamentally dislocated the non-agricultural village—based economy. Women had formerly participated in a wide range of small scale enterprises, they processed foodgrains and oil seeds, made bread, shoes pottery, nets and ropes, raised cattle and repaired various things; all these activities declined. In Bengal the female dominated household industry of rice husking was replaced by mechanized threshing machines. When machines were introduced, men replaced women as rice huskers. The new mills allocated menial jobs to women but the norm of female seclusion precluded Bengali Hindu and Muslim women from accepting this employment.[28]

In the process of modernization, the profession of teaching and medicine were now open to a few women and factories, mines and plantations employed significant numbers of women but under the harsh conditions; it was difficult to view this employment in a positive notion. Poor-Women often found employment in exploitative industries. However, the women leaders ignored this reality, instead they focused on education, franchise and legal rights. Their vision in the field was arrested in higher castes women only, who sought employment as victims of unfortunate circumstances. They were not concerned about the women of lower castes, as they considered lower castes women's work was taken for granted. Class distinction played very crucial role in the minds of women leaders unconsciously.

The decline of female economy as employment in Jute Mills, in addition to other related factories was due to increased mechanization, as it was discernible since 1930.[29]

Education

In India as it has been recorded in world, the literacy rate is the lowest resulting in more than 50 per cent people are illiterate. But the position of Indian women as regards literacy is quite admirable. According to census report, the literacy rate of women in 1991 was 46. 01 per cent and it has enhanced to 60.22 per cent in 2001 and particularly in Kerala State the percentage has raised in 2001 to 90.92 per cent (Bahujan Nayak, 15th April 2001). Despite recording the greater degree of talents in women the Indian society tame women according to the sweet will of the men in almost all sections of society. This is really a stigma on men dominated Indian society. The educational status of women has failed to improve their social status. Daily news-paper contains enormous reports of atrocities on women in the country. International organizations on protection of human rights and creation and maintenance of amicable relationship in human society. Continuously have been preparing various devices to grant equal rights to women with men have been proved a farce, since condition of women in Indian society has not changed an inch. The coercive dominating attitude of men against the women has made them submissive to men in every field. In urban area most of the families females between age group of 18 to 25 years are more educated than males; even then the higher educated wife has to act on the tune of her lower educated husband. The practical happenings in a large number of families depict the coercive state of domination of husband over a wife. If one studies the proceedings of divorce cases, he will come to know the degree of cruelty practised upon women. Education alone cannot save the women from men's atrocities, here is an instance of a rape case committed by a blood relation in Sehore Districts of Madhya Pradesh upon a girls hostel student recently. Despite the higher literacy rate of women than men in India a Unicef report confirms that among the entire world's population of prostitutes or flesh market, Indian ratio is 6:1 (Danik Jagaran dated 14th April, 2001). We frequently read in news-paper the police atrocities on women like rape in custody, nude parade etc.

The education imparted on the women from the books written by the men make the female a special and peculiar character than human creatures. These writers have been more attentive to make the women alluring mistress than efficient wives and rational mothers. Understanding of the sex has been so excelled by the spacious homage that the women of present days with a few exceptions have become anxious to inspire love when they should cherish a nobler ambition and deserve respects their virtues and abilities. The wrong system of education creates an inferior feelings in female children from the initial stage. The disparity between male and female children starts at home and further enhanced by education institutions. Thus equality of status and rights is marred at the very starting stage of development. In the introductory statement of Mary Wallstonecraft in her book "A Vindication of the Rights of Women" very passionately mentioned—

> "One cause of this barren blooming I attribute to a false system of education gathered from the books written on this subject by men who considering female rather as women than human creatures, have been more anxious to make them more alluring mistresses than affectionate wives and rational mothers; and the understanding of the sex has been so bubbled by this specious homage, that the civilized women of the

> present century with a few exceptions are only anxious to inspire love, when they ought to cherish a nobler ambition and by their abilities and virtues exact respect."[30]

In India the electronics media is playing an important role to educate the masses by projecting various programs through T. V. Most of these programmes display the techniques and arts of developing delicacy in women. The portrait with artful movement of limbs of the female is displayed to create physical passion in opposite sex attributable to eroticism. Naturally the women gradually absorb those notion and became inclined towards such characteristics which make them feel as distinct object of beauty and pleasure. So they forget about their energy and ability to excel in other fields and compete with opposite sex. By stimulating their energy to become an alluring and lovable object they become psychologically weak and develop the physical weakness. The prolonged tradition of observing the distinction and subordination the females have created a separate ambit of their activities which is not only attributable to male's domination but also to their own choice though education supplements it.

Women's Own Reaction

In the accurate examination of the reformists' drive for social reforms, the effect of common population and the reaction of women themselves for whose emancipation and improvement they made endeavour, we are told or confronted with such situation and evidence that the women themselves in several occasions opposed the reforms. Geraldine Forbes writes that women themselves were not partners in the scheme created for their regeneration; more often they were portrayed as opposed to their own liberation. Without first hand accounts by these women, their reluctance to change in the ways prescribed by husbands and fathers could be read as nascent feminist resistance, an intelligent reading of their true interests or plain and simple opposition to any change, Sudha Majumdar has related her mother's opposition to Sudha becoming a "boarder" at St. Theresals School for Girls.[31] In her words she narrates as follows:—

> "She felt that my being a boarder would result in many complications and make if difficult, if not impossible to give me in marriage when the time came ......To prevent me from becoming a permanent liability on the family, dependent on my brothers in old age, she recommended that to ensure my economic independence it was paramount importance to execute a deed before hand in my favour granting me the rights of a substantial portion of my father's estate.[32]

The women's self opposition to their better future and development of status to achieve equality of rights and equal status with men can further be observed in the discussion in succeeding paragraphs. The discussion elucidates many examples which show that women themselves vehemently opposed the devices for their betterment.

The Vigilance Association wanted abolition of brothels but wherever this happened, prostitutes began soliciting on the streets. When reformers and government officials of India wanted to control and abolish "devadasi" practice of adopting girl children Devadasies reacted by forming organizations and responded to institute reform from within and protect their way of life. But the agitating reformists who wanted abolition of devadasies made the issue focus of discussion, they called this system a masked prostitution. Thus in 1947 Devadasi Act passed to abolish dedication of girls to temple service, barred temple dancing and declared that any bogam, Kalavanthulu Sami, Nagavasulu, Devadasi or Kurmapuvalu woman who danced was a prostitute. The framing of regulations which set maximum hours of work, prohibited women from working in night, disallowed child labour and mandated maternity benefits, though intended to improve the condition of women but indirectly had an adverse effect on them immediately. So women for whom these regulations meant, themselves opposed it. Limitation in working hours was with a view to give them rest but the prevailing condition of that time needed provision of food to survive and that needed more pay.

Thus the regulations for providing rights were not the solution. Only rights do not help improving the status. An woman who had no means to survive except labouring can not understand the importance of education, health care and maternity benefits because before all these she needs money to subsists.

Since nineteenth century there had been numerous struggles for improvement of social status of women and different legislative measures adopted for giving them better social status. But in reality even the women of nationalists group and reformists were making all efforts keeping in view the social customs and the conditions of women of higher castes and middle class. The picture of Indian lower class or labour class and low castes women was not kept in view. The self-opposition to the measures meant for the women of factory and mill was due to their want of bare necessity of livelihood and the caste systems and customs prevailed over them.

Without removal of the caste discrimination and customary distinction among the women themselves and making provisions for livelihood, the strive for equality with men and providing similar working avenues to women that of men will be of no avail. Why women themselves oppose the reformists proposals for their betterment? Now it is the time when our leaders, reformists and learned people should think it deeply. We have seen the condition of women engaged in prostitution or live in brothels or become devadāsi. If these are to be abolished the society must first think over their proper settlement in society with dignity but the religious faith, customs and the conservatism of men do not provide the facility and impose restrictions, therefore, for their survival they oppose the move, even though that meant for their betterment in reality.

The present condition of women even after two centuries or 55 years of independence if compared with the British period, has not improved much. Even today, Indian women are not equal in themselves. Does one find any impact of the women's organizational work on the women of lower castes, landless labourers? After a lapse of nearly two centuries after evolution of women's struggle in India, whatever we find the advancement and modernization in women population are limited to the royal family, aristocrats and higher castes. These struggles for social reforms had no effect on lower classes untouchables, who were living in different world devoid of bare necessities of human life. Now the democrats of India are advocating for special rights to women in politics. What do they mean to produce out of political rights of women population. As I believe the women of higher castes and higher social strata are competent to make room for them in politics even without any privilege. Whereas, even the men of low castes and lowest social strata are not able to contest against the women of higher castes. When men of lower classes or castes cannot claim equality with female of higher social strata, what results can be achieved by women of the lower castes out of special privilege in politics?

In the existing disparity among women of different castes if political reservation is granted to women irrespective of keeping demarcation or distinction of castes and classes, then only women of already advanced class will encroach upon the rights of other women and disparity will increase manifolds.

Servile Mentality of Women

The Indian social structure has been erected in such a way from the time immemorable that, women themselves weaken their capability. They develop incapacity, insecurity, shyness and gradually loses enthusiasm.

The moment they get a chance to demonstrate their intelligence, bravery and sense of responsibility, hesitate to avail the opportunity of aggrandisement. Some of the Indian women are plunged into religious dogmas and taboos so deep they consider themselves as an object to be offered for the comfort of male and procreation to keep continue the clan. Some of the Hindu women are found to be made for worshipping male and to fulfil their unreasonable desires. In the field of economy these women press themselves hard to save the balancing state of economic stability of the family, while the male members become extravagant in their daily expenses.

As regards progress in educational field, it is prevalent in Indian society that when the parents and teachers aspire for an excellent career of a female students according to her performance in lower academic duration, she recoils herself either for her lack of confidence or due to the social taboo. Most of female youth have been found to love feminish move and to be more inclined towards the characteristics of prudent submissive personality. They very often become victim of sexual exploitation due to their own impulses and fallible imagination.

In an essay Lindsay (Lendsey) Harlan stated, "women's genres inevitably take account of representations of heroism made in men's genres.[33] That means the women in general accept and believe the superiority of men. They extol the men's valour and vigour. Thus they accept the inborn superiority of male and fails to claim equality with them. Equal opportunity and equal status are not the same in literal as well as practical sense. Equal opportunity may provide some means of improving the status but will never be the element of equality with men.

Lindsey Harlan in her essay "Heroes Alone and Heroes at Home" has very clearly depicted the shrivelling attitude of India. She says the Indian women especially of the Rajput community maintain shrines and the images, they perform regular poojas and know the appropriate offerings. They are infect incidentally concerned with heroic narratives. They are least concerned about the greatness of the heroic deeds but tend to focus on ritual. They are mostly dependent on men (husband/father or brother or in-laws). Because they lack interests in outside world. Women by nature tend to keep themselves within four walls. The women have a national tendency that, what happens outside home like warfare, politics etc are of the men's concern and women have nothing to do with them. Detail of martial and political manoeuvres abound in men's accounts of heroic struggles but they are hard to find in women's accounts. Lindsey also mentions in her essay that, where she carried out her research on women in Rajasthan she pointed out that girls education was not considered important; even those who sent their daughters to schools only aspired for better prospect for marriage. She found families who wanted educated daughters-in-law who can teach their children well but don't want daughter-in-law to be independent and employed having suitable academic or professional qualification. Even in these modern days the Indian Rajput mothers want homely girls. Harlan also mentions, though the purdah system in Indian higher caste Hindu families have been reduced considerably but the sense of distinctiveness of male and female is strictly observed by female. The mentality of women of the higher caste Hindus become crystal clear from the following statement—

> "Good women still "know their place" and eagerly distinguish themselves from lower caste women who must work in public and career especially feminist who make a virtue of outside employment."[34]

Political Interest

In the political field Indian women are though being accepted now but very few, because the stages a politician has to pass through from the day of joining the party generally does not suit a female instinct. Scarsely enough the rural guardians approve political participation of their female children. On the other hand there are pretermitted remarks prevalent in society against the female who engender political enthusiasm and enfranchisement, which quite often discourage female to take part in political activities.

The other side of political backwardness of women is due to the political stalwarts attitude towards women. It is glaring defect in political parties that only the affluent members or the one who has political family backgrounds are given political avenue. Hence female from the mediocre family spontaneously loses interest in politics. To develop the political interest women should develop education, will power and courage.

References

1. Mahesh Chandra Deb's "A sketch of the Conditions of the Hindu Women" (1839) (Geraldine Forbes' Women in Modern India, Cambridge UNI Press Ed-1996, p. 15.
2. Geraldine Forbes' "Women in Modern India", Cambridge University Press, p. 16.
3. Uma Chakrabarti's "Whatever Happened to the Vedic Dasi Recasting Women (Women in Modern India p. 16).
4. Geraldine Forbes' "Women in Modern India" (p. 17).
5. Isvarchandra Vidya Sagar, "Marriage of Hindu Widows" (Calcutta K.P. Bagchi and Co. 1976) p. 108 and 109.
6. Janice Wood Wetzel's "The World of Women—The Macmillan Press Ltd, London-1993 (p. 88).
7. Janice Wood Wetzel's "The World of Women" The Macmillan Press Ltd., London-1993 (p. 89).
8. Women in India by Geraldine Forbes (Cambridge University) (N. Delhi 1996, p. 22).
9. Women in India by Geraldine Forbes (Rosalind O'Haulon's Issues of Widowhood; Gender and Resistance in Colonial Western India, p. 22).
10. Geraldine Forbes' "Women in Modern India (p. 20).
11. Mandakranta Bose's "Faces of the Feminine in Ancient, Medieval and Modern India, p. 114.

12. Mandakranta Bose's Faces of the Feminine in Ancient, Medieval and Modern India, p. 114.
13. Durga Saptasali 6. 2.
14. Nuruttara Tantra 6. 4.
15. Kularnava Tantra 11. 64.
16. Mandakranta Bose's "Faces of Feminine in Ancient, Medieval and Modern India, p. 115.
17. Mandakranta Bose's "Faces of Feminine in Ancient, Medieval and Modern India, p. 115.
18. Shakti Sangama Tantra Chapter 2, 13. 43-49.
19. Faces of Feminine in Ancient, Medieval and Modern India, p. 271.
20. Footnote on p. 4 and 5 of Invented Identities, edited by Julia Leslie and Mary McGee.
21. Foot note on p. 7, Invented Identities edited by Julia Leslie and Marry McGee.
22. Dr. Sushila Mehta's "Revolution and Status of Women in India"
23. P-36, Louies Dumont's "Women and Social Change in India.
24. Cynthia Cockburn's "In the Way of Women" (p. 124).
25. Cynthia Cockburn's "In the Way of Women" (p. 124).
26. Maethreyi Krishanraj and Karuna Chanana's "Gender and the Household Domain", p. 31.
27. *Ibid.*, p. 32.
28. Mukul Mukherjee's "Impact of Modernisation on Women Occupation".
29. Dagmar Engels' "The Changing Role of Women in Bengal" (p. 169, Women in Modern India)
30. Marry Wollstonecraft's "A Vindication of the Rights of Women (1992 Ed., p. 1).
31. Geraldine Forbes' "Women in Modern India", p. 27.
32. Sudha Majumdar's Memoirs of an Indian Women edited by Geraldine Forbes.
33. Invented Identities edited by Julia Leslie and Mary McGee, p. 232.
34. Invented Identities edited by Julia Leslie & Mary McGee, p. 235.

Five

Political Reservation and its Meaning

Late Sardar Gyan Singh (Meerut) mentioned in his article titled "Nari Rajniti Aur Arakhan" that, on 26 July 1997 a Women Seminar on Women—Politics and Reservation was organized at Bombay Bazar, Meerut. The bill of 33 per cent reservation for women was though introduced at the beginning of the Parliament Session in 1997 but it could not be passed because, some MPs suggested modification to grant quota to Schedule Castes, Scheduled Tribes and Other Backward Communities women proportionate to their population. The women who organized the seminar expressed their displeasure on this suggestion for allotment of SC, ST and OBC quota in the bill. They, thus upheld that women are only women (one identity). They also declared that if the Parliament fails to pass the Bill of 33 per cent reservation for women before 15th August, 1997, they would resort to agitate on the street.

Now it is a matter of concern for the women of SC, ST and OBC communities in India that, when our benevolent patriotic political stalwarts are very anxious to give political rights to women so that they can improve the status of women, then what is harm if proportionate quota is allotted to SC, ST and OBC according to population. The declaration and expression of anguish by women in the seminar of Bombay Bazar at Meerut can be considered as the result of perpetration of savarn ruling class because, on the one hand they consider SC, ST and OBC women as women but cannot give them their dues.

In reality our upper castes leaders do not want to give equal rights to women nor do they want to improve the status of women in society. This 33 per cent reservation for women has a different intention. It is worthy of mention here a statement of a lady (Chandra Prabha Solanki) of the Seminar held at Meerut. She said, "I consider women's demand for reservation a wrong notion, because the reality is that the reservation for SC has not benefited the dalits as only the shrewd and affluent dalits have been benefited by it, similarly reservation for women will benefit the savarna shrewd and rich ladies. The common women will not be benefited. Therefore we should demand for all round facilities for development." The statement of Prabha Solanki gives vent to the real intention of the political magnates. The intention behind the women's reservation is to capture parliament by installing upper caste women by reducing the reserved seats for SC/ST. The present state of Parliament compact them to formulate policies and programme taking into consideration the interest of lower castes people. But if they can form the absolute majority by their oun men then they can fulfil their desire by depriving 85 per cent population of India (SC/ST/OBC and Minority) whom they consider their born enemy.

This reality has been clearly proved in the same seminar by instigating two little girls to say that, by giving reservation to SC, ST and OBC illiterate uncivilized women in politics and public administration should the nation go to dog?

The upper caste former speaker of the Lok Sabha B. Rai has vehemently, supported the women's reservation but supported allotment of proportionate quota.

Whenever the sufferers of backwardness demand their right the manuwadi elements oppose it either on the pretext of unity or religion. When our generous savarn women consider that women are all one, there is no distinction then why they perpetrated innocent girls to abuse dalits and backward class women calling them illiterate and uncivilized. Suppose the reservation bill was introduced by BJP with a generous thought of providing equal rights to improve the condition of women then proposal for allotment of proportionate quota according to population to SC, ST and OBC should have been accepted by them. But when it is vehemently opposed at every level up to their reach, it is crystal clear that in the name of women they want to bag the seats for savarna politicians. Savarna women only will get the chance to be elected by contest since backward women are still not in a position to compete the upper castes women, not because of their lack of capability and intelligence but because of their lack of unfair means like criminal force, money, immoral practices and shrewdness to apply.

Women themselves are confused about what they are going to achieve out of the reservation. Savarna women if succeed in getting 33 per cent reservation, have to submit to the cruelty of partymen of their own caste. They will have to work as proxy of the male. Their independent opinion will have no say. But without reservation when a woman wins a poll she can maintain her entity to a larger extent. Reservation also will play all those defective roles which they put to refute the suggestion of allotment of quota. Even if 33 per cent reservation without quota for SC, ST and OBC women is allowed, capable and intelligent women leaders who really love the country will not find place in parliament because the vaidik politicians appreciate stooges and become worst inimical to able personalities.

Present Hindu political tendency is never a women's supportive one. Hindu religious doctrine teaches to make the women their slaves. This has already been explained under the heading "Position of Women in Hindu Society" in Chapter 3.

If these politicians really respect the women, they should have first discarded those religious taboos and teachings which degrade women before men. The Hindu religion teaches women to worship men and to be always busy to provide comfort to their husbands and male relations in the family. Hindu religious philosophy teaches—

"Pujiye Vipra Sheel Gun Heena
Na Hee Sudra Gun Gyan Praveena
Dhol, Gavar, Sudra, Pashu, Naree
Ye Hain Sab taran Ke Adhikari".

Upper castes Hindu political leaders have the same view that is why, they will not treat the women colleagues with respects. This reservation will give them opportunity to strengthen the upper caste in parliament. They will be able to pass the bill easily in parliament with full support, despite the fact that, the bill may be against the interest of majority population of the country. Therefore, Women's Reservation Bill can be termed as Second Device to establish permanent supremacy of upper castes, the first one being "Review of Constitution". The provision of the existing constitution prevent the upper castes ruling class from doing arbitrary act and its amendment is also not easy for them because of reserved seats for SC/ST in parliament. Hence if 33 per cent reservation can be given to women without allocating seats categorically for SC, ST and OBC, 1/3rd majority will be easily be with them. Thereby they will be able to amend the constitution according to their whims. When one demands quota in women's Reservation Bill the savarn women oppose it on the plea that women have no separate identity, all are women only. But where this advocacy vanishes when a Hindu woman hate a Muslim, Kori, Chamar, Bhangi, Mushaior Mahar. Why they cannot sit together and eat together? When a question of right arises this shrewd section wants to encroach upon the rights of others on the pretext of equality and similar identity.

An important question may arise here that, were not our constitution makers competent to examine and understand the Indian Society? If they were learned and expert politicians then why the provision of reservation for women was not incorporated in the largest constitution of the world when provisions of reservation for SC/ST and even OBC were incorporated. If our predecessor politicians thought it expedient for the country then they would have done it since there were many renowned woman politicians very active Sarojini Naidu, Vijay Laxmi Pandit, Sushila Kaur, Hansa Mehta etc. at that time. Even a woman Prime Minister remained continuous in power over 10 years but never felt its requirement.

Women are not outside the caste hence the caste quota served the Women's interest. However, if our politicians are so concerned about the interest of women they should provide reservation according to the caste quota or the reservation should be given out of residual seats after allotment of reserved quota to SC/ST/BC and minority. In this context I would like to warn the SC/ST/BC and minority about the real intention of Women's Reservation Bill. Draw your attention to the parliamentary events of the past; when Dr. B.R. Ambedkar was Law Minister he brought a Hindu Code Bill, this bill was a clarion call for emancipation of women from the cluster of man's atrocities. The bill incorporated enormous rights for women like equal rights to wife and sons on one's property, marriage according to own choice of the bride, divorce, adoption of child by widow and so on. But not a single Indian women of that time supported the bill against the will of the political stalwarts and now their present generation is shouting for reservation. It is all farce show to deceive majority population.

Women who have courage and skill need not special privilege to show their capability in any field. Politics also is a part of human social activity and it depends upon the liking of a particular woman whose inborn qualities are developed according to the environment she lives in or brought up. Therefore reservation in a particular field does not encourage a woman if she is not otherwise mentally prepared to enter into it. On the other hand a woman who has political instinct in her, always remains inclined towards politics, no adversaries can suppress her desire and activities. It would not be irrelevant to mention that Indian society especially in Hindu and Muslim communities women have not been given equal position with men; there are so many roles in family, village, society and nation as a whole. Women have to perform but the religious doctrines have put them in inferior position to men. Yet we have before us numerous examples of unique skill and chivalrous character of women who did glorious deeds without any special sanction and support. Take the instance of Rani Lakshmi Bai of Jhansi who rebelled against the British Raj and led the Army herself in 1858. Every one of Indians regarded Rani Lakshmi Bai as the leader most likely to prevail against British.[1] Even the British official Sir Hugh Rose, against whom Rani had fought had appreciated her as the ablest and most valiant. To explain her bravery it would be justifiable to quote a few sentences from the book of S.M. Burke and Salim Al-Din Quraishi, "The British Raj in India".

> "Clad as a man, the Rani personally led her troops to battle and died fighting valiantly outside Gwalior (17 June)."
>
> "Of the rebel leaders, the ablest and the most valiant was the Rani of Jhansi, Sir Hugh Rose against whom she fought, acknowledged that she was the best and bravest military leader of the rebels."

Merits and Demerits of Women's Reservation Bill

In the succeeding paragraphs the merits and demerits of the women's reservation have been discussed in the context of Government's or the ruling party's real intention and its indirect implication upon the majority of population in India. The points discussed have to be taken into consideration by the readers and critics keeping in view the larger interest of major population and the unity, integrity and prosperity of the Nation, as a whole. It would also be the responsibility of the learned men of this country to think about the devices to bring all citizens (male and female) at parity for the development of the nation. Therefore, readers and critics are requested to form their opinion about the Women's Reservation Bill based on the description given under the headings 'Merits and Demerits'.

(a) Merits

Merits of this Women's Reservation Bill as per the government's show are quite pervasive and of greater importance in national progress. The ruling party advocates grant of equality of status to women with men and all other avenues which can be achieved by women on getting special privilege in politics. However, according to my conscience and belief the merit goes to the ruling class only. This political reservation will make the upper caste permanent ruler of the country. Majority in parliament can be formed by upper caste by placing their candidates on 33 per cent reserved seats for women. The women will get chance to excel in politics. The reservation will ensure their participation in formulation of laws of the country. The interest of the women population could be protected. But this is the virtuality of the women's reservation in principle. Practically the upper castes ruling class especially Brahmins who introduced varnashram or varnavyavastha in society to become the permanent ruler, will be benefited. Whatever they lost during British regime and after independence will soon be restored back by their one act play of supremacy in Parliament. Gradually the allies of Brahmin will also lose their dominant role in Government of the country. Though people belonging to many castes who consider themselves superior to SC and ST will find opportunity to sit in parliament but will soon find themselves under the claws of brahminism. The strategy the government in devising, though initially will benefit all upper castes but in the long run only the Brahmins will be benefited. This bill is the primitive stage of establishing Brahmin Raj in India. Other upper castes will gradually be adversely affected after some time as is evident from the past history of Aryan.

Women's reservation drastically curtails the rights of SC,

ST and BC and minority and protect the absolute interest of upper castes. All those women who vehemently advocated in favour of women's reservation are savarna and are well versed to deceive others. Real intention of caste Hindus is not to give reservation to women but to lead their own women ahead to capture and control administrative machinery and impose slavery upon women as prevailed in the past.

(b) Demerits

Reservation for women without allotment of quota for SC, ST, BC and minority will not be beneficial to all women but only to a particular class. Women are not equal in every class. The dalit women have not yet received the basic education to improve their personalities. An illiterate women cannot compete with a literate. Similarly dalit women being economically deprived can also not compete with an affluent woman. A beautiful woman cannot always be defeated by a moderate beautiful or ugly woman. The conditions of dalits ST, BC sections of women are worse than that of upper castes Hindu women. Upper castes women are educationally advanced, they are more beautiful because of their comfortable life free from hard labour, protection from sun and rain and possession of modern appliances of comfort and rest. These inequalities will never allow any benefit of equal reservation to SC, ST and BC women.

Dalit women cannot incur expenditure for beautification and development of delicacy. Thus they cannot develop their health properly and look ugly. Political parties as a general trend, enrol beautiful and glamorous women candidates, as such women of the backward classes can hardly stand against the savarna women in competition. On the other hand money gives men of the modern days all the courage and strength to undertake any venture, which SC, ST and BC women lack. Thus savarna women find themselves in better position to defeat the dalits in every field.

The prevailing untouchability in India makes the dalit women mentally feeble in front of savarna women; hence equitable reservation for them will be meaningless. Education which has the most important role to help them reach at the peak of advancement, is lacking in dalit women. As stated earlier the educationally, economically and socially backward women cannot properly comprehend the meaning of policies and programmes decided by the party high command. Hence the interest on their own community or class cannot be safeguarded by them even if they find a place in party or in parliament.

On the other hand when quota for SC, ST, BC and minority women is not allotted, almost all the seats will be contested by savarna women suppressing the rights of others, and finally bagged by them. Consequently the parliament will be captured by savarna. Even if the caste Hindu legislators be pleased to improve the status of women, they will take into consideration only the interest of savarna women and not for the common category. Normally men's atrocities are suffered by low caste women but they never get justice because they have no representative of their own in Assemblies and parliament to safeguard their interest.

As stated earlier woman is not a caste and Indian society is caste ridden. Therefore, all women cannot be taken at par. Their problems are different in one caste from that of another caste. Hence uniform treatment as regard reservation will not help lower caste and minority community women to ameliorate their grievances. Castism in India occupies every field of human activities. Hence women's progress in the field of education, employment, economy, socio-culture and politics depends upon the progress of their own caste. As such if the caste based quota is not allotted to women, lower caste women's interest cannot be protected against the prejudices of savarna women and men. Low castes women's position can only be improved if they themselves can seat in parliament to high-light their problems.

Reservation for women without allocation of quota to SC, ST, BC and minority women will certainly defeat the aim of improvement of common women and make a permanent supremacy of higher caste women over lower castes and minority. It will not at all prevent atrocities on women in lower strata of society by men of every class or castes.

If the aim of political reservation for women is to improve the status of women in society then women of different communities and castes should be first made equal to each other in status then only they can compete for equal status with men. When all women are not equal in status or social position then how can they be treated at par in politics. The intended bill of reservation for women treats all women equal, which is contrary to the existing norms of the society. When society has not yet accepted all women equal irrespective of castes and religion, then how the politicians can consider them equal? The reality goes against the advocacy of the ruling political party. At the present condition of women in India, the political reservation for women without allotment of specific quota to SC, ST, BC and minority women will not bring equality between men and women but will further increase the disparity among women of different classes and castes resulting in deprivation of rights of women of the weaker sections. Thus Women's Reservation Bill has an indirect blow against the progress of weaker sections.

Reference

1. S.M. Burke and Salim Al-Din Quraishi's "The British Raj in India" (Oxford University Press, 1995, p. 33).

Six

Atrocities on Women

General

In Indian society women are prone to men's atrocities. The atrocities on women which can otherwise be termed as devil acts of men upon the women, are of several kinds. The most heinous act of this kinds is rape. The next in order of cruelty is violence (manhandling) which frequently occurs in illiterate and rural families. Then we find some religious superstitions and dogmatic practices which are made applicable only to women in family and society.

On the basis of reports published in daily newspapers in India it is clear that the women are victims of social change and economic exploitation in India. This is pointed by thrust upon our attention due to facts indicating crimes against women are increasing at an alarming rate in the country to-day. From the media news it seems, the rape is becoming a fashion in daily occurrence in cities, towns and rural areas. What is worst, it is not only the goondas or anti-social elements who indulge in this kind of crimes.'

Even policemen who are supposed to be guardians and protectors, rape women under their custody. Teachers who are expected to have ideal character, rape their girls students. The politicians who are the policy makers of the country and reformers of the society often found involved in crimes against women. The rich and high castes young men find their past time and amusement in teasing and raping young girls and women of the poor and low caste strata of the society. It has become a trend of the country to commit all sorts of crime against low caste and poor women of the society. Women of the low caste only are becoming the victims of crime in routine nature. The social phenomena rapidly developing confrontation between the 'haves' and 'have-nots', the rich landlords and poor tenants, the upper-castes and the lower castes groups. In the ever increasing deep rooted caste discrimination in India, the ensuing fight of the upper caste landlords and the aristocrats to curb the low castes agitations for right to equality, mass rape of low castes women has become common event in the country. It has become a common phenomena in rural areas of the country that the dacoits or goondas loot the village and after they leave, the policemen would come at the end and in their turn harass the women to elicit information and even hospitality. The rape of innocent lower caste women is quite often used as an instrument of class war between the rich lords and the poor tenants. It is the last instrument used by feudal overlords to assert their supremacy and authority over their revellious under-lings. Sometimes when a policeman, who is scorned and deprived of his self respect by his superiors, rape the woman under his custody insanely to prove to himself and the society his authority. A burning instance of this nature is the famous Mathura case in which two police constables raped a fourteen year old tribal girl Mathura, in their custody simply to assert their authority and intimidate her men.[1] In fact the atrocities of women are used as malignant desire to stigmatise another human beings in society. The double standard morality makes a raped woman unfit for marriage. Thus she remains as damaged property, no longer acceptable in respectable society. Here we find the curious irony of social norms in Indian society which can not provide protection to its women against rape or male brutality and shamelessly call her sinner and debar her from any respectable status and role in social life!

The society puts heaps of injustice on women as a result of insult on rape to such an extent that she is forced to prostitution for all her life.

I am constrained to say that Indian society has not much changed from that of the ancient India. The women's atrocities knows no bound in Indian society as the daily happenings confirm. There is not a single day when we are not met across an incidence of rape. The incidence of women's atrocities specially during the communal conflicts after independence are heart breaking.

Rape of Women

Whatever the atrocities committed on women in society, the most heinous act is the rape. Some of the instances of rape of women which took place in Indian society are discussed as follows.

There are several instances of rape committed by responsible people of the society like teachers, politicians and government officials including the police personnel, who are supposed to be the protector of honour and dignity of human beings and maintain law and order of the society. The rich and high caste people who are considered to be the model of civilization frequently found to be oppressors of women. They indulge in raping young girls and women of the poor and low castes working under them for subsisting only for their amusement. The rape of women and innocent young girls in the villages or rural areas has become a terrible proposition for the criminal elements to terrorize the men into submission. It has become a common cause of oppression by higgher castes landlords on the low caste to deter them from demanding right to equality. It is the last instrument used by feudal over lords to assert their supremacy and authority over their rebellions. The rape is not committed just for sexual pleasure of the rapist. It has become a device of the rich, powerful and higher caste people to suppress the poor to enslave them and to compel them to live at the mercy of the powerful and influential people of the society. It is such a heinous and malignant device by use of which one person or family stigmatize the victim family and the women in the society with a view either to take revenge or to depress morally so that the victims find it impossible for her/them to live in the human society. It was and also is the ethics of Indian society, "Once raped becomes a spoilt stocks of the society". The raped women can never expect to live a respectable life in society. No respectable society is ready to accept her fit for marriage. This is the irony of social norms of Indian society. Indian society is men dominated it cannot provide protection to its women against rape or male brutality; on the contrary it condemn women calling them sinner after they are raped. Thus male dominated society make the women's lives a living hell. They are debarred from being a respectable wife, mother, sister or a daughter in the society. Although reformists, politicians, lawyers, thinkers and learned men of the country make vociferous statements about the dignity and reverence of women but the reality shows a vicious picture of society relating to the status of women.

Dr. Sushila Mehta very rightly quoted the instances of rape in Mahabharata to reveal that seeds of rape and crimes against women lie deeply rooted in Indian social structure and ancient culture. She indicted men of Indian society for having perverse pleasure in insulting or degrading women. In fact Dr. Mehta is right to comment as above because even the prevailing criminal phenomena of India supports her view. We find the incidence of rape even during the communal conflicts. There is not a single day when we do not read any incidence of rape in daily news.

In 1980 there was a fantastic incident of rape by policemen of a married woman Mrs. Maya Tyagi, who was made to walk naked through the streets of Baghpat town of Uttar Pradesh while large crowd watched the scene in mute silence.[1] Whatever the jengoist Hindus might say about the mistreatment of women throughout the country speak volumes on our attitudes towards the despicable status of women in society which lie deeply embedded in our cultural values.

Keeping in view the above discussion as regards men's atrocities on women, the rape is the most heinous and despicable act of men in a civilized society. Such an act on the part of men clearly indicates that women have no regards and honour before the male population. Women are looked down by the men in society. The former's status in society is like a chattel or the object of male's lustful satisfaction. There are several other forms of atrocity on women besides the rape in Indian society which directly or indirectly degrade women and make them submissive before the whims of male. Some of the atrocities of those kinds are discussed in the succeeding paragraphs.

Atrocities on Women other than Rape

There are several types of cruelty or harassment done by male population upon the female population irrespective of religions and castes, in Indian society. The daily news report clearly shows that the women are victims of social charges and economic exploitàtion in India. The alarming rate of increase in the crimes against women in India has drawn the attention of public in India as well as foreign countries. Women's atrocities in India attracting the attention of the world and reputation of India as a sovereign democratic republican country is stake before the developed countries. Women of the low castes and poor classes have become the object of amusement of higher caste rich spoilt youngsters. The air of money earned clandestinely is spoiling the youths of this country; criminal activities are openly made and go unabated. This has direct impact up or the women's morality and character. It has become a trend of the country to commit all sorts of crime against the women particularly of the low castes and poor society. Cruelty on women are not limited to low castes and poor it also occurs in high castes and rich families. There are so many instances of Vaishya and Rajpoot families where either women are treated as the property of men's occupation. Women are made obedient to their husbands and in-laws due to cruel attitude of male members of the family. Even before marriage in parental home also the females are governed by father brother and male relations. In some cases females remain as the household servants (maid) of the male. Quite often it is found that they are treated like the machines for procreation and kitchen tools. Even the educated employed women are compelled to maintain household and kitchen solely, in addition to their job for earning the livelihood. On the other hand males are found making all sorts of social nuisance and spending money earned by the females. In the service also women suffer humiliation of their male colleagues and the superior officers based on sex discrimination; some time to the extent of sexual exploitation.

Recently Dainik Bhaskar, Bhopal in its report published on 15/4/2002 relating to the atrocities on women police employees. In that a woman employed in the police department on compassionate ground following death of her husband stated that every body (male) among her colleagues wants to take undue advantage of her being innocent helpless heavily burdened of the family. However she refused to express the specific attitude of her colleagues towards her, though she hinted that women in police service are not safe from the misbehavior of male especially when they are widows or unmarried girls from poor families. She said misbehavior of male employees towards female has become a routine nature. A police sepoy Farida Sultan says that, she joined the police with an aim to become a sub Inspector but she has lost all her hopes and charms of her life in the department in last eight years service. According to her, the charms of the uniform and her hobbies both are buried under miseries. She asserts, what the police department seems to be, it is not in reality (police mahkma Jaisa dikhta hain, vastav mey vaisa hain nahin). Her husband is also in police service. She states that, being a woman she has to suffer more from the family burden and the service which male police employee never has to. Some women sub inspectors also asserted that they not only suffer from the cruelty, humiliation and maltreatment of their husbands but also from the maltreatment and humiliation from the department. Even some IPS officers also agreed that women police have more problems than employees of the other departments. Thus it is widely accepted that police women are victims of sex discriminations and unwanted behavior of male police. It is very unfortunate to note that a democratic country has not yet been able to maintain care free environment of its citizens and failed to protect the honour of women in society. It is a disgusting picture of Indian nationalism and morality.

There are endless humiliation on women in family but so far nothing has been done by our politicians, social reformers and legal experts to eliminate women's atrocities in society. On the contrary in one pretext or the other male's domination in society is upheld by all and sundry. Therefore, I am constrained to say that, Indian society has not much changed from that of the ancient India. Still women are beaten by men scorned and scolded every now and then in family as well as in society. As a daughter she suffers administration of parents and relatives so as to make herself a feeble and meek person. As a wife she is supposed to perform in household like a maid and to tolerate all sorts whimsical acts of her husband up to the extent of sexual assaults and mental torture. As a mother she has to tolerate insults and indignified behaviour of her children at old age but cannot impose her authority on her children. This is a mortifying state of life which always reminds her past to repent for the present but finds no way out.

The women in India are usually subjected to men's atrocities are quite established tradition. It has lastly been accepted by the government also and due to the rising pressure of women's organizations, government has agreed to bring a bill to the Parliament on prevention of women's atrocities as reported in Dainik Jagaran, Bhopal dated 7th December 2001.

Men's atrocities on women in Indian society becomes

further clear from the statement of former sarpanch Kala Bai in a state level meeting of women Panchayat Representatives held at Bhopal. While expressing her deep feelings and experience during her speech she said—

> "I don't know what does the 'dalit' means? We are called by the name 'chamar' or 'Basore'; misbehaved and treated as untouchables. If there happens to be a member from the 'Mehtar' community then she is not allowed to enter the Panchayat office or meetings. Even she is not heard by the Panchayat. Till to date women of Mehtar community in her area are compelled to carry human excrements on their head".

Causes of Atrocities on Women

Most of the crimes against women are due to commercialization and industrialization. The social order of the old days is completely broken. The socio-psychological pressure of Kinship or even the joint family system is no longer operative. On the other hand the modern emerging social controls, rules, regulations and even the penal code or laws are not generally accepted and abided by the people. Besides these in modern society there are many other factors and forces which contribute to enhance the number of rape cases in the country. The social phenomena rapidly developed confrontation between the 'haves' and 'have nots', the rich landlords and poor tenants, the upper caste and the lower castes groups. Violent conflicts erupt every now and then.

In the ever increasing deep rooted caste discrimination in India, the ensuing fight of the upper caste landlords and the aristocrats commit several atrocities including rape a woman to curb the agitations of low castes for rights to equality. Mass or gang rape of low caste women have become common event of the country. It has become a common phenomena in rural areas of the country that the dacoits or goondas ransacking the villages the policemen harasses the women to elicit information about the incident. Women are maltreated in society only because the attitude of men towards women is mean. The laws or the legal procedures alone cannot protect the dignity and honour of women in society; even without statutory low women can live respectable life if the nature of the men towards female remains reverential, honest and pious. The present state of the society in relation to the safety of women's modesty is worse due to overall neglectful and suppressive behaviour of males.

The richness and lordships also are responsible for oppression on women in society. The rich men and feudal overlords assert their supremacy and authority over the poors and low castes members by adopting all sorts of evil nature of activities and women become the most victims of atrocities.

Behaviour of men supposed to be the protector of law and order of the state are quite often involved in outraging the modesty of women. The policemen's attitude towards women is most despicable. Sometimes it is found that when a police man is scorned and admonished by his superior officers, rape the woman under his custody insanely to prove to himself and to society his authority. A case of tribal girl Mathura of this nature has been discussed under the heading "Rape of women" in the preceding paragraph. The causes of increasing rape as pointed out by the police investigations revealed, one as the most that, it is the local politicians and rich landlords who give shelter and encourage dacoits and unemployed youths to indulge in these criminal activities. The films also play a major role to misguide the young men by displaying several objectionable vulgar sexual scenes in the film show. As a result young men play and lionize such anti-social activities like rape, teasing and abusing women. Rape is not committed just for their sexual pleasure. In fact it is mostly used as a malignant device to stigmatize and suppress the opponents in society. This has become a political arms now-a-days to lay down one another in political games.

Religious culture and the legendary instances which the Hindu scriptures contain have great impact upon the society to degrade the women by committing several kinds of atrocities. Dr. Sushila Mehta has quoted instances of rape of women from Mahabharat to reveal that seeds of rape and crimes against women lie deeply rooted in Indian social structure and ancient culture. She indicted men of Indian society for having perverse pleasure in insulting or degrading women. In fact Dr. Mehta is right to comment like this because even the prevailing criminal phenomena of India supports her view. She says—

> "There is the classical example of Draupadi the great heroine of the epic Mahabharat who was raped by Duryodhana in the midst of an august assembly of men. The act was committed before the very eyes of all the respectable men of society, surprisingly enough none of the great men uttered a single word of condemnation of Duryodhana nor did they raise their little fingers to save the honour of Draupadi; Perhaps the august audience found some perverse pleasure in seeing a women made naked against her will".[3]

The incidence of women's atrocities specially during the communal conflicts after independence are heart breaking. The women's atrocities are the result of men's discriminating and repressive behaviour. Men of both Hindu and Muslim communities have the same regards for women, they create different artificial scenes to moleste or rape or humiliate women. The communal riots in Bengal, Punjab, Bihar, Uttar Pradesh and Maharashtra have several times had created hell on Indian earth for women after the independence.

The recent riots in Gujarat have witnessed the plight of muslim women. The criminal elements backed by the politicians, administrative authorities and the nobles of the state have brutally raped and killed the women. The Hindu religious orthodox and demagogues exaggerated lot about the prestigious position of women in India and especially in Hindu social structure. But it is strangely unbelievable that they could do the acts like that of in Gujarat. It is a despicable state for women to believe on the generosity and dignity of men dominated society. The sufferage of indignation and humiliation of women is deep rooted in Hindu ancient culture. The study of Hindu ancient scriptures, men's behaviour and attitudes towards women become crystal clear. Since the time immemorial women had been under subjugation of men; they never given equal status with men in family. Though women are called "ardhangini" but that was limited to the religious rites. In actual practice men treated women like property to be disposed off at the sweet will of their men. The very instance of this kind we find in scripture when a respectable man like Yudhishthira, who was considered to be the model of truth and honesty did not hesitate to use his wife Draupadi as pawn in the game of gambling! Rama, who was the model king and super most man (purushottam) did not hesitate to abandon his wife to forest in order to secure his own power and prestige. The Ravana who is highly glorified in some parts of the country raped his daughter-in-law Rambha! The truthful king Harish Chandra sold his wife Taramati for a paultry sum of money.[4] There are several such instances in ancient Hindu scriptures. The detailed study of Indian scriptures will reveal that women were not at all treated by men as human beings. The reasons behind such inhuman behaviour of men could not be pin-pointed. However, taking into consideration the inclination of people towards the religious faith and the position of women depicted in scriptures, it can be concluded that religion, religious culture and practices are mainly responsible for degraded or subordinate condition of women in human society of India. The people's attitude which to a larger extent is influenced by the religious dicta and cultural practice, is attributable to women's degradation and disrespect in society. So to change the attitude of men towards women, religious reform is inescapable. But in Indian society it is a difficult task to carry out.

Men's cruelty on women in Indian society is also attributable to women's biological structure, their physical weakness and differences in shape, colour, look and usual behaviour. Taking into consideration the prolonged struggle of women for equal rights and the changes took place in our society, it may well be observed that, despite all efforts to provide security to women through law yet they are victims of men's cruelty because of their structural discrepancies and physical weakness. Though all other aspect of human criminal element can be checked and equality could be provided but physical equality cannot be created. This aspects of women's inability will last and create problems of social status.

As stated earlier, the women's degradation and atrocities are attributable to religious cultural practices and scriptures. How can a woman find a safe place for her dignity and honour in India, where the religious sanctions permit her immolation. An instance of religious sanction can be found in Brihad Aranyaka Upanishad. A section of this Upanishad which is often left untranslated by scholars is fourth Brahmana of Sixth Chapter. Two Slokas which sanction use of force to fulfil man's lusty desires for sex may be translated as under[5]—

> "Thus verily indeed, is loveliness among women, when a woman has removed the soiled clothes of her impurity! And is beautiful, one should approach and invite her.
>
> If she should not grant him his desire he should bribe her. If she still does not grant him his desire, he should hit her with a stick or with his hand and overcome her, "with power, with glory, I take away thy glory, thus she become inglorious."

Thus the Hindu religious scriptures sanction cruelty of men over women allowing the former to outrage the modesty or immolate the latter to fulfil the carnal desire of the former.

This is a clear evidence of women's subordination and helplessness in men dominated society. The Hindu religious morale encourages men's air of superiority and chauvinism towards women in Indian society! Whatever the Hindu scriptures incorporated in it undoubtedly depict man as the lord and the master, he can use or abuse the woman for his own pleasures as a piece of property, without any consideration of her liking and disliking.

There is no doubt about the women's position as a chattel of her man according to the religious scriptures of Hindu mythology. This position become very clear from the instance we find in Mahabharata. The story runs as –"the King Pandu was under a curse which spelled instant death on his sexual intercourse! So he urged his senior wife Kunti to sleep with sundry Brahmins in order to bring forth brave sons! When Kunti demured politely, Pandu quoted the example of sage Uddalaka and his son, to convince her. He narrated "one night Uddalaka's son saw a guest leading his mother towards the bed room, he protested. His father explained that it was his "dharma" to ask his wife to entertain his guest sexually as in all other ways! Thus Kunti was persuaded by Pandu to seek fathers for her children and bringforth great sons like Yudhishthir, Arjun and Bhim."

The cultural value of Hindu religion which had been accumulated in the Indian society for times immemorable, brought about perpetuate physical, mental, intellectual and even spiritual slavery for women. For, even a woman's own concept of self, as clarified by sociologist Cooley, is an amalgam of man's concept of the woman and society's assignment of her social roles. In such a despicable culture how can women claim equality or human rights in a rigid social structure so much tilled towards male domination that they seem to have forgotten about her being a human or she could have a personality or her own will like or dislike! The cultural male domination has resulted women's downfall to slavery which had the outcome of most despicable ideas and ideas leading to the terrible custom of 'Sati'. Due to this custom of 'Sati', the status and role of women in Indian society was degenerated to such an extent that, an ideal woman is called 'Sati'. That is to say, in Hindu Society Sati is worshipped because Sati depict a woman character who can tolerate infinite insults, any amount of beating by her man and live a beastly life of drudgery and subordination without uttering a single word of resistance. The word 'resistance' could not be found in women's dictionary. Unfortunately, in Indian society absence of this resistance to men's cruelty gives further impetus to more cruelty and abuse till the poor woman dies the death of a beast. The cultural value in Indian society is based on ancient religious philosophy, which are Brahmacharya for men, Dharma' of "Pativrata Sati", for women.

Indian Politics and the party forces are also responsible for women's degradation and slavery. To elucidate this view we can take into consideration the daily occurrence of atrocities on women. The reports of gang rape of women are sometime investigated in casual manner or the criminals move freely due to the dereliction of police men or due to the political pressure, i.e., the interference of political party high commands. No one can deny the fact that, although media and the investigating authorities do not disclose the findings of the investigations, quite often politicians also found directly or indirectly involved in the rape and murder of women. It is the politicians who shelter the criminals. Even sometimes culprits are set free immediately after the arrests. Molestation, teasing, abduction and selling of young girls or beautiful women are increasing day by day because the criminals involved in these cases are all and sundry absolved of the crime either due to political support or the police support. In fact, although several Acts of women's security have been enacted by the Parliament but its implementation is not done properly and in its strict sense.

Even where the police authorities honestly discharge their duties, the legal value of the laws under which the criminals are prosecuted, is at bargain between the parties to the case and the lawyers, thereby justice is denied to the plaintiff. The present state of women's degradation, thus is also attributable to lawyers' professional mischieve. Atrocities on women in Indian society is in its rancour state not only due to political inter-play and dishonesty of police officials and lawyers but other administrative machineries and business class are also responsible. Thus at large the public posture is responsible. Indian male folk do not have respect for women, they never ready to accept women as their equal and complements in society, on the contrary consider them as the property or object of whimsical play.

Caste Based Atrocities on Women

The caste based atrocities on women has made the condition of women belonging to Scheduled Castes and Scheduled Tribes deplorable. Though sex disparity in India is prevalent in every sphere of social, educational, economic and political arena yet the women of the lower caste is much exploited and harassed in comparisons to women of the higher castes. The Times of India dated 24 February 2001 reported a case in which a tribal woman in Nalgonda district of Andhra Pradesh was gang raped in custody by five constables of Central Reserve Police (CRP). The statement of the 23 year old victim, a Lambada tribal woman of Porelegadda village reveals that she was going in jeep along with her six-year old niece and others at around 3 P.M. on February 16 while the police personnel stopped the jeep near Guddimalkapur village and forced her to alight and wait near a Community Hall. Soon after, on the pretext of interrogating her, five CRPF constables gang raped rendering her unconscious.

In another case a police party while carrying out a raid in a village Divar Kanchan have assaulted Shri Ram Ratan Jatav, a scheduled caste and tried to outrage the modesty of female members of his family. But the police station refused to lodge FIR against the police party. The matter was being concealed by the higher castes influential persons of the village in favour of the police. (*Dainik Jagaran,* dated 24/03/2001).

In Madhya Pradesh tribal killing has become a routine nature. Even the administrative machineries are sometimes involved in tribal killing, which can be considered as the caste based atrocity of ruling class. The Times of India dated 25/4/2001 reported a case of tribal killing in the Bagli block of Dewas district in Madhya Pradesh, in which four tribals were killed during police encounter. The Chief Minister Digvijay Singh also announced a compensation of rupees one lakh each to the families of the tribals who were killed. It is very surprising to note that we do not find instances of similar killing of higher castes people either in police encounter or by criminal gangs. Thus, such type of killing directs any one to conclude that there might be some conspiracy behind the act.

The case of low caste women's rape has become more prone to the rural as well as urban society. A case reported in *Nav Bharat*, Bhopal dated September 6, 2001 which says that in Nuzirabad Police jurisdiction, a married woman of 20 years while cutting grass in the field, was forcibly raped by a youth named Shimbhu Singh.

Mr. Vimal Thorat writes about the exploitation of dalit women under title "Dalit Mahila Shoshan Ki Rup Anek". He rightly says, the exploitation of dalit women is quite different from that of in the case of others. Because, some of the women's problems are in the dalit community only in India. The other women of the upper castes do not face the same problems. Why the problems of dalit women are different from women of the upper castes? This question need to be examined in details in the context of social tradition, customs and religious mandates.

In the social context the dalit community is in the most backward state in education. The dalits being in the lowest step of social ladder according to Hindu religious mandates they are poor and deprived of education. When the entire community suffers educational backwardness the position of dalit women is much backward in comparison to other women of higher castes, who are not the victim of caste distinction and religious suppression. Due to poverty the dalit women are mostly found to be struggling for earning livelihood in rural area as unskilled labour or bonded labour. The survey carried in 1991 it was found that almost 71 per cent of agricultural labour were dalit women and only 43 per cent were from other castes. This 43 per cent were all having some rights on the land they worked on but less than 20 per cent of the dalit women labours were classified equivalent to that of the other castes women mentioned above (43 per cent). The more drastic condition of dalit women labour is that they remain almost without work during the year because the agricultural work is time bound seasonal. Moreover the unemployment problem in rural area with the dalit women is four times greater than that of the upper castes women. One more noteworthy fact is that where the labour rate is high the dalit women workers are less and where the rate is less the number of dalit women are more. This trend is the creation of caste disparity in Hindu society. In every respect dalits are suppressed by social tradition and upper caste anti-dalit tendency.

In the modern days the most uncalled for notion is that in India still the women of dalit community are supposed to carry the human excrements and filths on their head just to manage their livelihood. Due to their engagement in such filthy work, they quite often remain without work as they are treated as untouchable by majority people in society especially the higher castes. The higher castes women also refrain themselves from the dalit women.

Why the illiteracy among the dalits is like a huge mountain? The attributable factors to illiteracy in dalit women are many. First the poverty— instead of going to school the dalit girls are compelled to work. The literacy rate of the rural dalit women is the lowest in the country, for instead of joining schools the number of dalit girls leaving schools before completion of the session is far greater than the upper castes girls. Almost 60 per cent of dalit girls students leave the school before completion of primary education. This is due to poverty and mostly as a result of caste based atrocities on them. In the course of higher education, though very limited members reached to that stage, the dalit girls meet several forms of humiliation.

In Indian Hindu society there are several religious and social dicta, the victim of which are only the women of lower castes viz., "Devadasi Pratha" (Custom of God's maid or mistress). This custom and tradition compel beautiful women of the lower caste to fulfil the lusty desires of priest and upper castes rich men of the locality in the disguise of religious celebacy. This is nothing else than compelling the low caste attractive girls to prostitution in the name of religious obligation. The vicious scene of such an obnoxious custom appears in the report of Scheduled Caste and Scheduled Tribe Commission of Andhra Pradesh. The 28th report of the Commission recorded the presence of 10,000 jogins (woman saint) in only one district Nizamabad of Andhra Pradesh. According to survey carried out upto the end of 1987 about 15,000 jogin were found in Barad district of Andhra Pradesh of whom more than 78 per cent were dalits village girls whose marriage were celebrated with the deity of the village under the pressure of religious orthodox and later the higher caste Zamindar rich men and the priest class used them to satisfy their carnal desires.

Deity marriage custom has been introduced by these higher castes people keeping in view to satiate their lust. This practices of recognized prostitution are in vogue in Telangana region of Andhra Pradesh and adjacent states Karnataka and West Maharashtra where Devadasi custom prevails. Tamil Nadu and Orissa are also not stain free in this respect.

Another caste based atrocities which the dalit women suffer from is persistent violence and inhuman cruelty which has been termed "atrocities on dalit". These atrocities are classified by the Home Ministry into four kinds – killing, severe injury, set on fire and rape. Although there have been preventive measures yet the incidents are increasing day by day. The study of the cases of atrocities reveals that though all kinds of atrocities are committed on dalit women but the cases of rape are the highest. Though women of upper castes also became the victims of rape yet the dalit women became the victim in larger number. For on the one hand they are poor and dependent on upper castes, on the other hand they are looked down upon. So, they become more victims of their lustful desires or sexual exploitation of high castes than the women of non-dalit communities. During 1981 to 1986 the cases of rape were about 4000, i.e., about 666 per year. In 1993 this was increased by 198 and in 1994 this number raised to 993, approximate three dalit women were raped daily. The cases were more in U. P. and Rajasthan. A report of the Home Minister of Madhya Pradesh in the year 2001 is more deplorable. There were 4154 rape cases in Madhya Pradesh from January 2001 to 30 June, 2001, i.e., 23 women were raped daily. On investigation into the causes of rape it was found that mostly the dalit women's rape occurred due to economic dependency of dalits on the upper castes rich men and Zamindar. Similarly dalit women who are engaged as casual in constructional work or agricultural labour in the field, they quite often became the victim of sexual exploitation of higher caste landlords or contractors.

There is still the practices of bonded labour in Bihar, Orissa, U.P., M.P. and Maharashtra. The dalits are compelled to work by the use of force. They cannot escape because the Zamindar or landlords have their own private force or goonda to watch them.

From the above description of the facts any prudent man can conclude that the injustice met to women of dalit community is far greater in degree and number in comparison to upper caste women. Thus all women are not equal in status in India. Since equality among the women could not be established so far in Indian society, then how could we expect equal status of women with men. Until the caste discrimination is abolished even all women cannot claim equality among themselves. Similar is the case with men; they are also not getting equal rights and status among themselves due to caste distinction. In the prevailing circumstances equal status of women with men cannot be imagined in Indian society. The political power or special privilege and educational facilities will not be able to equalize women with men without abolishing of castism. Castism is the root cause of inequality in men and women both. So the equality between men and women cannot be expected.

References

1. Dr. Sushila Mehta's 'Revolution and Status of Women in India', Metropolitan Book Co., (P) Ltd., New Delhi 1982 Ed. (p. 201).
2. Dr. Shushila Mehta's 'Revolution and Status of Women in India', Metropolitan Book Co. (P) Ltd. New Delhi 1982 (p. 202).
3. Dr. Sushila Mehta's 'Revolution and Status of Women in India', (p. 202).
4. Dr. Sushia Mehta's 'Revolution and Status of Women in India', Metropolitan Book Co. (P) Ltd. New Delhi 1982 Ed. (p. 202).
5. Dr Sushila Mehta's 'Revolution and Status of Women in India', Metropolitan Book Co. (P) Ltd., New Delhi, 1982 Ed. (p. 203).

Seven

Women's Organisations

Indian and International Organisations

In the course of national liberation and revolutionary struggle of the countries like Vietnam, China, Korea, Bulgaria, Yugoslavia, Poland, Czechoslovakia, etc., women's organizations were formed which together with progressive women of France, Italy, Belgium and other countries were the first to create a genuinely international broad based democratic women's organization after the Second World War. The active role in the creation of this organization was played by the women of the Soviet Union, the country that made a decisive contribution to the victory over fascism.[1] On December 1, 1945 Women's International Democratic Federation was born as a result of thousands of women's participation in the struggle against German fascism and Japanese militarism and holding the Internal Women's Congress in Paris on the date. This Federation declared that its goal would be to consolidate the peace that had been won at so great a cost to struggle against any reappearance of fascism, to battle for the national independence of the world's people, for the rights of women and the happiness of children.

Women's organization in socialist countries have founded peace funds and participated in their activities. The women of the socialist countries greeted the onset of detente in Europe, the treaties signed between the Federal Republic of Germany and the U.S.S.R. and between the F.R.G. and the Polish People's Republic and the annulment of the notorious Munich Agreement of 1938 which betrayed interest of Czechoslovakia.

The women's movement in Asia was not uniform. Asian countries have reached different levels of socio-economic and political development, they have different national traditions and different history. But what was typical problems with many of them is their economically subordination in the system of international capitalist division of labour, the exploitation to which they are subjected by the foreign monopolies and the resultant economic and cultural backwardness. In the country like India women's organizations considered it their primary responsibility to study the conditions for female labour in industry, the level of the working women's general education and professional training and the efficiency with which the literacy programme is implemented among the adult population. Many of women's organizations in India have started playing more and more role in the political and economic life of the society and the other democratic organizations are making their efforts to further the development of democracy and social progress. In the past they had played very important role in the freedom struggle. The activity of the women's organizations in India is an example to the point that they have greatly contributed to the national liberation movement with their people. Now almost eighty years they have been active in political life of the country. In the year 1930 they responded to the address of the national liberation movement leader M.K. Gandhi and took part in famous March to Dandi.

The struggle for Indian working women was led by National Federation of Indian Women (NFIW), the largest democratic women's organization in the country founded in the year 1952. The Federation united over 2, 00, 000 women industrial workers, peasants, representatives of the intelligentia and the middle class. To strengthen its unity and cooperation with other democratic organizations, the Federation made efforts for fundamental socio-economic transformation for the development of the public sector of economy, a radical agrarian reform. The Federation held an annual congress, organized massive demonstration of working women and meeting of protest, demanding higher wages, women's full employment in industry and an extensive programme of social insurance of workers. One of the basic programme of the Federation is to defend the working women's rights.

The principal demands of the Federation were:-

(1) No women to be dismissed from the factories and mines
(2) More women to be employed in those branches of industry where female labour can be used.
(3) ILO's convention No. 100 to be strictly observed.
(4) The Maternity Benefits Act to apply to all categories of working women including those working on hire (in towns and villages).
(5) Crèches and day nurseries to be opened at enterprises for the children of the female employees and the existing child welfare establishments to be improved.
(6) Stable minimum rates to be set for women working in various branches of industry.
(7) A definite percentage of vacancies to be reserved for women in the textile, jute and food industries or plantation etc.
(8) The National Award Scheme for labour (if paid at the given enterprise) to include women employees.
(9) Price on essential commodities to be reduced.
(10) Food stores with fixed price to be opened.
(11) A women's Advisory Council under the Ministry of Labour and Employment and so on.

Indians working women under the Federation took an active part in the struggle of the working class for their rights and against the policy of wage freeze soaring prices and jobbery in food stuffs. In 1967, when difficulties arose in supply and prices on foods and essentials went up, the Federation addressed an appeal to all its local branches, to other women's organizations and to all women of India to start a collection of money in aid of the starving districts. With the money collected mobile soup kitchens and stations were organized in Bihar, Orissa and the other States where the food shortage was the most acute. The Federation demanded from the government that it should find the means to solve the food problem and introduce strict planning of production and consumption of food stuffs. In 1967 in confirmation of the demand and on the initiative of Federation representatives of 22 women's organizations and trade union section of the jute and textile industries came out for a hunger strike in the State of West Bengal. A similar march took place in the same state later in June 1968.

Indian Major Women's Organizations and its Objectives

After 1910 national and provincial women's associations were started by women who had experience in local women's association. These organizations are *Bharat Stri Mahamandal* (BSM) founded by Sarala Devi in 1910, its local branches were in Calcutta, Lahore and Allahabad and later in other Indian cities. Women's Indian Association (WIA) was founded in 1917 by Annie Basant, Dorothy Jinarjadasa and Margaret Cousins. The centre of the association was Madras although branches were in many other cities. Bombay Presidency Women's Council (BPWC) was founded in 1918 by Lady Tata and others who had been active in war work. This association coordinated the activities of women's associations in the Bombay Presidency and later joined the National Council of women in India (NCWI). The National Council of Women in India was founded in 1925 by Lady Aberdeen of the International Council of Women, Lady Tata and others from the BPWC. All India Women's Conference (AIWC) was founded in 1927 through the efforts of Margaret cousins and others. *Bharat Mahila Parishad* (BMP) was founded in 1904 with the main objective of communications net work among women, which was the main factor contributing to the new stage of organizational development of women's movement. Another association which facilitated communication among women was the Senate of the Indian Women's University. The association assisted both the success of WIA in its early stages and to the establishment of all India women's conference in 1927. The aims of the WIA were as follows:—

(1) To present to women their responsibilities as daughters of India.

(2) To secure every girl and boy the right of education through schemes of compulsory primary education including religious instructions.

(3) To secure the abolition of child marriage and other social evils.

(4) To secure for women the vote for Municipal and Legislative Councils on the same terms as it is or may be granted to men.

(5) To secure adequate representation of women in Municipalities, Taluks and Local Boards, Legislative Councils and Assemblies.

(6) To establish equality of rights and opportunities between men and women.

(7) To help women to realize that the future of India lies largely in their hands, for as wives and mothers they have the task of training, guiding and forming the character of the future ruler of India.

(8) To band women into groups for the purpose of self development and education and for the definite service of others.[2]

The above aims of the WIA and the functioning of the AIWC form its date of establishment till the independence of India have a broad base to conclude that these organizations were mainly engaged in political activities though social affiliation was their pre-condition for working. Moreover, the social changes took place in Indian society from the day of their coming into existence till independence also proves that Indian women have achieved a great deal of political rights. Whereas, the most important factor of their improvement in status, the equal opportunities in every walk of life with men have not yet granted to them. The right to property, inheritance, religious equality with men and equal status in family have not yet been granted to them in any of the religious communities of India.

Most discriminating aspect of the women's organization was that none of the organizations has ever adopted a resolution of abolition of castes or to create casteless equality. Thus although certain amount of equality prospect is granted to women but that is limited to or availed only by the upper castes elites and women of noble families. The majority women population in India are still in the deprived category in almost all fields of social, political and economic sphere.

Even after 55 years of Indian Independence the people of Scheduled Castes and Scheduled Tribes (depressed class) have not been able to merge with the mainstream of Indian civilized people. Why this condition prevails, no reformist or the leaders of Women's Movement ever thought. The members of the noble family or elite group can precautiously think over the problems of their own. How can they experience the pains the lower deprived classes suffer from. That is the reason why despite a considerable improvement in the political and social status of women of the higher castes, the Government of India is vehemently advocating for political reservation for women without any distinction of caste and religion. This reservation will be farce dream for the women of depressed class who are still leading the life of destitute. No special efforts are being made to bring them to the status of women of the upper caste and elites. It is quite easy to comprehend the social condition of Indian Scheduled Castes and Scheduled Tribes who predominantly reside in remote agrarian environment where even in the advanced scientific era they are living without basic amenities. Political equality of women of depressed class with men in general is not at all imaginable till such time they are economically and educationally backward. The women's organizations from the very beginning have not paid attention towards the caste discriminations prevailed in Indian society while planning different strategies for social reform. The Indian social phenomena of the present days is the evident in support of existence of caste discrimination. Due to this discrimination there is vast gulf between the women belonging to Scheduled Castes/Scheduled Tribes and women of the upper castes.

The analytical studies carried out by various historians and social thinkers have revealed that women of depressed class or oppressed class are lagging behind in education, economic stability due to caste discrimination they are also psychologically losing heart in the struggle for advancement having suffered the caste based atrocities of upper castes. I do not understand how the government is planning to grant political reservation for women without making any effort to uplift the women of deprived classes to the position of women belonging to upper castes, who are already in a position to contest with men in every field.

Involvement of the Organisations

Open Door International was an organization led by Mrs. Wienfrel Le Sveur which advocated absolute equality between men and women workers. They opposed special regulations for example, limitation on loads carried, as unnecessary restriction that would lead to retrenchment.

Godavari Gokhale (later Parulekar) and her friend Miss Bhalerao formed the Women's Fellowship of Service as a Women's wing of the Servants of India Society. Godawari focused on labour, teaching, sewing promoting labour unions, organizing domestic workers and developing adult literacy programme. Due to her own radical experience she was driven towards a greater appreciation of the Communist Party. She had a special interest in women as industrial workers and believed their concerns could be integrated into organized labour demands for justice.

All India Women's Conference (AIWC) was a major women organization which was committed to examine the working condition of women. In 1933 the AIWC appointed a committee of three women to visit mines in Bengal and Bihar and suggested how to implement the Whitley Report and recommendation to abolish female labour in mines.[3]

Mrs. A. Chatterjee, Mrs. Renuka Ray and Miss Iris Wingate toured seven mines in Raniganj and Jharia. In their report to AIWC, they argued forcefully for termination of underground works for women. Finding the poor condition of works in mines for women, the AIWC earmarked a village on experimental basis for upliftment of women. National Vigilance Association was an organization, which kept watch on the exploiting life of women. It collected letters, sketches and translated statements about and from women in rescue home with a view to highlight the misery of women to bring sympathy among the people for this kind. The Vigilance Association wanted abolition of prostitution. The organization set up rescue homes to train prostitute to earn their livelihood in some other way. The rescue homes also tried to recruit these women with their families and caste people.

The women's organizations became more involved with the abolition of devadasis (maid or mistress of God or the women married to God according to Hindu customs and traditions) than with the abolition of prostitution. There was general acceptance of prostitution as a necessary evil, and many of those women who fought for abolition, for example Charulata Mukherjee and Ramola Sinha in Bengal, devoted their energies to rescue homes.[4]

Following the publication of Whitely Committee report the National Council of Women in India (NCWI) formed a Study Committee on labour and the Bombay Council

Scheduled a three-day conference on women and labour. In the meantime AIWC decided to broaden its mission to include social issues and appointed a member of Sub Committees in 1930. After visiting mills, collecting datas on conditions in the factories, AIWC in 1931 approved the recommendations of Whitely Committee for reduction in working hours, provision of women inspectors and medical practitioners, maternity benefit and prohibition of women working underground in mines. The Women's organizations approached the government to pass legislation and made efforts to get in touch with women and child labourers. They organized a three-day conference in Bombay to enlighten their members on labour issue and bridge the gap between themselves and women labours. They conducted lectures on focusing the need of nutrition, cleanliness and education of women labourers. Also lectures on employer-employee relations and labour legislation were conducted. These efforts have encouraged the middle class women to visit the workers line and know about the living condition. As a result of the conference the participants of the conference decided to form study circle and made efforts to improve the lines of women labourers.[5]

AIWC's demands for social insurance, maternity benefits and other measures to improve the working condition of women probably had international influence. Therefore by and large they ignored the warning of Rajkumari Amrit Kaur against the special legislation. The Bombay council on the other hand showed keen interest in the lives of real working women. They set up regional training centres offering medical services, sewing lessons, and literacy classes. They also arranged piecemeal works for the wives and children of labourers. Lectures and entertainment programmes were arranged. The factory women gradually developed interest in consulting medical personnel, listening lectures and attending literacy classes. They became so interested and valued so much these programmes of the Council that once when the Council ran short of money, the women workers collected money and paid the teacher.[6] Women's organization finally demanded for a Hindu Code that would remove the legal disabilities of women in marriage and inheritance. This position on Hindu Law reform was clearly influenced by the appointment of committees in Baroda and Mysore to consider the question. The AIWC in its 8th session in January 1934 passed a resolution for establishment of an unofficial commission to investigate and reform Hindu Law.[7]

In the year 1934 AIWC held an All India Legal Disabilities of Women Day under the direction of Renuka Ray.[8] The purpose of the day was to publicize the demand for a commission to investigate and ameliorate the legal position of women in personal law. There were public meetings at which lawyers spoke in favour of reform and the participants signed petitions. Although position of women in Islamic Law was discussed, the main focus was on Hindu Law. The purpose of the Legal Disabilities of Women Day according to Renuka Ray was to create public support for the AIWC's demand. However, the public opinion on AIWC conception was very narrow because the members comprised only readers of English language periodicals.

As mentioned in the discussion on women's organizations in the preceding paragraphs, most of the Women's organizations got its existence through the women of elite groups and noble families. Ms. Everett in her research study revealed that there was a general practice in women's organization that Indian women of nobility were invited to preside over the conferences and wives of British officials to be patronesses of the association. This practice also prevailed in the BSM during 19th century.

In this context it would be relevant to mention that Indian organizations of the present days who are mostly affiliated to the political group could not yet abandon the practice of British time. The influence of revivalism can be seen in the speeches delivered at the annual conferences. For example, in 1912 Sarala Devi spoke on the honored position of women during the Aryan period.

Women's Vigilance Committee founded in New Delhi in 1977. Its Bombay branch, Mahila Dakshata Samati efficiently opened its doors in 1983 in reaction to bride-burning dowry death. However, the grass roots members who worked with organization had been active in the field of women's liberation long before. They felt the necessity of working in coordination rather than in individual manner to achieve its goal. The Samati made decisions by consensus and remained unaligned with political parties and ideologies.

The Association for Women in Psychology (AWP) developed an International Feminist Mental Health Agenda for the year 2000 on the occasion of the Decade of Women world meeting. The organization intended to change the attitude of inferiority and powerlessness in efforts to promote women's equality worldwide. It made efforts to develop social and cultural standards and reject inequality, discrimination and the under-valuation of women as acceptable norms. To lessen or eliminate the devastating impact on their mental health, it is imperative for the organization to make programmes of supplying information to women for awareness and self perception to bring social, economic and political equality.[9]

Women's Movements

Participation of Organisations (Documentary Evidence)

All India Women's Conference (AIWC) publication included Proceedings of annual conferences and the AIWC journal "Roshni" (1940-1954). The Presidential addresses were included in the proceedings which provide a useful indication of the ideology espoused by women leaders. Roshni details the AIWC campaign for Hindu Law Reform. The Annual proceedings of the AIWC contained important information on

AIWC activities, organization and finances. British Parliamentary Papers, Government Reports, Indian Parliamentary debates, records of the constitution formulation process and census records provide useful documentation of women's movement and government attitude. Indian Social Reform Journals—Modern Review, Indian Review and Indian Social Reformer are evidence of organizations participation in Women's Movement. A journal of the British Women's Movement Common cause and Women's Indian Association journal 'Stri Dharma' are also sufficient documentary proof of women's organisations' involvement.

Women's movement in India was first raised for suffrage. Sources of origin and development of Women's movement organizations were western educated elite males, who instrumented the movement. It is evident from the statement by Jana Matson Everett in her book "Women and social change in India" as under:—

> "However, the present study has utilized substantially different sources in examining these topics. Maclay states that the Western educated elite males were instrumental in the emergence of an Indian women's movement, a conclusion with which the present study concerns."[10]

But Maclay did not say anything in details as to how the elite males were responsible for the emergence and augmentation of women's movement in India. Even it was not mentioned, how the women's movement fit into the political environment in the context of pre-independence nationalist upsurge.

In the opinion of Geri Forbes and Gail Minault the success of women leaders in India can be attributed to their skill in utilizing Indian traditions and religious values to justify their activities.[11] And this must be the probable cause, why the early participation of women in public life in India during the early 20th Century was accepted by their male colleagues.

Haunath Papanek had brought a point of segregation in her "Separate Worlds and Symbolic Shelter". She observed that sex segregation has identified a class of female professionals like doctors, lawyers, teachers to serve a female clientele has been necessary and socially approved. Women's movement in India had to face less hostility between sexes than Western countries because women grow up without depending on male approval in the development of their self-confidence.

The evidence of women's movement to reform Hindu society and Hindu Law has been present and mentioned in Harold Levy's famous work, "The Hindu code Bill in British India" a dissertation submitted to University of Chicago-1963. Levy briefly examines the role of women's organization in Hindu Law codification in his paper though his interest was not on group campaigns to influence codification.[12] However, we can believe that Hindu Law codification was influenced by the women's movement.

The educational development in the end of nineteen century and early twentieth century in India had created new women in the country. As a result the women started forming organization and joining it. Thus a new field of communication development among the women beyond the periphery of family was created. Moreover elite male guardians' encouragement to move with the times made an association of women concern. Gradually starting from small clubs the women joined Indian National Congress, National Social Conference and many other organizations that reflected women's concerns. In this way organization became the medium for expression of women's opinion and the training institute for women who would later take up leadership role in politics and social institution. But the model role was undoubtedly of the western ethics.

The first organizations for women were begun by men who belonged to the religious reform associations. In Bengal

Keshav Chandra Sen, the charismatic leader of the Brahmo Samaj developed educational programme, publication of women's journal, arranged prayer, meetings and established Bharat Ashram, where families lived together and emulated the life style of English middle class.[13] However, some members of Brahmo Samaj broke with Keshab Sen considering him to be more conservative, and established separate Sadharan Brahmo Samaj with the motive of male-female equality and formed new associations for women of their families.

As like Brahmo Samaj in Bengal the Prarthana Samaj did similar work in women's movement in Bombay. The Prarthana trio-G. R. Bandavarkar, Narayan Ganesh Chandravarkar and M. G. Ranade were mainly concerned with social reform, for improving women's status. Justice Ranade and his friends helped Ramabai Saraswati (wife of Ranade) to establish Arya Mahila Samaj in 1882 when she arrived in Western India, for upliftment of women. The Arya Samaj imagined the ideal woman as an efficient house wife, entering the public world will help the nation during natural calamities and epidemics.

Among the women's auxiliaries of general reform associations the prominent was *Bharat Mahila Parishad* (Ladies Social Conference) of the National Conference, which was formed at the third meeting of Indian National Congress in 1887 for the forum for discussion of social issues. Thus this organization was influenced more or less by political instinct behind it and Mahila Parishad was not inaugurated till 1905. When the participants in National Conference doubted their male colleagues about consideration of women's problems seriously, the *Mahila Parishad* was inaugurated separately. The first meeting of the *Bharat Mahila Parishad* was held where 200 women participated. Women had arranged this meeting in a packed hall barring men to attend.[14]

The meeting started with a prayer in Marathi and Gujarati and the President's opening address by Lady Balchandra. Ramabai Ranade, newly widowed was the first speaker. She encouraged women to work side by side with men for the regeneration of the nation. She suggested, they could devote their spare time to volunteer work; teaching, orphans, inspecting schools for girls and helping widows find respectable employment. Next speaker Mrs. Abbas Tyabji read a paper on Muslim women's education followed by lectures on philanthropic and charitable work.

Begum Jahan Ara Shah Nawaz a later prominent and influential member of national women's organization was the brain child of her uncle Shah Din. He had read about Sikh Conference in Lahore where 2000 women collected enough money to set up a high school for girls. Being fearful about the muslim women lagging behind, he ordered the women in his (Mian) family to meet twice a month to discuss female education and social reform. In 1915 women of the Mian family were playing a leading role in the All India Muslim Women's conference.[15]

Role Played by Women

Women in Struggle for Independence

The Indian famous historian Sumit Sarkar concludes that the ideology of the Swadeshi movement precluded women leaders but one notable exception was Sarala Devi, daughter of Swarna Kumari Devi.[16] She was influenced by Tilak's skillful use of Mahratta traditions in his Shivaji festivals (while living with her uncle Satyendranath of the ICS cadre in Western India). During Swadeshi movement in Bengal, she started physical culture clubs, began a Swadeshi Store for women's work and organized festivals which celebrated Bengali traditions. Despite apparent opposition to a young unmarried girl in a leadership role, she remained important among the Swadeshi movement leader until she moved to Lahore in 1905 after marrying Arya Samaj leader Ram Bhoj Dutt Choudhurani. During Sarala Devi's leadership several women's organizations took their form. However, all the organizers were from the narrow Brahmo community. In 1905 Sarala Devi, daughter of Durgamohan Das of the Sadharan Brahmo Samaj and Suniti Devi, daughter of K.C. Sen, who married Maharaja of Cooch Behar formed a local Mahila Samiti in Calcutta (now Kolkata). At the beginning of 1913 another Brahmo woman Saroj Nalini Dutt founded a series of Mahila Samiti in Bengali hinterland. Though Saroj Nalini was brought up in a western environment, but she was able to overcome opposition to her organization by appealing to traditional ideals. Another daughter of Swarna Kumari Devi, Hiranmoyi Devi organized the Mahila Shilpa Samiti, women's handicraft exhibition which inspired the Swadeshi movement from 1906 to 1908.

With the juvilant efforts of Maharashtrian Brahmins which included Sanskrit Professor R.G. Bhandarkar, Judge M.G. Ranade and N.G. Chandravarkar, all of whom were enthusiastic students of Indian history, Prarthana Samaj (a religious association) was formed after they met Brahmo leader Keshab Chandra Sen in 1867. This Prarthana Samaj's lectures for inspiration of women increased association in 1882 in the name "Arya Mahila Samaj" under the leadership of Pandita Ramabai. As an educated and publicly active Brahmin widow, Pandita Ramabai served as a symbol of progress to Prarthana Samaj leader Ranade, who had been involved in several efforts to improve the status of widows. However, she did not remain long with the Arya Mahila Samaj. In 1883 she travelled to Europe and America to raise money for women's services. While abroad she converted to Christianity and later founded a Christian girls' school and widows' home in Poona.

In the first decade of twentieth century women relatives of reformist-oriented leaders began to form local women's associations. These associations offered classes and provided special services for women and included the Hindu Ladies Social and Literary club (1902), the Gujarati Stri Mandal (1903) and Women's Zoroastrian Association (1903). In 1908 reformist-oriented leaders from various communities—Beharamji

Malabari (Parsi) Durgaram Gidumdal (Gujarati) and Ramabai Ranade (Maharashtrian) founded the 'Seva Sadan', a women's service organization open to the women of all the communities. Another Seva Sadan leader was Begum Nawab Misra a member of Muslim Tyabji family active in social reform. The early activities by Indian women in south India included a Brahmin Widow Home (1913) founded by Subbalakshmi Ammal and the Mahila Seva Samaj (1913) of Mysore. In North India Rameshwari Nehru edited an early women's magazine in Hindi "Stri Darpan" and organized a 'Mahila Samiti' in Allahabad in 1909. Amina Binte Badruddin Tyabji started a Muslim Girls School in 1895 in Bombay. Begum Nawab Misra ran a girls' orphanage and Shareefa Hamid Ali started a Nursing Centre. Some women members of Shafi family started an association in Lahore in early 20th century. In 1916 the Begum of Bhopal formed the All India Muslim Women's Conference. In 1917 Abru Begum, sister of A. K. Azad proposed a resolution against polygamy that provoked opposition from Muslims.

As a result of the role played by women's organizations in women's movement, in the 1926 elections women were eligible to vote in five provinces. But the percentage of women voting was low. However, there was increase in the female vote in the three provinces where women voted in 1923. The Madras Legislative Council had removed the sex disqualification for membership for the 1926 elections and the WIA supported the candidacy of Kamala Devi Chattopadhyay who was an independent. She was the only female candidate but lost to a congress candidate. The WIA had organized deputation to government officials demanding nomination of women to Legislative Council. As a result three women were nominated, Dr. Muthulakshmi Reddi in Madras, Mrs. Ahmed Shah in united provinces and Mrs. A. Kale in central provinces. Muthulakshmi Reddi, a WIA leader was chosen by her colleagues to be Deputy President of the Madras Legislative Council and acquired a distinguished reputation for her legislative work in the area of social reform.

International Issues and Women's Participation

The history of the past proves that women of the socialist countries first took part in social liberation movement, they fought for social liberation, freedom, independence, peace and social progress. They raised in the spirit of revolutionary traditions and were ever faithful to the principle of proletarian internationalism. Shortly after the Second World War Soviet Women's Committee (until 1956 the Anti- Fascist Soviet Women's Committee) began its activities to repel the fascist aggressors. During those days Soviet women helped to consolidate and strengthen the forces battling fascism by creating an anti-fascist people front.

On September 7, 1941 the women of the Soviet made a ringing appeal to their sisters all over the world to combine their efforts in the battle against the Nazi aggressors. The world-wide women responded to their appeal. From Great Britain, Australia, India, USA., and other countries women expressed their solidarity with the Soviet people in their struggle and made known their desires to contribute to the victory over the evil enemy of mankind. It is noteworthy of women's history of valour that Central and South Eastern European women were in first contract with Soviet women to fight against the fascist and occupied territory. Many Bulgarian, Yugoslav, Polish and Chechoslavak women took part in the armed struggle as members of guerilla groups and army units. Women of Vietnam, China and Korea fought for freedom and independence of their nations, against the Japanese militarists and foreign colonists.[17]

In the year 1930 on the call of the leader of national liberation movement Mr. M.K. Gandhi women's organizations of India in massive strength took part in the famous march to Dandi. This campaign was stirred up by the unfairness of the established British Colonial authorities forbidding Indian people to engage in evaporation of salt from sea water. The campaign was headed by Sarojini Naidu, a veteran of the women's movement in India. They waged struggle also for the preservation of national cultural traditions, national dress among them. Thousands of women got down to weaving as an effort to provide the country with sufficient cloth made in India from Indian cotton; the aim was to revive the national textile industry. It was a historical record of women's participation in national movement that over 20, 000 women were subjected to arrest and imprisonment for participation in the March to Dandi and other mass actions of the people against the British domination.

Modern Role of Women

The ecclesiastical conceptions of the question of women's rights ignore and under estimate the class and social roots of question of difference in burgeois. The complex question involves the social and political system of the society which burgeois investigators consider the question of relationship between man and woman, while the cause of women's inequality in the society is said to be the ancient views that, men hold the reign of women. The most reactionary of these views even go further and advocate theories showing the biological inferiority of women, their mental backwardness and so on. Under the influence of certain transformatory factors which have accelerated the process of women's involvement in social life, the views on the issue of women's status have undergone some evolution and this has affected the stand and nature of the demands advanced by feminist organisations.

Many feminist organisations have included some important social demands as the real access of women to public and political life, the provision of employment for female work force, equal opportunities for education and preservation of peace. Referring to the low level activity of women in public and political life the feminist and pacifist ideologists have rightly observed that, the degree of this activity does not correspond to the level of their participation in production.

They pointed out the reasons for women's lagging behind in social and political activity lie either in the women themselves or men. Women are said to be not interested in politics and men do not allow women to indulge in politics. Therefore every one of the reformists and thinkers propose equal opportunities for women to obtain education, the greatest possible liberation from house and so on.[18]

Women's Movement for Social, Political and Educational Rights

For the women's education and participation in public life women leaders preferred the strategy involving utilization of traditional ideals of Indian womanhood. Both Hindu and Muslim women appealed to the associations of women with religious faith to legitimize participation.

The women movement in India before independence influenced the elite group of Hindu and Muslim women because from the beginning the Indian women's movement was oriented towards elite representation and not towards mass mobilization. The caste disparity which the Hindu religion sanctions and strengthens did not allow the elite women of India to consider the problems of low caste women. The members of the movement at the beginning were from handful of families prominent in associational politics of the urban, educated elite and a large gap between the elite and the masses remained.

The women movement in India by and large had an intention to achieve political power. Even the research carried out by Jana Matson Everett reveals that from the beginning the Indian women's movement approched suffrage campaign as a means of achieving social reform. The leaders believed that the enfranchisement of women would mean additional support for reform legislation. The women's delegation appealed before Montague on December 17, 1917. Their memorandum asked for women's franchise on the same basis as men in the new constitution and improved facilities for women's education and health care. Here it is significant to examine the position of Indian society and evaluate the role of the women movement played in improving the status of women. The first point one has to find, whether the demand of the women organisations for suffrage at all affected the women of oppressed class? Were the improved facilities for education meant for women of every community or class? What sort of health and care the women leaders intended? All these questions if examined in details in relation to prevailing condition of Indian society of that time, will spontaneously give them reply to negate any efficacy of the above on the women belonging to depressed class, who were in far below the state of human. Similarly recent endeavour of the ruling political party to provide reservation for women without ascertaining quota for different sections of oppressed people will result monopoly in parliament of the higher castes or elite group of Indian population. Which will help them to safeguard the interest of upper castes at the cost of deprived or depressed class (dalits).

The women's movement campaign had two phases; in first phase (1917-1928) the issues were female enfranchisement and eligibility for the legislature; in the second phase (1928-1937) the issues were liberalization of the terms of enfranchisement and increasing female representation in legislatures. In both phases the extent to which the interests of the women's movement and those of the political authorities coincided, was the main factor determining the outcome of the women's movement demands. The interests of the women's movement and those of the political authorities coincided after a short period of divergence during the first phase of the campaign.[19] Thus it can be concluded that women's movements aims were mainly political. The women leaders were able to gain the support of the Indian political elite. Members of the women's delegation mostly WIA members – lobbied at the provincial and national conference in 1918. They had no difficulty in getting their resolutions considered by these organizations. Representatives from all of the important political groupings testified in favour of women's suffrage at the hearings of the Joint Select Committee on the Government of India Bill in 1919. Women's movement was supported by British Women's Organisations. While in Britain Sarojini Naidu, Annie Besant, Herabai and Mithibai Tata spoke at many public meetings and were enthusiastically supported by British Women's Organisation, which also promoted the cause of women's suffrage in India.[20]

Although the women's movement demands were for women to be eligible for the franchise and in the legislature on terms equal to those applied for men, those demands were presented as a measure for women's upliftment and the support for these demands in provincial legislature by liberals and conservatives did not necessarily mean that the legislators believed in the sex equality. Moreover, while the women's movement was very successful in influencing the British and Indian political elites it failed in mobilizing women to vote. The WIA visited the homes of newly enfranchised women and administered questionnaires to the candidates on social reforms. But there is no evidence that, any large scale efforts were made by women's organization to reach those who were enfranchised as an attempt to electoral activity. Women of both Hindu and Muslim communities were related to women organization of social reform as well as political movement. The women organization AIWC played a significant role to maintain unity among the Hindu and Muslim women, although political party (Muslim League) insisted on muslim women baring AIWC to maintain communal electorate.

Following are the prominent muslim women who participated in women's organization and represented the women in the fight for upliftment and human rights, claiming equal social status with men. Jahan Ara Shah Nawaz, Qudsea

Rasul, Sarifah Hamid Ali, Kulsum Sayani and Hajra Ahmed, who worked with women organization till 1940. Among the problems the muslim women faced, most of them were similar to those of Hindu women except the problems of purdah and most of the women organisations considered it as a muslim problem. In the politics also the leaders talked about women that, "all women were equal" and they supported from behind, for universal franchise but no body dared to condemn purdah system. The politicians who could ignore the problem kept silence about the purdah system and left the matter as religious issue not to interfere with.

The regulations or segregationists, a group dominated by government officials and the police in the abolition of prostitution and rehabilitation of women to earn their livelihood were much worried about the problems. They wanted brothels and prostitutes contained in designated area to facilitate administrative supervision, the maintenance of order, sanitation and medical supervision. A number of influential educationalists and medical men supported this position. Therefore the women's organizations transformed these issues to incorporate rhetoric of Indian womanhood and nationalists aspirations. Thus when the Bengal Legislature discussed the suppression of Immoral Traffic Act in 1931, Mr. S.M. Bose called attention to the women's petition with 16000 signatures. He said, "Women of Bengal are no longer asleep, they are keenly aware of the danger that threatens their womanhood. Muthulakshmi Reddy tied the devadasi issue to the national project.

Muthulakshmi Reddy was a woman doctor and legislator from South India. Sushma Sen who encouraged women members of the educated Bengali families to participate in public life. Begum Shah Nawaj provided much needed information on Muslim perspectives towards women's issues and nationalists issues. All the above women were active in the women movement in India. Jana Matson Everett writes that speeches of Sarojini Naidu and Annie Besant were valuable in the early stages of women's movement as she examined.

Even the English writer has pointed out that there is inequality among Indian women in terms region, time and the scarcity of leaders in the movement. In the context of regional inequality it is said that upto 1920 women's movement organizations in Hindi speaking region of North India were very scare. But we find the evidence of women's movement for Hindu law reform in the records of AIWC journal "Roshni."

Women's India Association was an organization which also undertook women's political and social movement but details of the same could not be obtained by Ms. Jana Matson Everett as she stated in her book 'Women and Social Change in India' based on dissertation submitted by her to the University of Michigan in 1976.

Under the influence of fundamental changes that are taking place in the world today, a section of the feminist movement is cooperating with the democratic women's movement over such issues as world peace, the implementation of women's economic, political and civil rights, the health, upbringing and education of children and so on. A whole series of international feminist women's organizations took part in such major international women's forum convened at the initiative of the WIDF. As the World Congress of Women (Copenhagen 1953), the World Congress of Mothers for the Defence of Children from War, for Disarmament and International Friendship (Lausanne 1955), the International Assembly of Women on the 50th Anniversary of International Women's Day (Copenhagen 1960), the World Congress of Women (Moscow 1963) and the World Congress of Women (Helsinki 1969).

As a result of women's movement or the feminist struggle the question of women's right assumed an important position, taking into consideration the present condition of women, by social democrats. The communists over the issue of women's right indissolubly linked the struggle for emancipation of women with the struggle for social transformations. Right Wing Social democrats have admitted that the women's question in capitalist countries is unresolved; they said the question depend on the social and economic structure of the society and also the political course adopted by the countries. They recognize the struggle for the economic and civil reforms that affect the status of women in the society and the family but only within the framework of the existing system. Female members of Social Democratic parties and women's organization of 24 countries had come together to form the International Council of Social Democratic Women (ICSDW) which in turn formed part of the Socialist International.[21] The ICSDW had a membership over 2 million women in the seventies of twentieth century, who made an effort towards publicizing the ideas of democratic socialism and the rights of women.

Role of Reformists and the Condition of Women in India

Justice Ranade in his social reform advanced through the organization 'National Social Conference (began in 1887) it was firmly believed that India had enjoyed a golden age, when women enjoyed a higher status than in his time and blamed the Smriti writer for the fall. He argued that, evolutionary change was inherently Indian, outside forces could act as a stimulant but true impetus for change came from the inner resources of the society itself.[22] Ranade described the society he hoped to see changing from constraint to freedom, from credulity to faith, from unorganized to organized life, from bigotry to toleration, from blind fatalism to a sense of human destiny.

The historian Sumit Sarkar has argued that these reformers were concerned primarily with modifying relationship within their own families and sought only limited and controlled emancipation of their women folk.[23]

While male-inspired and male-guided organizations for women did invaluable work in educating women and providing them with their first experience with the public work, they also imposed some limitations. The male reformers specifically regarded household as the primary focus and fundamental arena of activity for women. They visioned the households run by modernized women who are imbibed with scientific ideas about hygiene and child rearing very helpful for the society. But they had no intention in reality, to give equal status to women with them though they wanted to improve the status of women. The historian and the writers concerned about the life of women in India in early twentieth century have mentioned about the desire of male social reformists in their writing that, men wanted their wives to take part in activities outside the home; social work to help the unfortunate and relief work when disaster struck. Their wives could assist in nation building not through the political activities but by building institutions to ameliorate the worst situation arising from social customs. The association were useful to young women who attended meetings of the organization, gradually found themselves free from the dominance of the older conservative women of the household but they hardly found any place at that time, where they could compete with men. Men domination prevailed in society. Even the present modern civilized society in India is not free from this trend. Modern politicians and reformists even after 55 years of independence and 52 years of democratic republican set up have not come out of the social customs and bondage of ancient and medeaval times.

We can justify the past and present condition of widows in comparison with a past instance of Bengal.

> "Haimavati Mitra a child widow from Bengal sought out leaders of Brahmo Samaj to help gain an education, they looked for a bridegroom. In a conversation with her friend Sarojini Haimavati said that, all she wanted

> to do was to study. Sarojini's retort was, "you should study after you have got married". Haimavati, by now rather cynical about Brahmo promises said, "The future depends on God's will, of course."[24]

The above instance make us to feel that the real emancipation of women were not the aim and object of the reformists, though they wanted to improve the social condition of women but not to grant equality with men. If we take the revelation of the present social research the picture of women in society will not be so different from the past.

As regard upholding the dominating position of men over women, the outspoken opponents of British rule in India also approved the decision. English Court in which, when an educated girl who was married in childhood refused to go to live with her old husband on attaining puberty, was ordered by the court to submit herself to husband or to go to prison. Mr. Tilak approved this decision of the court on the plea that, British law in deciding the case, was upholding the dharmashastras. It will be more clear about the women's position in India from the statement of Pandita Ramabai, wife of social reformist and Justice M.G. Ranade. She said in anger—

> "The government advocated education and emancipation but when a woman refused to "be a slave", the government comes to break her spirit allowing its law to become an instrument for reverting her chains".[25]

The Indian society provide no opportunity for recognition of a woman's work as an independent individual. The recognition and award for any distinguished work was limited to men only, women were not recognized or rewarded at all.[26]

Keshab Chandra Sen who pressed for a law of legalize cross-caste marriage within the Brahmo community and to raise the age of marriage for female to 14 and for male to 18 years later disregarded this law and married his 13 years old daughter to the Maharaja of Cooch Behar according to

Orthodox Hindu rites in 1878. Although K. C. Sen advocated for female education he did not believe that girls and boys should have same type of education. He believed that the goal of female education was to make women better mothers and opposed higher education for women.[27] Swarna Kumari Devi's novel "An unfinished song", offers many insights into the attitudes of Brahmo as the preface states that the novel portrays life among "the reformed party of Bengal", whose members have become outwardly westernized but retain the inner nature of the Hindus.[28] From the above illustrations the clear character sketch of male reformists can be drawn. Yet further in the words of Everett position of organizations for social and Religious Reforms become clear. She writes—

> "Very few women were approached by early Brahmo women's associations, and social opposition to reformists ideas concerning women continued to be high."[29]

Women Faced Opposition

There has been tremendous opposition in society to women's progress. Though many struggles carried on world wide for human rights and improvement of women's status but the Indian society hesitated to treat women with dignity and honour and to provide opportunities for personality development of women. Many national leaders also vehemently opposed women's struggles for rights. Some of the instances of opposition faced by women in their struggle for personality development are stated as under.

Opposition to Women's Education

The first and foremost step towards personality development is to acquire education. The women of India faced greater impediment on their way to acquire education. In the mid nineteenth century in Bombay Presidency the elite reformists from three communities Parsi, Gujarati Brahmins and Maharashtrians participated in Students' Literary and Scientific

Society where they discussed the position of women in society. The discussion inspired efforts to educate women in each of the three communities. As a result girls schools were started in Parsi Community and a women's magazine "Stri bodh" was published in 1857 and by 1863 a girls high school was opened with an English educational curriculum Alexandra Institute". On the contrary Gujarati and Maharashtrian Brahmins encountered stiff opposition from orthodox leaders and were not successful in changing social practices affecting women.

Bal Gangadhar Tilak who was an extremist Congressman publicised the Ranade's efforts to improve the status of women and widows in contradiction. He bitterly opposed the girls school, NSC and the age of consent legislation.

Muslim opposition on women's education was also very bitter. Sheikh and Begum Abdullah faced bitter opposition in 1906 when they started a girl school in Aligarh. Atiya Begum and Miss Sakhawat Hossain faced the same fate when they tried to be admitted to All India Muslim Educational Conference in 1926.

Although constituent assembly was eager to frame clauses guaranteeing sex equality in political and economic spheres, there was strong opposition to sex equality in the sphere of marriage and the family.[30] This opposition from the major politicians clearly indicates the thoughts of Indian male that though the women are granted equality with men but will remain subordinated in the family status and marital status. Thus the superiority of male can be maintained in society even after granting equality to women.

The demands of various women's organizations for a long time has brought into existence a proposal for Hindu Code Bill containing provisions for upliftment of women's position in society. However, in its process there were tremendous arguments between the proponents and opponents. The arguments justified their position in terms of three major issues.[31]

(a) furthering democracy
(b) strengthening Hinduism
(c) serving the public interests

Even at this stage of global upliftment of women and scientific development, the women of India are not given free and easy access to educational institutions. The Indian society irrespective of religious community impede women's progress and shining in the field of education. Still in rural area women's public appearance and girls acquiring education are not considered honourable dignity. Hence most of the rural girls remain illiterate despite nation wide endeavour and publicity of literacy enhancement. It is very surprising to note that even the rural women themselves resist women's education and upliftment.

Opposition to Women's Movement

When the women's associations tried to reform Hindu Law, they were vulnerable to the charge that they did not represent the masses of Indian women. Surendra Nath Banerjee opposed women's suffrage and his moderate party differed with him when representation from all of the important political groups testified in favour of women's suffrage at the hearings of the Joint Select Committee on the Government of India bill 1919.[32] The supporters included Tilak, Besant, V.J. Patel, U.P. Madhava Rao, Jinna and Yakub Hassan.

When the Congress became more militant in its strategy and goals the British policy towards it became more repressive. And late in 1929 when Gandhi insisted on a pledge that forthcoming Round Table Conference would formulate a plan for immediate dominion status for India, the Viceroy refused to accept the demand. Therefore in January 1930 Gandhi launched a massive civil disobedience campaign. As a result of this campaign women's participated on a much larger scale than Non-cooperation Movement. But Gandhi opposed the participation of women keeping in view the sex discrimination in the Salt Satyagraha and stated that women's role in civil disobedience should be limited to picketing liquor and foreign cloth shops and spinning. After Gandhi was arrested Sarojini Naidu directed the Salt Satyagraha until her own arrest. Here lies the truth how the Mahatma treated the women. The above facts clearly state the position of women in Indian society according to the opinion of elite politicians and the political magnate of the period. Gandhi never allowed in his life full liberty to women. He farcely advocated equality. Sex equality he never could tolerate. It is evident that after him there was no equivalent potential leader to lead the Salt Satyagraha except Sarojini Naidu yet he never treated her equal to Nehru, Patel and any other male political leader. In fact he intended to impede the progress of women in Hindu Society.

However the Congress Party expressed gratitude to women for their participation in civil disobedience movement. It was in this atmosphere that Congress adopted a "Declaration of Fundamental Rights" which included sex in its guarantees of equality before the law and no discrimination in employment or office and pledged that there would be universal adult franchise.

References

1. N.A. Kovalsky and Y.P. Blinova's Women Today-Progress Publisher-1975 (p. 97).
2. Jana Matson Everett's Women and Social Change in India 1979 Ed. Heritage Publishers New Delhi (p. 72).
3. Aparna Basu and Bharati Ray's Women's Struggle (A History of the All India Women's Conference).
4. Geraldine Forbes' Women in Modern India (The New Cambridge History of India) Cambridge University Press 1996 (p. 185).
5. Geraldine Forbes' Women in Modern India (The New Cambridge History of India) Cambridge University Press 1996 (p. 172).
6. Geraldine Forbes' Women in Modern India (The New Cambridge History of India) Cambridge University Press 1996 (p. 173).
7. Jana Matson Everett's Women and Social Change in India, Heritage Publishers, New Delhi 1979 Ed. (p. 148).
8. Renuka Ray's "A Plea for a Commission on the Legal Disabilities of Women.
9. Janice Wood Watzel's "The World of Women (The Macmillan Press 1993) (p. 178 and 183).

10. Jana Matson Everett's "Women and Social Change in India", Heritage Publishers, New Delhi 1979 Ed (p. 34).
11. Geri Forbes' "Social Service and Politics, Bengali women in the Independence Movement (Paper presented at the 9th Annual Conference on Bengal Studies, Columbia University, New York 1973) ; Minault: Parda Politics: The Role of Muslim Women in Indian Nationalism (1911-1924).
12. Jana Matson Everett's Women and social change in India, Heritage publishers, New Delhi 1979 Ed. (p. 35).
13. Geraldine Forbes' Women in Modern India (The New Cambridge History of India) Cambridge University Press 1996 (p. 173).
14. Geraldine Forbes' Women in Modern India (The New Cambridge History of India) Cambridge University Press 1996 (p. 66).
15. *Ibid.*, p. 68.
16. Jana Matson Everett's "Women and Social Change in India" Heritage publishers, New Delhi 1979 Ed. (p. 57).
17. N.A. Kovalsky and Y.P. Blinova's book "Women Today" (p. 96 and 97).
18. *Ibid.*, p. 15 and 16.
19. Jana Matson Everett's "Women and Social Change in India Heritage Publisher, New Delhi 1979 Ed. (p. 102).
20. The Common Cause (London) 1918-1919: p. 107 of Everett's Women and Social Change in India.
21. N.A. Kovalsky and Y.P. Blinova's "Women Today" (p. 16 and 17).
22. Geraldine Forbes' "Women in India", p. 26.
23. Sumit Sarkar's "The Women's Question in Nineteenth Century Bengal".
24. Women in Modern India, p. 69.
25. Letters and Correspondence of Pandita Ramabai edited by A.B. Such (p. 69, Women in Modern India).
26. Revolution and the status of Women in India by Dr. Sushila Mehta, p. 206.
27. Suniti Devi—Maharani of Cooch Behar, The Autobiography of an Indian Princess (p. 52 Women and Social Change in India).
28. J.M. Everett's Women and Social Change in India, p. 54.
29. *Ibid.*
30. Jana Matson Everett's "Women and Social Change in India (p. 161).
31. *Ibid.*, p. 163.
32. Parliamentary Paper 1919 (p. 132) (p. 105, Jana Matson Everett's "Women and Social Change in India").

Eight

Women's Consciousness

To evaluate and examine the potentiality of women in forming the human society and shaping the nation, it is pertinent to find out the effect of consciousness and the extent of its presence in women. Therefore I have made an endeavour to find out, the level of consciousness in women and how it can be enhanced. The following discussion supported by comments and statements of sociologists, anthropologists and the learned men especially the historians, will clarify the position of women in India in this context.

"The feminist consciousness relies on the discourse's capacity to demonstrate that women are capable of being creators of history that, they are active autonomous subjects in their own right". (Subaltern Studies, Vol. VI, p. 100). The above statement clearly indicates that women's entity in any continent or the country depends upon their consciousness and not the political power what the present Indian ruling party (BJP) thinks or tries to inculcate upon the women population of India.

There is evident of the research work of prominent historians about the position of women in the world that, search for the sovereign female subjects and its attempt to define the autonomy of the Third World women, feminism gets entangled with nationalism and orientalism. Unfortunately in the fight of feminists and imperialists thought cross at the very point where feminism aims to distant itself from these discourses. At this point the half silent murmur of orientalism becomes audible in feminism. If such is the global trends of women folk how the political power will help them to establish their equal entity with the male in a male dominated Hindu majority society of a country like India where women is treated like a property possessed and maintained and protected by male.

We talk much about the liberty of women in fact even our elite group do not accept full liberty and equality of women; they also value the cultural tradition of rest of the Indian population irrespective of religious belief on cultural tradition.

There are instances of the opinion of Indian writers, historians and sociologists incorporated in Subaltern Studies edited by Ranjit Guha, which confirm that feminism and imperialism has become increasingly sophisticated so the tactics used alienate one from the other is very lengthy process. Yet it is not limited to the feminist discourse generated from western countries nor does the sign does it entirely depend on different set of meanings of feminism based on geography and ethnicity. Western feminism which somehow different from the Indian feminist culture is taken to be sign of liberation of women in the context of the Indian society. However, that signifies limitations and shortsightedness from a shared cultural background. Thus the Western women in their society also face some barriers to understanding their own culture. Similarly Indian women face lot of barriers in the case of their westernization or alienation from own culture. Thus they tend to be equalized with men in society like the Western is not mentally accepted in Indian prevailing tradition. The political rights will not at all change the status of women in society without changing the mentality of Indian society and changing mentality needs overall change in civilization which comprises religious belief, education, social inter-action economic state and political atmosphere. In this context it is relevant to mention the statement of one of the famous Indian writers Madhu Kishwar. She writes:—

"Those of us wish to combat or reject these cultural

ideals of womanhood have however, been largely ineffective because we tend to do so from a totally "Western Modernist" stand point. The tendency is to make people feel that they are backward and stupid to hold values that need to be rejected outright. We must learn to begin with more respect for traditions which people hold dear."[1]

The position of women in Indian society can be viewed from the statement of renowned writer and commentator Ranjit Guha's statement quoted below, which make us to believe, there is vast difference between the Indian women and the western women is nationalist view or as far as the nationalism is concerned. Guha states:—

"Western woman has an additional meaning specific to Indian nationalist thought. This complicates an Indian feminist strongly shaped by nationalism because of the rejection of "The West" including Western women, has been part of a nationalist tradition. While the nationalist construction of the Western women is a separate study, some comments made by Vivekananda in his lectures in America provide a useful illustration of the blueprint of Indian versus Western womanhood."[2]

As per the statement of Guha what were the comments of Vivekananda appeared in a newspaper report as under:—

"(Vivekananda) stated that in India the woman was the visible manifestation of God and that her whole life was given to the thought that she was a mother and to be perfect mother she must be chaste. No mother in India ever abandoned her offspring, he said, and defied any one to prove the contrary. The girls in India would die if they, like American girls were obliged to expose their bodies to the vulgar gaze of youngmen."[3]

From the above statements we can bring into an analysis on the point of present BJP led NDA government's motive and suitability of political 33 per cent reservation for women in India. At the outset if we take the family for example in Hindu society, as per Swami Vivekananda, the women's primary role is to be a perfect mother, which in fact the Indian womanhood believe to be their moral obligation. Even after modernization of India due to industrial revolution and advancement of science the women have not become mentally prepared to abandon this obligation. Education and right to equality in every field bestowed upon them by the statutory law have not been able to change their morality. Then how the government speculate that the political reservation will bring change in women and what they are deprived of in society could be achieved by political rights? To become a perfect mother what they need is proper respect, education, well maintenance and human rights equal to men. They should not be put under any subjugation by men. These requirements of women in society can be met by men by changing their attitude towards women and it need not specific political reservation. Women in India have been in politics since the struggle for independence started, but they never thought of discrepancies in politics due to lack of reservation. The competent women politicians are never debarred from contesting. What the actual events in Indian politics occurred since the independence were, certain class has controlled the politics and others were wanting due to capricious manoeuvre of this class, so either men or women from other classes got very limited share in politics.

If the case of rearing up of offsprings is taken into consideration, we find Indian women in many cases that being in all respect competent to perform dynamic role in politics fail to do so because of their responsibilities towards their children. They prefer caring their children to making political career. Hence Swami Vivakananda's statement is practical and true in majority of women in India. Thus we cannot overrule that, Indian women first to become a perfect mother then to meet any other challenge of life. Many people advocates "Naari

Shakti" (women's strength) is required to bring a good shape to the government. I must ask certain questions to the readers in this context—

(1) What we mean by Nari Shakti?

(2) How Nari Shakti shape the government?

(3) Is the politics only way to use Nari Shakti?

(4) Is there no other way to use Nari Shakti else politics?

(5) Does our present government think that, government cannot be shaped better without definite percentage of women's participation?

About the fifth question, if answer is negative then we have a clear view about the present ruling party (BJP) that its leaders should take the charge of other fields of women's activities and place women in politics compulsorily. Moreover, when 33 per cent seats seem to be essential for women then why don't they reserve it from the residual quota after providing reserved quota for SC, ST and OBC, since women in politics are found from the upper castes. There is rare woman politician from the reserved category. When the reservation is provided in statutory provisions of the constitution with a view to bring equality in status of the deprived class with the possessed or affluent class, separate reservation for women should also define the quota for deprived section in proportion to their strength of population. Here it is relevant to bring to the notice of the public that Indian population is as under:

Brahmins	3.5 per cent
Kshatriya/Vaidya	5.5 per cent
Vaishya/Kayestha	6.0 per cent
Other Backward Classes	52.0 per cent
Minority (religious)	10.0 per cent
Scheduled Castes	15.5 per cent
Scheduled Tribes	7.5 per cent

So women's reservation of 33 per cent in politics should be distributed in above mentioned proportion. Deviation from the proportional reservation entails giving special privilege to upper castes; because to achieve political position one has to be educated, economically sound and free from the family burden which only the affluent class can do. On the other hand deprived or oppressed class in Indian society, due to slavery for thousands years is still in hand to mouth condition, lagging behind in education and social habitation. They have no settled house even for living, no fixed monthly income to subsist. How can a woman from a family with all these deficiets can think over the national interests and join politics. Hence a layman can easily conclude that women's reservation in politics will be nothing else than giving an extra privilege to the ruling class of India, that is to say that the democracy will be controlled by the aristocrats of India and its real meaning will vanish for ever. Our politicians and social magnates should now consider the matter deeply before taking a final decision. The statement made by me in this book will be a document for verification of the future political state of India. I am giving some of the clues for future changes in politics of India illustrating the contingencies in various other chapters.

Women Suffer Discrimination

The social trend of India leave the vestige of sheer discrimination of sex. Women in Indian society irrespective of religion, territory and language suffer from sex discrimination and find themselves placed in subordination of men. They become the men's possession or property. This sex discrimination has been deep rooted in society from time immemorial.

But further more drastic condition of women is in the society of low caste people. The women of the low caste suffer double discrimination—one of sex and the other is of their caste. Thus the position of all women of India is not the same in society. The problems of a woman of dalit community are not the same as of a woman of Brahman community.

I am going to discuss here in this Chapter the discriminatory attitude of the society based on caste, which the women suffer in India in the following paragraphs and heading.

Caste Discrimination

In India sex disparity is not so worse than that of the caste disparity floating in Hindu Society. In Hindu Society even the individuals of the same sex and same power, position and capability are not treated at par if their castes are not same. There are many glaring examples of caste disparity at high level society and administrative machinery. Even the social and cultural institutions follow it. Here I would like to quote an instance to authenticate the statement. There is a custom of nominating the Prime Minister of India as the Professor of the Vishwa Bharati University since the Prime Ministership of Nehru. But when the peasant leader Mr. Charan Singh, a jat by caste was elected, Prime Minister of India then Managing Committee of the Vishwa Bharati University had convened a meeting and decided not to nominate further any political leader to be the Professor of this University. This decision was influenced by the heart core decision to avoid low caste person to be appointed as Professor.[4]

Here it is noteworthy to clear further the Hindu Social trend on caste disparity that, the Vishwa Bharati Vishwa Vidyalaya was established by Vishwa Kabi Rabindra Nath Tagore, who was a member of Brahmo Samaj and his ancestors were inhabitants of Khulna district of East Bengal and belonged to Scheduled Caste by birth (this was disclosed in an exhibition held in Hanseshwari Temple at Banshberia in Hooghly district in 1960s). Thus we see that Hindu higher castes never allow any lower caste to a prestigious position even though the position is created by a low caste. The same instance occurred in the case of Kali Mandir of Dakshineshwar—the temple was constructed under the sanction and financial management of Rani Rashmani but she was refused entry into the temple at the time of inauguration of the temple, for she was a low caste by birth. The priest Ramakrishna an abnormal and illiterate man did not allow the Queen, to enter into the temple who borne the expenditure on construction and maintenance of the temple.

So one can very well imagine from these examples, how can different sex be treated alike when there is caste system alive? Women in all respects-sexuality, body, bearing and cultural heritage and habitation, are subordinated in the male dominated society. Even in the castes structure women of the low castes are oppressed by women of higher castes, then how can we expect equality between men and women. As the Indian Government (present ruling party BJP and alliance) advocates for political reservation for women to grant them equality and to improve their status, we can logically put a question—when they are so generous to grant equal status to women with men why don't they try to equalize all men of different castes? Why don't they take any step to abolish the castism and grant special privileges to economically, educationally and socially backward class of people to reach equal position of higher castes or possessed class?

The caste systems have influenced all citizen of India belonging to Hinduism. One of the scholar of Women's Movement and Social Status of University of Michigan, J. M. Everett states in her book about the existing and influence of caste system in India. She writes:—

> "....hierarchical world view is grounded in the caste system under Hinduism, it operates at the level of social segments of castes unequal in ritual status; membership is ascribed ...... there are norms governing the behaviour of members of each jati. According to Louis Dumont, the system of values in the caste system is based on the fundamental opposition of pure and impure—one jati ranked higher than another if it is ritually purer than the other. In this value system of

caste there is an absolute distinction between religious authority and political power".[5]

Even the Buddhism is not freed from the influence of castism, as is evident from the day to day behaviour of the neo-buddhists in India. The Buddhism is also not completely free from the caste distinction or varna system in principle. In Thailand though the casteless Buddhist norms co-existed for centuries with an ideal kingship derived from India, the famous historian of Cambridge University Susan Bayly states in her "Caste, Society and Politics in India" that, hereditary Brahmin ritualists still serve the Thai royal house and the classified hero Rama is still the model for Thai rulers as for the former Khmer Kings of Cambodia in their capacity as protectors of faith and righteousness.[6]

Even in Sri Lanka the ruling Sinhalese who are Buddhists undoubtedly have the feelings of superiority of race and caste as is evident from the treatment they give to the Sri Lankan Tamils, who are dalits or low caste Hindus. Thus Buddhists or Buddhism is also not free from the caste distinction. In India Buddhists (Neo) being all from the dalit community are not directly the protector of castism. Muslim rulers to relate people of different ideals of Jati and Varna which apparently reduce human experience to arbitrary stereotype high and low, clean and unclean 'pure' Brahmin and impure untouchable. In the period of Mughal conquest to the early stages of colonial rule, the caste or the caste like conventions which had come into being in different regions equipped both the weak and strong with a means to maximize assets and protect themselves from loss. This often involved naked coercion; the new ruler and other elite frequently involved Jati and Varna principles in attempt to assert authority over dependent cultivators and other subordinate or weak groups.

The social phenomenon of India clearly shows the caste disparity in every walk of life. This can be well verified and confirmed from the following facts and circumstances. The women students who became boarder and stayed together without observing the caste rules had to face grave consequences of breaking these rules. Despite being good professional doctors they could not help their brothers, sisters and cousins suffering public indignation. Due to non-observance of caste rules the girls medical students had to endure public taunts when they travelled to and from classes even if they chose to live in private home instead of boarding.

Where there is separation in society either in religious norms or social culture, equality can never be established. In India the separatist attitude of Brahmin is visible every where. Even the foreign historians have noticed and recorded in their writings this distinctive attitude of Brahmins in India. In this context we can refer the statement of Susan Bayly:—

> "India's specialist Brahman priesthoods and ascetic preceptoral corporation tended to retain a considerable degree of separation and independence, even from very powerful rulers and their courts. Elsewhere in Asia, most notably in pre-modern Japan and China, both the Buddhist clergy (the monkhood or Sangha) and its Confucian equivalents were often significantly more closely tied to state power than was the case for their Indian counterparts."[7]

Castes or caste like grouping of Indian population in Hindu society has created great disparity in cultural and ethnic history. The Brahman is raised to a status superior to that of the reigning king. A very large portion of subordinated population have been culturally, morally and even biologically, from the Brahmin and ruling class have been labelled as 'tribal' and untouchables. It was first made an endeavour by the pre-colonial.

Discrimination Based on Race, Culture and Religion

Susan Moller Okin in her essay "Inequalities between the sexes in Different Cultural Context" has very clearly stated that, while middle and upper class feminists are alleged to have been insensitive not only to the problem of women of other races, cultures and religion but even to those of women of other classes then their own. Thus she says that Gender is a problematic category, unless qualified by race, class ethnicity, religion and so on. Even she has pointed out those are often called an essentialists whom Ruth Anna Putnnan adopting the term to her own purpose calls "Substitutionalist" feminist, allegedly commit the mistake of subsumming all women under the category to which they themselves belong. They put the experience they had, while middle and upper class women as the substitute for that of all men. The same situation exists in India in the present days in the political, cultural and social aspect of women. The politicians of India highlights the problem of women only of the environment of higher classes women. The remedy they devise to eradicate these problems is never given any comparative analysis of the problems of women of all other races, culture and religion. Thus the policy they frame or intend to frame always results in wrong achievement and creation of further several different problems related to the previous one. It can be taken as granted and considered the notion of human acts that the privileged or the superior class never have the idea of the miseries of the lower class or the category one does not belong. Similar case is also with European race. If any one is writing about women in Western Country the privileged women will talk about themselves and their own problems; there will be little chance to say about the situation of poor women in poor countries that may differ from that of the European countries.

Not only in India, in other developed countries also have the practice of racism. We can find the instances of racial discrimination on women in Britain in the following statements. Cynthia Cockburn writes in her book, "In the way of Women", a book comprising the elements she found in her deep research that—Sexuality is only one of fields in which women bodies are politicized. Another is "race". The scientific research of the past aimed at demonstration of identifiable races on the basis of psychological characteristics and to assign them superiority and inferiority. But after the Second World War the concept of "race" grounded in the idea of fixed typologies and based upon certain phenotypical features such as skin, colour and skull shape does not have any significant scientific meaning or utility. Even UNESCO document put it "for all political social purpose 'race' is not so much a biological phenomenon as a social myth.[8]

However, it cannot be denied that racism operates systematically in labour market. To illustrate the practice of racism Carole Pateman mentions:—

> "the buyer is never indifferent to the sex of the owner of property in the person. He contracts for jurisdiction over a masculine or feminine body."

Likewise the buyer of the labour power is never indifferent to ethnicity or skin colour. The purchase of labour power is not only a contract for the use of mental and manual skills at the lowest possible wage. More than this, it is also a purchase of the services of a particular kind of person, some one with a previous status (may be high or low) certain cultural attachment and certain looks, to all of which ethnicity and skin colour are genuine. The system of male power equipment which almost all the organizations in Britain operate employ majority of men out of white male power and the culture of management is almost solidly a white monoculture identifying and excluding all other groups. The majority of work force comprises men, however, where the sex stereotyping involves an active preference for women in certain jobs, the white employers tend to negate black women. White person is preferred for most of the jobs if not all, even for the unskilled manual jobs.

The joint efforts of employers, trade unions and white workers have created in Britain an ethnically – stratified work force with a particular distinction between white and black. A rigorous quantitative survey of workers (Asians, West Indians and white men) in mid seventies of twentieth century, reveal beyond any doubt that, black workers were concentrated within the lower job level that could not be explained by lower academic or job qualification. Even in broadly comparable jobs they had lower earning than white. Thus the position in the labour markets of black women is of course doubly subordinated. As we find in the survey report (Smith 1977) that the black men had to make twice as many job applications as whites before being accepted for a job. They often did shift work, yet their shift work premiums did not succeed in raising their earning above those of whites. And the black men were much more vulnerable to unemployment. So the position of black women were very worse. They suffered manifold disadvantages of the women at work plus the discrimination and stereotyping accorded to the black groups. Even there are differences between the group of non-white women like West Indian women, who are more frequently self supporting and more likely to work full time. Black women suffer from patriarchal control in the family and exploitation in waged work.[9]

Though black people are not strangers to Britain but they are quite often represented as being strangers. The history of Britain proves that African Soldiers came here with the Roman legions several hundred years before either Angles or Saxons landed on British shores. Some came as a slave; some came as merchant sailors. Large number of blacks were living here before the Second World War. The black population however increased by West Indian and Asian immigration after 1945. Thus exploitation of black immigrant labour had become gradually a strategy of capital accumulation in West European country and substantial number of migrant communities gathered in major cities where they rapidly became the subjects of white racism (Miles and Phizacklea) 1984.[10]

Despite the black workers majority in unions they failed to check the exploitation of black and the racist bias of the

Immigration Act 1971. White workers continued to see blacks as cheap labour in every field. Moreover raising cost of British labour power together with growing worker, militancy in which migrant groups joined, brought about a change in the strategies of inter-action capital. The increase of multinational due to stimulation of labour movement from one country to another it was found profitable to shift capital investment in the exporting processing zones of Third World Countries where they were able to exploit labour especially the female workers whose discipline was guaranteed by repressive governments. Racial discrimination reached its height by formulation of new laws in Britain which declared the West Indian and Asian immigrants and their British-born offsprings as "unwanted " in Britain. The media represented widely the black people as the cause of lawlessness. Thus many black people were indeed angry at the treatment of white and were fearful about the safety of their communities.[11]

References

1. In search of Answer: Indian Women's Voice from Manushi (London-1984) Edited by M. Kishwar & R. Vainta (p. 46).
2. Ranjit Guha's Subaltern Studies Vol. VI (p. 103).
3. The Complete Works of Swami Vivekananda, Vol. III. p. 506.
4. Article "Prasanga Vishwa Bharati Jaat Chetna", written by Prachal Bairagi-Bahyan Nayak 17th Feb. 2002 issue from Kolkatta.
5. Jana Matson Everett's "Women and Social Change in India (New Delhi 1979) (p. 36).
6. Susan Bayly's "Caste, Society and Politics in India" (New Delhi-1979) p. 28.
7. Susan Bayly's "Caste, Society and Politics in India (p. 29) (New Delhi, 1979 Ed.).
8. Cynthia Cockburns "In the Way of Women" (p. 173).
9. Cynthia Cockburn's "In the Way of Women" (p. 175).
10. Cynthia Cockburn's "In the Way of Women" (p. 177).
11. Cynthia Cockburn's "In the Way of Women" (p. 178).

Nine

How to Improve Women's Status

The past experience of Indian politics proves that political reservation for women is not essential to improve the status of women. Even without reservation we had many dynamic women politicians in pre-independence and post-independence period in India. Sarojini Naidu, Vijay Laxmi Pandit, Annie Vesent, Sushila Kaur, Hansa Mehta and later Indira Gandhi, Vijay Raje Scindia, Jayalalitha, Sushma Swaraj, Uma Bharti, Mayawati, Mamta Banerjee and many other renowned women politicians who established their identity in politics without reservation. After Pandit Nehru, Mrs. Indira Gandhi remained in power for longest period. History of social, political, economic exploitation on Indian soil proves that, being a woman Prime Minister having longest tenure could not improve the status of women and save them from atrocities in male dominated society. Hence it can be concluded that neither equal status can be achieved nor persecution may be reduced by political reservation for women.

Even without political reservation women in Indian society can improve their personalities and achieve equal status and rights in every field with men only when they become competent in education, will-power, courage and adaptability. These aspects are discussed as follows:

(a) Education

History of civilization of the world has proved that education is the first and foremost requirement of human development of personality and status. Hence women can equalise themselves with men if they excel in education. Without proper education even if they enjoy the rights and facilities will hardly be benefited. Only the educated people can properly utilise the rights granted to them for their benefit. What does the political right mean, when one does know why he votes for? The present state of women population in India clearly indicates that they need education first. If they are provided with necessary facilities to develop their educational state especially in rural areas, their status will automatically be improved. Education helps the women to maintain high morale character and warns them against the ensuing oddities. Mental faculty develops with educational development and our own common experiences says that education helps in improving the economic status also. Education not only improve the personality of a woman herself but it has great impact upon her entire family. Educated women is more capable to manage her family in better way than the illiterate does. Children of educated mother prosper fast and maintain social etiquette better than others.

Taking into consideration the above discussion on education, it can be concluded that our women at the prevailing circumstances should demand for special facilities for them to acquire education and not the political reservation. The present issue of political reservation for women does not really aim at improving their status. On the contrary it is a device to dupe majority population on the pretext of women's right.

(b) Will-power (Determination)

Next to education is the will-power or determination which can make a person improved and able to raise status equal to others. If Indian women create will-power i.e. the power of determination in them they can reach to a peak of elevation. Determination is an element without which no person can succeed in any venture. Hence women cannot aspire for betterment without determination. The woman who has no determination cannot be benefitted by the political reservation but who has determination or self-confidence to be a political leader can be succeed even without reservation. Mamta Banerjee, Mayawati, Uma Bharti and many other women politicians are example, who became leaders without reservation. They possess will-power to the fullest extent. Therefore, our women should develop will-power or self-confidence in themselves instead of demanding reservation. Reservation alone cannot help them to improve their status in society, who lack will-power.

(c) Courage

In India due to the influence of ancient traditions & practice in Hindu as well as Muslim societies specially in remote areas, women lose courage from the childhood and become dependable on man. The parents discourage their female children to take part in strenuous activities; this make them mentally feeble and gradually lose courage to act independently. In many occasions women are found displayed indomitable courage and valour which in no way less than a man can play. This genius is common in all the females but the surrounding environment suppresses them from development. That is why the female children gradually become dreaded, insecure and dependable on male. Therefore the women of the day need to develop their genius not by suppressing the genius but by generating in them the bravery. A brave child can undertake any venture he likes, similarly a brave woman can flourish in any field she chooses. Thus a successful woman is a self reliant and does not need special privilege to improve her status. A successful woman herself can create a high status for her in society without any body's grace or support.

(d) Adaptability

The last but not the least important quality a woman should have, is her adaptability in the environment she face or suppose to live in or work for. We find women feel discommoded at a new place or in an unfamiliar situation. This is because as a common habit women are used to remain within certain limited area of activities. Thus they become inclined to those usual habits and environment. Moreover, they are indolent or reluctant to accommodate themselves in the new disposition.

The success or failure in any field depends upon the acquiescence one shows by his acts. As such if a woman is adaptable to the situation she faces in her activity, she will be sure success. Her adaptability to the new environment or condition will give her courage to display her genius on the task she is entrusted upon and achieve the results. Thus adaptability helps encouragement and make a person successful. Therefore, the women should develop in them adaptability because, as I explained above adaptability contributes a lot to a person's success and a successful woman in all respects commands reverence, dignity and high status in society equivalent to man. Reservation or special privilege has nothing to say for a successful self reliant woman. Therefore, instead of reservation the Indian women should develop adaptability to become self reliant.

Conclusion

Based on the details I have given in the Introduction, the position of women in India and their role in shaping the civilization of the country, their future course of action regarding the pending reservation bill needs to be forecasted and analytically discuss the merits and demerits of the bill in question. My discussion after introduction was concentrated upon the position of women of the backward classes (SC/ST/BC and minority) and to what extent the bill will be beneficial to them. I have clearly painted the picture of lower castes society and their women and have to say that political reservation alone will not improve their personalities and status at all. Moreover, the reservation for women without allocating quota for SC/ST/BC and minority will be a device of depriving these women from the real rights they need. The bill as it was introduced in Lok Sabha will be beneficial only to upper caste women.

The foregoing entire discussion comprehensively states that Women's Reservation is not in reality an intention to grant equal status or rights to women in India but it is a malafide device to bring perpetual supremacy of upper castes in Parliament. I have amply clarified how the women can improve their status without reservation. Now what our women should do is to either oppose the Women's reservation bill or vehemently demand allotment of quota in the bill for SC, ST, BC, and minority in proportion to the strength of population. If the bill is passed in its ppresent form without modification lower castes population especially the SC and ST will again be the prey of Brahminical Social Order as the upper caste people will be able to establish majority permanently in Parliament and act according to their sweet will to their fullest interest.

Therefore I suggest all the aboriginals of India should oppose the bill to avoid a political suicide of SC/ST. The lower castes women population should be made aware of the need to improve their education. They should develop courage, will-power, adaptability and self reliance. These aspects of their character if could be developed, their economic status will be improved and will get a place of reverence in society. Political reservation without allotment of quota will never help them to enjoy all those rights which upper castes women enjoy. Hence the time demands from women of the lower castes (aboriginals) to improve their personalities through education, will-power, courage and adaptability. These are not only the requirement for the time being but it should always be upheld and not only by lower caste women but also by other women of the country. These are key to personal prosperity of the women.

Bibliography

The information given in this book and the thoughts provoked and the opinion formed are all based on the following sources of information.

Case Study of A. I. R. 1976 SC 490.

Case Study of A. I. R. 1981 SC 746.

A.I.W.C. Proceedings (1932-1951).

A.I.W.C. Roshni (Magazine) (1940-1954).

Allen, M. The Hindu View of Women 1982 Ed.

Ambedkar Mission Patrika, Published by Ambedkar Mission, Chitkohra, Anishabad, Patna (Bihar).

Aparna Basu and Bharati Ray Women's Struggle of (A History of the All India Women's Conference).

Aqil Ahmed, A Text Book of Mohammedan Law-1993 Ed.

Asian Women's Resource Centre on Culture and Theology.

Association for Promotion of the Status of Women (1988).

Association for Women in Psychology (1985) (An International Feminist Mental Health Agenda for the year 2000).

Anderson H., The Social Evil, Calcutta.

Acosta Vargus, Gladys with Normagamarra Sedano (1988) "The Rights of Women in Political Constitutions".

Austin Granville, The Indian Constitution: Cornerstone of Nation; Clarendon Press Oxford (1966 Ed.).

Bagal, Jogesh Chandra, Women's Education in Eastern India; Calcutta (1956 Ed.) (World Press Pvt. Ltd.).

———, Women in India's Freedom Movement; Modern Review June and July 1950.

Baig, Tara Ali, Women of India; New Delhi (1958 Ed.).

Balfour, M. I., The World of Medical Women in India; London (1929 Ed.).

Banerjee, S., National Awakening and the Bangabasi; Calcutta (1968 Ed.).

———, Marginalization of Women's Popular Culture in Nineteen Century Bengal.

Bahujan Nayak, (A weekly News –paper in Bengali), Published from Calcutta-47.

Barrett M., Women's Oppression Today; London (1980 Ed.).

Barrnett, Stephen A., The Structural position of a South Indian Caste (1970 Ed.).

Berlin Sharon, The Women Question: Does Social Work Have An Answer? (1982 Ed.).

Beteele A., Caste, class and power; University of California Press, Berkeley (1965 Ed.).

Bhasin Kamla, The Position of Women in India; Srinagar (1972 Ed.).

Bhowmik Usha, The Dowry System in the Context of Present Social Order and the Need for Social Structure Based on Equality, Liberty and Peace; Upanishad Monograph; Bombay (1988 Ed.).

Binodini Dasi, Amar Katha (Bengali); Calcutta (1912).

Blakey Virgina, Women's Health and Family Planning (1955 Ed.).

Bose Mandakranta, Faces of the Feminine in Ancient, Medieval and Modern India (Ms. Madhu Khanna's Essay "The Goddess-Women Equation in Sakti Tantra").

Bose N.K., The Structure of Hindu Society; Delhi (1975 Ed.).

Burke, S.M. and Salim Al-Din Quraishi - British Raj in India; Oxford University Press Delhi (1995 Ed.).

Caton, A.R., The Key of Progress; London (1930).

Chakrabarti, Uma, Whatever Happened to the Vedic Day Recasting Women.

Chaudhurani Sarla Devi, Jibaner Jharapata (Bengali) Calcutta (1975 Ed.).

———, A Women's Movement, Modern Review October 1911.

Chattopadhyaya, Kamala Devi- The Awakening of Indian Women; Every Press, Madras (1937 Ed.).

Cochrane, Susan H., Education and Fertility: What Do We Really Know? (1979 Ed.).

Coupland, Reginald, The Indian Problem: Report on the Constitutional Problem in India; Oxford University Press (1944).

Cousins, Margaret, E., The Awakening of Asian Womanhood; Ganesh and Co., Madras (1922 Ed.); Indian Womanhood Today –Kitabistan Allahabad (1941 Ed.).

Cynthia Cockburn, In the Way of Women; the Macmillan Press, London (1991 Ed.).

Dagmar Engels, Beyond Purdah? (Women in Bengal 1890-1930) ;Oxford University Press, Delhi (1999 Ed.).

Dagmar Engels, History and Sexuality in India: Discursive Trends (1990 Ed.).

Dainik Bhaskar, Bhopal Ed. (a daily Hindi News-paper).

Dainik Jagaran, Bhopal Ed. (a daily Hindi News-Paper).

Dalit Voice, (a fortnightly English Magazine) published from Bangalore.

Davis Susan, Personal Interview (The Ford Foundation) Dhaka, Bangladesh (1989).

Deb, Mahesh Chandra, A Sketch of the conditions of the Hindoo Women (1839).

Derrett, J. Duncan, M., Hindu Law Past and Present; A. Mukherjee and Co., Calcutta (1957).

Dewan, Paras, Law of marriage and Divorce, Universal Book Traders, Delhi (1997 Ed.).

Dorai Swamy, S., Educational Advancement and Socio-Economic Participation of Women in India; Directorate of Non-formal Education, New Delhi.

Duley, Margot and Mary, I. Edwards, The Cross-Cultural Study of Women – A Comprehensive Guide; Feminist Press; New York (1976 Ed.).

Dumont Louies, Women and Social Change in India.

Edgar Thirston, Caste and Tribes of Southern India, Vol. V (1975).

Ellman, M, Thinking about Women—Harcourt, Brace and World; New York (1968).

Engels Dagmar, The Changing Role of Women in Bengal.

Epstien Susan, International Labour Organisation Information, U. S Ed. (1988).

Estates, Richard, J., Trends in World Social Development; New York, Praager (1988 Ed.).

Everett, Jana Matson, Women and Social Change in India; Heritage Publishers, New Delhi (1979 Ed.).

Fairchild, J. E., Women, Society and Sex; Sheridan; New York (1952).

Finlay, J. M., Transcending Equality Theory: A way out of The Maternity Debate; Columbia Law Review (1986 Ed.).

Forbes, Geraldine, Women in Modern India; Cambridge University Press, New Delhi (1996 Ed.).

———, The Ideals of Indian Womanhood.

———, Social Service and Politics (Bengali Women in the Independence Movement) Columbia University, New York (1973).

Gadgil, D.R., Women in Working Force in India; Asia Publishing House, Bombay (1965 Ed.).

Gandhi, M. K., Women and Social Injustice; Ahmedabad (1942 Ed.).

Gangopadhyaya Abha, Amaderi Ekjan (Bengali) Calcutta (1951 Ed.).

Garskot, M.H., Role Women Play; Readings towards Women's Liberation Brooks Cole, California (1971 Ed.).

Gdenn, Evelyn, N., Racial Ethnic Women's Jobs: The Intersection of Race, Gender and Class Oppression (1985 Ed.).

Gedge, Evelyn, C. Choksi Methan, Women in Modern India; D.B. Tarawala Sons & Co., Bombay (1929).

Glover Jonathan, A Study of Human Capabilities Clarendon Press, Oxford (1955 Ed.).

Glazer, Malbin, N., Women in a Man Made World; Rand McNally, Chicago (1972).

Goldstein Rhoda, L., Indian Women in Transition (A Bangalore Case Study) ; Scarecrow Ney Jersey.

Gordon, Leonard, A., The National Movement 1876-1940; New York, Columbia University Press (1974 Ed.).

Guha, R., Subaltern Studies Vol-I-VI (1981-1985), Delhi.

Heinsath, Charles H., Indian Nationalism and Hindu Social Reform; Princeton University Press (1964 Ed.).

Haynes, Karen, S., Affecting Chang : Social Workers in the Political Arena; New York Longman (1986).

Heisel, Donald, Women and Population – NGO Committee on the Decade for Women (1989).

Hudson, K., Places of Women in Society; Ginn Mass (1970).

Hyman Rodman, Marriage, Family and Society; Rondom House, New York (1965).

Cynthia, Cockburn, In the Way of Women.

Janice Wood Wetzel, The World of Women; The McMillan Press Ltd, London (1993 Ed.).

Jeffery, Patricia, Frogs in a Wall : Indian Women in Purdah; London Zed Books Ltd (1979).

Jones Kenneth, The Arya Samaj in the Punjab- -A study of Social Reform and Religious Revivalism 1877-1902; California University, Berkeley (1966).

Julia Leslie & Mary McGhee Invented Identities.

Kamle, N.D., Atrocities on Scheduled Castes; Ashish Publishing House, NewDelhi (1981).

Kane, P.V., History of Dharmasastra; Dhandarkar Oriental Research Institute, Poona 1974.

Kapadia, K.M., Marriage and Family in India. Oxford, University Press, Bombay (1966).

Kapur Promilla, Love Marriage and Sex; View Publishing House, Delhi (1973).

Kaur Manmohan, Role of Women in the Freedom Movement; Sterling Publishers Delhi (1968).

Keer Dhananjay, Dr. Ambedkar: Life and Mission Popular Prakashan, Bombay (1962).

Lazarus, Hilda, Sphere of Indian Women in Medical Work In Geraldine Forbes' Women in Modern India.

MacKinnon Catherine, Difference and Dominance: On Sex Discrimination in Feminism; Cambridge (1987).

Majumdar Sudha, A Pattern of Life, The Memoirs of an Indian Woman; New Delhi (1977 Ed).

Martha, Nussbum & Janathan Glover, Women, Culture and Development. Clarendon Press; Oxford (1955).

Mary Wollstonecraft, A Vindication of Rights of Women (1992 Ed.).

Kesari, U.P.D., Modern Hindu Law.

Krishnaraj, Maethreyi and Karuna Chanana, Gender and the Household. Domain.

Kishwar, M. and R. Vainta, In search of Answer: Indian Women's Voice from Manushi; London (1984 Ed.).

Kovalsky, N.A., and Blinova, Y.P., Women Today; Progress Publishers, Delhi (1975 Ed.).

Materson Jan, Human Rights: Questions and Answer, New York (1987).

Mayer, A. C., Caste and Kinship in Central India; Routledge, London (1960).

Mechintosh, M., Gender and Economics: The Sexual Division of Labour and the Subordination of Women; London (1984 Ed.).

Dr. Mehta, Sushila, Revolution and Status of Women in India; Metropolitan Book Co. Pvt. Ltd, New Delhi (1982 Ed.).

———, Rural Sociology in India; S. Chand and Co., New Delhi (1980).

Misra, Lakshmi, Education of Women in India (1921-1966) ; Bombay (1966 Ed.).

Morris, M.D., The Emergence of an Industrial Labour Force in India, Berkeley (1965).

Mukherjee, S.N., Raja Rammohan Roy and the Status of Women in Bengal in Nineteen Century.

Mukul Mukherjee, Impact of Modernisation on Women Occupation.

Murthy, Nirmala, Bring Health Service to Where Women Are: Women in Development United Nations; New York (1985 Ed.).

Nanda, B. R., Indian Women: From Purdah to Modernity (1976 Ed.).

Nurullah, Syed and Naik, J.P., A History of Education in India, Bombay (1951 Ed.).

Papanek, Hanna, India's Dowry Murders Mark Rise in Violence Against Women; The New York Times (February 11, 1989).

Riddles in Hinduism by Dr. B. R. Ambedkar.

Ranganathanda Swami, Indian Ideal of Womanhood; Ramakrishna Mission Institute of Culture, Calcutta (1969 Ed.).

Reddy, M., Autobiography of Dr. (Mrs.) S. Muthulakshmi Reddy (1964 Ed.).

Risley, H. H., The People of India; W. Thacker, Calcutta (1908).

Rogers, Barbara, The Domestication of Women: Discrimination in Developing Society, London, Tavistok Publication (1980).

Rowbothan, Shiela, Women Resistance and Revolution; Pantheon Books, New York (1973 Ed.).

Sarkar, Sumit, Women's Question in Nineteenth Century Bengal.

Schur Edwin, M., The Family and the Sexual Revolution; Allenand Unwin, London (1966).

Sengupta, Padmini, Story of Women in India; Indian book Co., New Delhi (1973).

Shukla, V.N., Constitution of India (1994 Ed.).

Spark, Coroline, H. and Bat-Ami Baror, A Social Change: Approach to the Prevention of Sexual Violence Toward Women (1985).

Suburannessa Vs. Sabdue A. I. R. 1934 Cal 693 (A case study).

Sudha Majumdar, Memoirs of An Indian Women edited by Geraldine Forbes.

Susan Bayly, Caste, Society and Politics in India; New Delhi (1979 Ed.).

Thammakku, (A bimonthly English Magazine) Published from Madurai (T. No.).

Times of India, (English Daily News-paper) Delhi Edition.

Ting Vs. Texas, (1940) 310 U. S. 1417 (A case study).

Trivedi, H. R., Scheduled Caste Women Concept; New Delhi (1976 Ed.).

Verma, B.R., Mohammedan Law.

Vidya Sagar Iswarchandra, Marriage of Hindu Widows K.P. Bagchi & Co., Calcutta (1976 Ed.).

Index